Military Jeep

4823478

Military Jeep

Enthusiasts' Manual: 1940 Onwards – Ford, Willys and Hotchkiss

Pat Ware

Crécy
www.crecy.co.uk

Crécy Publishing Ltd

Originally published by Haynes in 2010. This revised and expanded edition published in 2022

A CIP record for this book is available from the British Library

Printed in Turkey by Imak Ofset

ISBN 9781800352551

Crécy Publishing Limited
1a Ringway Trading Estate,
Shadowmoss Road,
Manchester
M22 5LH

www.crecy.co.uk

FRONT COVER: Members of the US Army's 101st Airborne Division, 327th Glider Infantry Regiment, pause for a spot of sightseeing in the Bavarian Alps, near Berchtesgaden. *David Doyle*

BACK COVER MAIN: US Army military vehicles attempting to make progress through a shattered Italian town. The photograph is dated 1944. *Warehouse Collection*

BACK COVER INSETS (TOP TO BOTTOM):
Bill Padden's superb ghost drawing of the Jeep shows exactly how the main components of the vehicle are arranged; to buy copies of this drawing, visit www.williampadden.com. *Bill Padden*

Sectional view of the four-brush 6V starter motor. *Warehouse Collection*

Jeep bogged down and abandoned on 'The sands of Iwo Jima'. *Warehouse Collection*

PAGE 1: Licence-built by the French Hotchkiss company between 1955 and 1966, the M201 remains every inch a military Jeep. *Christophe Muller*

PAGE 2: With the iconic cut-away radiator grille and prominent overflow expansion vessel, this Jeep emulates those used by units such as the Special Air Services (SAS) and Long Range Desert Group (LRDG) in North Africa. Note the jerrycans of mixed British and German origin strapped to every flat surface. *Simon Thomson*

ABOVE: The 'C' prefix to the registration number identifies this Jeep as belonging to the Canadian Army … the 'S' suffix indicates that it is radio screened. *Simon Thomson*

Contents

Introduction

'The Jeep...was America's greatest contribution to modern warfare.'

GENERAL GEORGE C. MARSHALL, 1945

The iconic military Jeep owes its existence to an American Quartermaster Corps (QMC) requirement issued in 1940 for a light, field reconnaissance car. More than 130 manufacturers were invited to bid for the development of a pilot model and to manufacture 70 pre-production vehicles. Only American Bantam, Willys-Overland and Ford chose to participate in the programme and, of these, only Bantam produced a prototype within the timescale. Bantam was also the only company to manufacture the required 70 pre-production vehicles.

BELOW: You could eat a meal off the flat bonnet of the Jeep, but it also lent itself to a number of tasks ... ranging from a makeshift altar, a map table, to a workbench. *Phil Royal*

When the standardised Jeep entered production in 1941, it combined elements of all three companies' designs, and yet was only produced by Ford and Willys. Despite having produced the original prototype, American Bantam was never involved in mass-producing what became the world's most successful military vehicle.

MECHANISATION OF THE US ARMY

The US Army had started to mechanise at the turn of the 20th Century, but it was on a rather haphazard basis. It wasn't until 1939 that the importance of standardisation was recognised, and the US War Department laid down five weight categories for logistical military vehicles ranging from ½-a-ton to 7½ tons. Although the motorcycle, often with a sidecar, was seen as fulfilling a need for a lighter vehicle, elements of the infantry believed that there was scope for a ¼-ton truck and it could be argued that the first step towards the development of the Jeep had already been taken when the US Infantry Board purchased an American-built Austin 7 pick-up truck fitted with oversized tyres for $286.75, in November 1932.

Produced under licence by the American Austin Company, later to become American Bantam, the little Bantam car was one of America's smallest automobiles, and the Infantry Board was hoping that the vehicle would prove to be suitable in the reconnaissance and messenger roles. Unfortunately, it was not the success that the Infantry Board had hoped and the next step in the process was the development of the so-called 'Howie machine-gun carrier', often described as the 'belly-flopper'.

In April 1937, at the request of Brigadier General Walter C. Short, Assistant Commandant at the Infantry School at Fort Benning, a specification had been prepared for a low-silhouette motorised carrier that could provide space for two men; travel, off-road, at some 3–5mph (5–8km/h); mount a .50-calibre machine-gun; and carry sufficient ammunition to fulfil various operational roles. The vehicle was developed, to Short's brief, but apparently without higher official sanction, by Captain Robert G. Howie, an instructor at the Infantry School's Tank Section. He was assisted in its construction by Master Sergeant Melvin C. Wiley and Sergeant G.L. Rush.

The 'belly-flopper' was powered by an American Bantam (Austin 7) engine of 753cc (46kW), and also incorporated the radiator, rear axle, and propeller shaft, perhaps salvaged from the same Bantam that had been purchased and delivered to Benning in 1932. There was no body, and the crew lay prone on the floor, steering through a lever arrangement. The vehicle was capable of speeds of up to 28mph (45km/h) and, at just 34in (860mm) in height, presented an extraordinarily low silhouette. On test, the 'belly-flopper' proved more than capable of carrying a variety of weapons besides the .50-calibre machine-gun, including an 81mm mortar, and a 37mm anti-tank gun. By late July 1938, Lieutenant-Colonel D.K. Mitchell, commanding the QMC, had stated that layout drawings for what was described as 'Project EDT No 29-8, truck, chassis, 4-wheel drive, ¼-ton capacity, (carrier, machine-gun)' were in the 'process of preparation'.

The little 'belly-flopper' was certainly a success within its limited terms of reference, but it had no real road-going capabilities, and there was never any question of volume production. Anyway, the QMC was presumably well aware that the lack of four-wheel drive would restrict the utility of the machine and began to consider how the gun-carrying role, so ably demonstrated by Captain Howie's machine, might be combined with the reconnaissance and messenger roles performed by the Bantam – with the addition of all-wheel drive.

Within little more than three months the 'belly-flopper' project had been closed and a new project established 'to construct a new three-passenger lightweight open body for this chassis, so that this vehicle can be tested in comparison with the three-passenger motorcycle'. Now, there are those who dispute that the 'belly-flopper' has any legitimate part to play in the Jeep story, but it has also been suggested that representatives of Willys-Overland were shown the 'belly-flopper' in March 1940 during discussions regarding the design of what was described as a new weapons carrier/reconnaissance car – in other words, *the Jeep*.

ABOVE: Bantam was founded in 1929 as the American Austin Car Company, and following bankruptcy and reorganisation resumed production in the mid-thirties with a range of six diminutive motorcars based on the Austin 7. One of these was considered as the basis for a military utility vehicle. *Warehouse Collection*

LEFT: In 1932, the US Infantry Board had purchased an American Bantam pick-up truck for possible military use. Despite being considered unsuitable, largely because of its lightweight construction, here a Bantam chassis – perhaps, the Bantam chassis – has been loaded with some 3,000lb (1,365kg), more than six times its specified limit. *Warehouse Collection*

ABOVE: Designed by Colonel Robert G. Howie, and constructed by Master Sergeant Melvyn C. Wilie, the eponymous Howie 'belly-flopper' was constructed using components salvaged from an American Bantam vehicle. *Warehouse Collection*

RIGHT: There is a strand of opinion amongst Jeep aficionados that claims the Howie 'belly-flopper' had little to do with the development of the Jeep. This US Army photograph of the two vehicles side by side would suggest that this view was not that embraced by officialdom. *Warehouse Collection*

BELOW RIGHT: With its very low profile, the 'belly-flopper' could literally hide in long grass but, clearly, it was never going to be considered as a serious road-going vehicle. *Warehouse Collection*

ABOVE: Hung about with kit and equipment, this high-level view of the Jeep illustrates just how small the vehicle is. Designed to replace the horse and the motorcycle and sidecar, the vehicle was a revelation back in 1940. *Simon Thomson*

LEFT: A pair of Bantam BRC-60 pre-production vehicles with suitably attired drivers. *Warehouse Collection*

LEFT: With its small size and relatively low profile, a well-armed and well-provisioned Jeep can be a formidable fighting machine. The Special Air Service Regiment (SAS), the Long Range Desert Group (LRDG) and Popski's Private Army all used Jeeps to penetrate behind enemy lines and to carry out interdiction raids on airfields and fuel dumps. It was essential in these operations that the Jeep carry sufficient supplies to permit extended operations. *Phil Royal*

LEFT: With little modification, Jeeps were small and light enough to allow delivery by glider and provided valuable mobility for airborne troops. *Phil Royal*

RIGHT: Although it is wearing over-sized tyres, this well-worn Jeep looks much as it might have done in 1944. *Simon Thomson*

Chapter 1

The Jeep Story

'The whole world knows the "Jeep", the tough scout car designed and perfected by Willys with the cooperation of the Army. It is built around the famous Willys "Go-Devil" Jeep engine, which is the fighting heart of the Jeep, and the source of its amazing power, speed, flexibility, dependability, and fuel economy.'

WILLYS-OVERLAND PRESS ADVERTISEMENT, FEBRUARY 1944

Following the end of the First World War, the abhorrence for war across the world was such that most nations slashed their defence expenditure. The United States was no exception and, although the US Army was alive to the need to mechanise, funds remained short. However, the Quartermaster Corps (QMC) was keen to find a replacement for the military motorcycle which, with its limited off-road performance, was not really suited to the reconnaissance and messenger roles that, hitherto, had been performed largely by horse and rider. This replacement came in the form of the Jeep.

What we would describe these days as the DNA of the Jeep almost certainly came from two relatively unknown vehicles – the American-built Austin Bantam car, and a one-off military device dubbed the 'Howie belly-flopper'. But the Jeep really shares very little with either of them in any physical sense.

THE DEVELOPMENT OF THE JEEP

In June 1940, William F. Beasley, Chief Engineer of the US Ordnance Department, was appointed head of the team that was responsible for setting out the basic requirements for what was to become the Jeep. He produced a simple free-hand sketch, signed and dated 14 June, which showed a small four-seat utility vehicle with a wheel at each corner, low

RIGHT: Looming out of the famed 'War & Peace Show' dust, this Jeep has been fitted with the A-frame device that allowed a pair of vehicles to be coupled together to tow a 105mm field gun. *Phil Royal*

cut-away sides, a removable canvas top, and a central machine-gun mount. The drawing included just four key dimensions: a ground clearance of 8½in (216mm); maximum height, with the top folded, of 36in (915mm); a front approach angle of 45°; and a rear departure angle of 40°.

At this point, the General Staff handed responsibility to the Ordnance Technical Committee and it seemed that the project was finally underway. A subcommittee was established to finalise the requirements and to draw up a complete specification. Alongside representatives from the infantry, the cavalry and the QMC, the committee included Major Howie, William Beasley, Bob Brown and Bill Burgan. One of the committee's first actions was to convene a meeting at the American Bantam Company plant in Butler, Pennsylvania. Here, they discussed the possibility of adapting a standard Bantam chassis with Harold Crist, Bantam's factory manager, and looked into Bantam's production capacity in the event that the modified standard vehicle should prove acceptable.

The QMC purchased three Bantam chassis and put these through a series of tests intended to determine their load-carrying capacity and off-road performance. Although they acquitted themselves well, it was obvious that a standard production vehicle, even heavily modified, was not going to be suitable. As an interesting aside, a year or so later Francis (Frank) H. Fenn, who by then was Bantam's Vice President and General Manager, wrote to the QMC suggesting that they conduct the trials again using the 'redesigned 1940 model' which, with its increased carrying capacity and three-bearing engine, he believed would be more satisfactory. The offer was not taken up.

Meanwhile, Crist and Brown had gone ahead and prepared a provisional document that was later to form the basis of the committee's 'official' specification. This tentative specification included the following features:

- all-wheel drive, with manual engagement of the front axle
- a more powerful engine than that used in the Bantam, in order to provide a maximum road speed of not less than 50mph (80km/h)
- high-efficiency oil-bath air cleaner
- two-speed transfer case
- hydraulic brakes
- fully-floating axles
- military blackout lighting
- simple rectangular body with a folding windscreen and three seats
- mounting for a .30-calibre Browning machine-gun, and provision for towing a gun or trailer.

Beasley's basic dimensions were retained, and in addition it was stated that the wheelbase should be 75in (1,905mm), and the weight should not exceed 1,200lb (545kg).

The bidding process

On 27 May 1940, the Ordnance Technical Committee in Washington ratified the specification, making just a few small amendments. The wheelbase was increased to 80in (2,032mm), and the front and rear track were specified as 47in (1,194mm); the maximum weight was increased to 1,300lb (590kg); and the vehicle was to carry a 600lb (272kg) payload.

The Committee recommended that the American motor industry be approached and that interested manufacturers

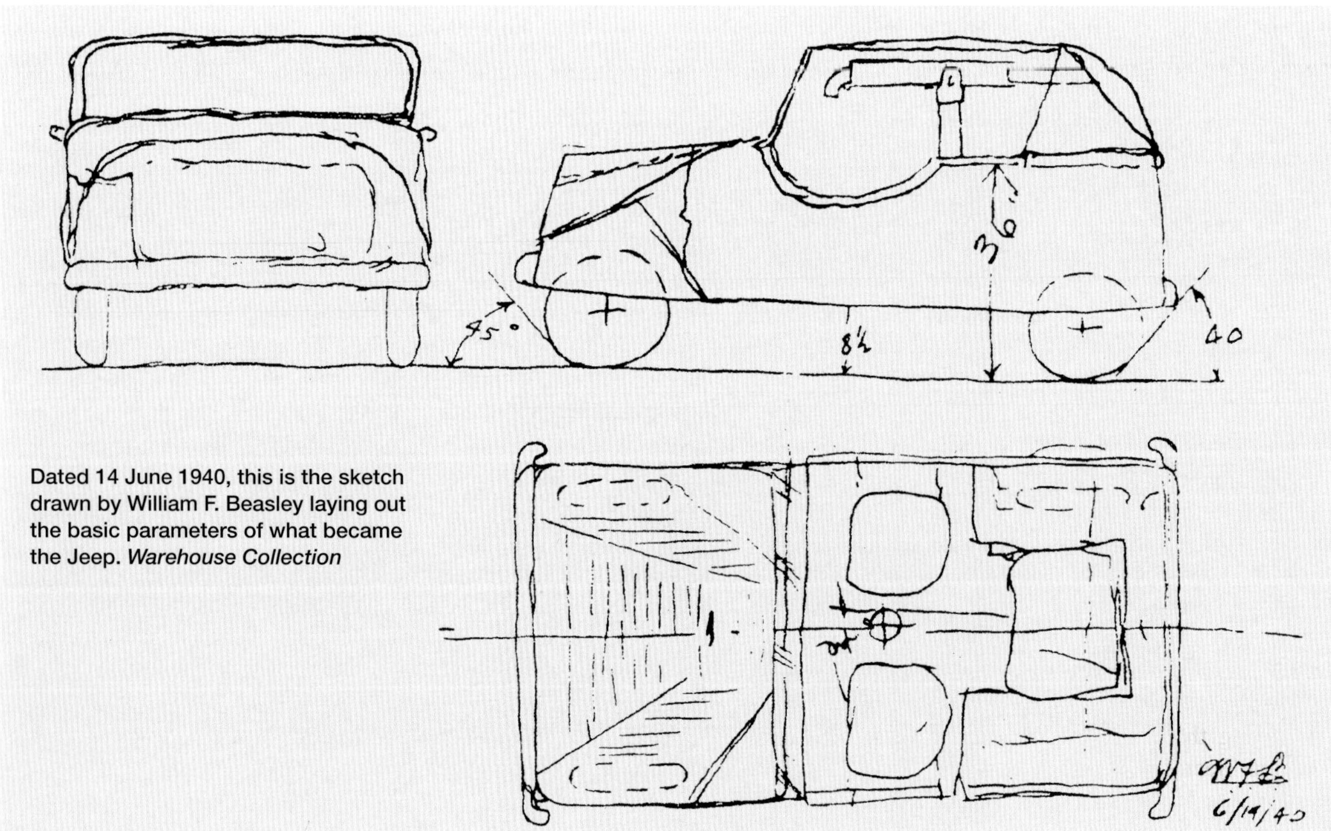

Dated 14 June 1940, this is the sketch drawn by William F. Beasley laying out the basic parameters of what became the Jeep. ***Warehouse Collection***

were invited to bid for the design and construction of 70 pilot vehicles for test, eight of which were to feature four-wheel steering. A sum of $175,000 was allocated for the procurement of the vehicles from the successful bidder. America had not at this stage entered the war, but the shadows were already lengthening, and it was clear that there was some urgency. The US Army was keen that the vehicles would be ready in time for the 1940 autumn manoeuvres, and for this purpose, 40 vehicles were to be allocated to the infantry, 20 to the cavalry, and the remaining 10 to field artillery.

In mid-July 1940, the invitations to bid were distributed, together with QM Drawing Number 08370-Z. The manufacturers were given ten days to prepare their responses and to compile the necessary documentation. For the successful bidder, there were just 75 days to produce a concept, draw-up detailed proposals, locate sources of major components, and build 70 prototype vehicles. However, since the first prototype was to be delivered to the Army within 49 days, this meant that just 26 days were available to construct the remaining 69 vehicles. The tenders were due at Camp Holabird, Maryland, by 22 July 1940, and the successful manufacturer would have to begin work immediately if there was to be any chance of meeting the 49-day and 75-day delivery deadlines.

The budget total of $175,000, which had been set aside for the project, gave a unit price of $2,500 per vehicle, but most of the 135 manufacturers who were approached felt that insufficient funds had been allocated to the project. Most also believed that the deadline and the weight limit were equally unrealistic, and only American Bantam and Willys-Overland expressed a desire to become involved. But, keen to get access to Ford's massive production capacity, it is said that the QMC had to indulge in some patriotic arm-twisting behind the scenes before Ford, too, eventually agreed to participate.

THE PROTOTYPES

Bantam pilot model

In 1940, like many smaller US car manufacturers, American Bantam was in trouble and saw the possibility of the QMC contract as a lifeline to help put the company back on its feet. Encouraged by their involvement in the June conference with the Ordnance Technical Subcommittee, which had been arranged by Harry Payne, Bantam's first response to the QMC, even before the bid procedure had been agreed, was to attempt to negotiate a contract for the manufacture and delivery of 70 Bantam reconnaissance cars using the outline specifications that they had helped to prepare.

The infantry was happy with this approach since it would almost certainly have meant that the vehicles would be available in time for the autumn manoeuvres. Unfortunately for Bantam, the Office of the Quartermaster General (OQMG) was decidedly unhappy, insisting that procurement should take place through a competitive bidding procedure, which they said must include the Ford Motor Company. Clearance for issuing the bid papers was given by the Office of the Assistant Secretary of War on 11 July, but it was to be almost another week before Bantam received the official bid documents. Although Bantam's financial situation remained unchanged, a considerable amount of speculative work had been done on the project in advance and the company believed that this work gave them an edge. However, they badly needed someone to lay out the vehicle on paper.

Francis H. Fenn, President of Bantam, approached Art Brandt, an ex-General Motors designer who at that time was working for the National Defense Advisory Commission, and asked if he could help. Brandt, who had been the first President of the American Austin Company and had helped to establish the Bantam factory, suggested that Fenn get in touch with Karl K. Probst, a freelance designer and engineer running an automotive design business in Grand Woodward, Detroit under the name Probst, Shoemaker & Merrill, or PSM Design Studio. Brandt had previously worked with Probst on a lightweight car project for GM and he volunteered to call Probst himself and to outline the task in hand, including the fact that if Bantam failed to win the contract, there would be no funds to meet Probst's fee. Unsurprisingly, it seems that Probst was not keen, but he suggested that Brandt ask Fenn to call him anyway, the following Monday. Fenn further discussed the project with Probst, who was still reluctant to become involved, and it was agreed that Fenn would call again when he had sight of the bid documents.

On 17 July, the bid documents arrived, and this may have been the first time that Bantam was aware that the QMC had upped the load-carrying capacity and the weight of the vehicle. Nevertheless, with the bid due back at Camp Holabird just five days later, it was essential that work should start immediately. Once again, Fenn spoke to Probst. In the meantime, the National Defense Advisory Commission had somehow become directly involved and Probst was persuaded that 'funds would be available if the vehicle was produced to the QMC specification'. Probst agreed that he would undertake the project and arranged with Fenn that he would be at the Bantam plant the next day.

The axles and transfer case had already been identified as the most urgent items, and Probst said that he would call in at the Spicer Manufacturing Corporation plant at Toledo on his way to Butler. Talking to Spicer's Bob Lewis, the two men agreed that, with the inclusion of constant-velocity joints, the axle of the Studebaker Champion would probably be suitable. They also agreed the basic parameters for the two-speed transfer case, and Probst left, continuing his journey east towards Butler, where, the following day, Thursday 18 July, he was introduced to Harold Crist, Chester (Chet) J. Hemphling, Ralph Turner, and two other key men who were to produce tools and parts for the project. Between them, these men created a formidable team and, although Probst has frequently been referred to as the 'father of the Jeep', and his contribution should certainly not be overlooked, as much credit should also be given to Crist, Turner and Hemphling.

Between them the men discussed the key problems of weight and performance. None believed that they could produce the vehicle that the Army was demanding within the 1,300lb (590kg) weight limit, but then neither did they believe anyone else would be able to. They agreed that the best thing to do was ignore the weight problem and concentrate on giving the Army the performance that it

LEFT: The team responsible for the Bantam pilot photographed with the finished vehicle at the Bantam factory in Butler, Pennsylvania. Karl Probst is leaning on the spare wheel, Harold Crist is in the driving seat. *Warehouse Collection*

wanted. The second difficulty was that of time. To develop a modern motorcar to the prototype stage takes somewhere around two years – Bantam was given just 49 days to produce the first prototype. The only course available was to employ as many existing components as possible.

A three-speed Borg Warner transmission had already been chosen and the axles and transfer case had been agreed with Spicer, which meant that the only major component remaining was the engine. It was clear that Bantam would not be able to use their own 753cc (46in^3) four-cylinder unit. Although it had been redesigned to incorporate a three-bearing crankshaft and a pressure lubrication system, with a power output of just 20bhp (15kW), it was not sufficiently powerful to meet the Ordnance Technical Committee's specification. The initial choice was between a Hercules engine, possibly the four-cylinder IXB, or the Ford 9N, one of which had been loaned to Bantam by Ford; but eventually, both of these were dismissed as being too heavy, in favour of a side-valve Continental BY-4112. With a capacity of 1,835cc (112in^3), and a power output of 48bhp (36kW) at 3,150rpm, it appeared more than suitable for the application.

Frank Fenn started to call major suppliers, checking component availability and transcribing key dimensions, while Probst started work at the drawing board. Although he was responsible for drawing up the plans, he should almost certainly not be considered as the ''designer' of the vehicle and it seems there were several substantial arguments over various design features, for most of which Crist prevailed. Nevertheless, legend has it that Probst worked at the drawing board for 18 hours, with breaks for sleeping and eating. By the evening of Friday 19 July, the team felt that the basic design work was complete. Probst apparently then went to the movies, but before retiring that night, dictated the list of parts required for the chassis. During Saturday, Fenn and Probst put together their estimates of cost and weight, and on Sunday completed the bid forms. Their best estimate of the weight of the vehicle was 1,850lb (841kg), against the QMC's 1,300lb (590kg) limit.

Together, Probst and Fenn drove the 200 miles (320km) to Washington to go through the documents with retired naval commander Charles Payne, who was their technical representative and liaison with the military authorities. The weight was a sticking point. Payne insisted that the bids should not be submitted with the 1,850lb (841kg) figure, suggesting that they bid below 1,300lb (590kg) and then request a variation once the contract was in the bag. Since the bids had not been typed on the correct forms, there was no disadvantage in changing the figures and a typist was brought to the hotel at 3.30am on Monday 22 July 1940 to retype the paperwork.

At 8.30 that morning, the two representatives from Bantam arrived at Camp Holabird to present the documents. At the same time, representatives of Willys-Overland, Ford and Crosley (not to be confused with the English company, Crossley) were also present, although neither Ford nor Crosley was making an official bid. Within 30 minutes, the Bantam and Willys people were called before the purchasing officer to be told that the contract was awarded to Bantam. Although the Willys bid price was lower, they had presented only a time and cost estimate, and had also asked for a 71-day extension on the existing 49-day deadline, bringing it up to 120 days. The extension would incur a cost penalty of $5 a day, which put the Willys price above Bantam's figure of $171,185.

Official notification of the contract was received by Bantam on 5 August 1940. The 49-day deadline meant that the first vehicle was due at Holabird at 5.00pm on 23 September. However, Bantam had not waited for the official notification and, as soon as the negotiations at Holabird had been completed, Probst had left for Detroit, where he lined up three engineers to work alongside him. Meanwhile, Fenn employed a fourth member for the team. Assembly work had already begun in earnest on 1 August, with Crist's men starting to make tools from Probst's sketches and layouts. The axles, which had to be adapted for four-wheel drive, proved to be a problem, and at one time it looked like the deadline would not be met, but Spicer made the delivery on 15 September and final assembly began, with the intention of having the prototype running within one week.

While the concept of the vehicle was an innovation, Probst and his team had no time to take chances with the design. The engine was front-mounted, driving to a unit-constructed gearbox and transfer case, and then to the front and rear axles, and the suspension used old-fashioned leaf springs. The chassis was a conventional ladder frame affair, with a non-stressed body bolted directly to it, and the scuttle, and perhaps the rounded front mudguards, were adapted from the Bantam motorcar.

ABOVE: Dated 3 October 1940, this photograph shows the Bantam pilot undergoing trials at Camp Holabird, Maryland. The original caption says that the vehicle was designed to carry 'three men, a swivel-mounted machine-gun and 3,000 rounds of ammunition'. *Warehouse Collection*

RIGHT: Although the body of the standardised Jeep perhaps owed more to the Ford Pygmy than to the Bantam, nevertheless, the vehicle still has that essential Jeep look to it. *Warehouse Collection*

On Monday 23 September, with Probst and Crist following behind, Ralph Turner set out in the prototype for Camp Holabird in Maryland, some 170 miles (275km) away. The vehicle had covered scarcely 150 miles (250km) around the Bantam plant, and as a precaution, the two engineers took with them heavier springs and a larger radiator, believing that these were the items most likely to give trouble. During the journey, they took it as easy as possible since the brand-new engine was scarcely run-in. However, if they made it to Holabird, Major Lawes would try to break the prototype in a tough 30-day test that would be terminated if the vehicle stopped for more than 24 hours. If the test were terminated, Bantam would have failed.

Probst, Crist and Turner arrived at Holabird and the test began immediately. With representatives of Ford, Chrysler and GM watching, Crist tried to create a little drama by driving the vehicle up a steep gradient in second gear. The assembled company was suitably impressed, and Major Lawes took over, thrashing the prototype around the Holabird test course. He returned, more impressed, apparently telling the exhausted, but no doubt elated, Bantam engineers that, based on just 15 minutes

LEFT: The test of the Bantam started on 27 September 1940 and continued until 16 October, by which time the vehicle had covered 3,600 miles (5,800km) across every type of surface that the Holabird facility could offer. *Warehouse Collection*

BELOW: Bantam BRC-60 fully in the air after cresting a rise, with the American 37mm anti-tank gun in tow and similarly airborne! *Warehouse Collection*

ABOVE: Classic 'little and large' comparison: the diminutive Bantam pilot is photographed alongside the Oshkosh Model TR artillery tractor. *David Doyle*

driving, his considerable experience told him that the vehicle was going to prove 'absolutely outstanding'.

But, there was still the hurdle of weight to overcome.

The vehicle was 730lb (332kg) above the QMC limit. It was Bantam's view that no more weight could be removed without sacrificing strength. At the bidding stage, Payne had tried to avoid discussion regarding weight, reasoning that they could better deal with the issue when the authorities had convinced themselves that the vehicle was what they wanted, but now the Bantam engineers felt that the question should be settled once and for all. A burly cavalry officer demonstrated, single-handedly, that it was possible to manhandle the Bantam out of a ditch despite it being 'overweight' and Bantam's view prevailed.

For the next 30 days and 3,600 miles (5,800km), the Bantam was put through its paces at Holabird as Captain Eugene Moseley, the Camp's chief tester, tried to break it, even apparently driving it off a 48in (1,200mm) high loading platform at 30mph (50km/h). With this kind of treatment, the vehicle inevitably suffered failures, including at one stage, a breakage of the chassis frame, but none put it out of the programme. The final report of the trials concluded that 'the vehicle had a good power output and met the requirements of the service'.

On 27 October, the vehicle was driven 466 miles (754km) to Fort Knox, Kentucky, where it was demonstrated to the Armored Force Board. It was driven across all types of terrain, including the heaviest brush, and only once had to be assisted when it became bogged down in deep mud. On two occasions the Bantam was coupled to the 'new anti-tank gun' and on one of these occasions, the vehicle was also carrying six passengers. All agreed that the performance of the vehicle was 'very favourable'.

Three days later, the Bantam started the return journey to Butler, Pennsylvania, with Ralph Turner and Mosley, the QMC test driver, on board – a journey that was cut short the following day after a 40mph (65km/h) collision with a telephone truck. Although the Bantam's front axle was damaged, the vehicle was able to make it back to Butler under its own power. This was the last time that the Bantam pilot vehicle was specifically mentioned in any reports on the project and its fate remains unknown.

Bantam BRC-60 and BRC-40

With the pilot vehicle back at the factory, the Bantam engineers set to work on changes to the design and specification, starting work on constructing the 70 'Model 60' – or BRC-60 – pre-production vehicles. The most noticeable differences between the pilot model and the Model 60 were deeper body cut-outs to improve access, the inclusion of a solid panel beneath the windscreen, and the squared-off front mudguards.

Bantam was the only one of the three manufacturers involved to actually complete the required 70 pre-production models.

ABOVE: Bantam BRC-60 equipped with a .50-calibre machine-gun on a mono-post mount, and clearly intended for anti-aircraft duties. The USA number (2015384) indicates that this was the 62nd pre-production Bantam from a run of 70 and it was retained at Camp Holabird for testing during 1940/41. *Warehouse Collection*

LEFT: This Bantam BRC-60 seems to have suffered some damage to the body side resulting in tearing of the sheet metal, which has deepened the cut-out. Seventy of these vehicles were constructed, eight of which had four-wheel steering. *Warehouse Collection*

BELOW: The fate of the original Bantam pilot vehicle is unknown, so life-long Texas Bantam enthusiast Duncan Rolls decided that he would build a replica. After 3,000 man-hours work this is the result, looking much as it must have done when it was driven into Camp Holabird on 23 September 1940. *Duncan Rolls, 2009*

But even before these were delivered, the company received a second contract for a total of 500, and then a further 1,000. Now described as the BRC-40 (derived from Bantam Reconnaissance Car, 1940), these vehicles were further modified in many ways including the use of the flat-topped bonnet pioneered by Ford. Bantam reduced the price of each vehicle by $50 to $1,123 for the first 500; the price was further reduced to $938 for the second 500; and if subsequent orders totalled 3,000 units, the price would reduce further to 'around $700'.

LEFT: In this rear view, the Bantam replica wears a reproduction of the trials licence plate shown in original photographs of the vehicle. *Duncan Rolls, 2009*

ABOVE: Following the successful trials at Camp Holabird, Bantam set to work building 70 pre-production machines, which were described as BRC-60. The figure of 70 was soon increased to 500 and then to 1,500, by which time the designation had been changed to BRC-40. A total of 50 of these vehicles had four-wheel steering. *Warehouse Collection*

ABOVE: For 30 days, Captain Eugene Mosely and his staff at Camp Holabird tried their damnedest to break the Bantam prototype – the little Bantam took it all in its stride. *Warehouse Collection*

RIGHT: Pre-production Bantam BRC-60 photographed at the Smithsonian Institute in 1944. Number 7 in the pre-production run, this is the only surviving BRC-60. *Warehouse Collection*

ABOVE: To modern eyes, the treatment of the front end of the vehicle is clumsy, the top is way too baggy, and the windscreen manages to look very flimsy. Nevertheless, the pre-production Bantam is unmistakeably a Jeep. *Warehouse Collection*

BELOW: Bantam BRC-40 armed with a 37mm M3 anti-tank gun. *Warehouse Collection*

ABOVE: Side elevation of the BRC-40 showing the longer step panel, the Ford-style bonnet and the deeper body cut-outs that first appeared on the BRC-60. *Warehouse Collection*

RIGHT: Rear three-quarter view of the production Bantam BRC-40. *Warehouse Collection*

LEFT: Bantam BRC-40 belonging to the British 6th Armoured Division. Note the unusual spring-balanced Bren gun mount on the passenger side. This was one of 1,000 vehicles supplied under contract SM 2262 in 1941. *The Tank Museum*

BELOW: Although the official news agency caption, dated August 1941, describes this as a 'Ford reconnaissance Bantam Jeep', it is clearly a Bantam BRC-40 but the use of the word 'Jeep' had clearly caught on by this time. *Warehouse Collection*

Willys Quad

Back in March 1940, Delmar 'Barney' Roos, Chief Engineer at Willys-Overland, had been invited to view the trials of the Howie 'belly-flopper'. Roos was shrewd enough an engineer to see that the crude machine contained the germ of an idea, and that the Army was already sold on the concept that was eventually to lead to the Jeep. Like Bantam, Willys was also in financial difficulties and, like Frank Fenn, Roos was equally keen that his company become involved in the bidding process for the Jeep project. Besides Bantam, Willys was the only company to respond positively. However, unlike Bantam, who already had a head start and thus pulled out all the stops to get their bid in, Willys did not believe that a prototype could be made ready in the time allowed by the QMC.

Having not even tried to put together a layout for the vehicle, all that Willys submitted on 22 July 1940 was a time and cost bid. Their price estimate was $250 per vehicle below the Bantam figure, but they were asking for more time to construct the first vehicle. The penalty clause of $5 per day put the Willys price beyond that bid by Bantam – and Bantam got the contract. The QMC ruled that Willys was disqualified. Nevertheless, confident that the Bantam would not survive the 30-day trials, Willys pressed on with the completion of their prototype, apparently at their own expense. With hindsight, this was a wise move, because although the Bantam did survive the test, the QMC did not believe that the company had sufficient production capacity to produce all of the Jeeps that would be required, and were keen to also secure alternative sources of supply.

It now seems inconceivable in what was effectively a competitive bidding situation, but not only were representatives of Willys present when Probst and Crist brought their prototype to Holabird in September 1940, but they were given every opportunity to examine it – and to sketch whatever details they felt would help them. Copies of Bantam's drawings were handed over to both Willys and Ford, leading Harold Crist to complain of unfair practice. But it was to no avail. The QMC argued that the vehicle had been paid for with US Government funds and they would show it to whomsoever they chose. So, some 50 days behind Bantam, Willys produced 2 prototypes, which the company had dubbed the 'Quad', one of which was fitted with four-wheel steering.

In a letter written to the purchasing officer at Holabird, Major J. Van Ness Ingram, Eugene M. Rice, Director of Fleet and Government Sales at Willys, quoted a price of $1,581 for each of 1,500 vehicles equipped with two-wheel steering, and $1,677 per vehicle for four-wheel steering.

BELOW: Front three-quarter view of the Willys pilot vehicle – the Quad. With a total weight of 2,423lb (1,101kg), the Quad was still way over the Army's limit. *Jeep Eagle PR*

RIGHT: Rear three-quarter view of the Willys Quad, dated October 1943. According to the official caption, the vehicle has been 'rebuilt'. *David Doyle*

BELOW LEFT: Willys Quad, showing the clumsy headlamp treatment, the very heavy front-end treatment, and the somewhat cobbled-together appearance. *Jeep Eagle PR*

BELOW RIGHT: The passenger seat of the Quad was arranged to swivel to one side and both front seats featured folding back-rests. *Jeep Eagle PR*

The first vehicle, which bore more than a passing resemblance to the Bantam, was delivered to Holabird on 11 November 1940. Like the Bantam, it was also over the QMC weight specification, weighing in at 2,420lb (1,099kg). However, by using the company's powerful 2,199cc (134in^3), 65bhp (48kW) Go-Devil four-cylinder side-valve engine taken from the contemporary Americar, the Willys prototype had a far higher power-to-weight ratio than the Bantam. The engine was a six-year-old design and although it had originally earned a very poor reputation, Roos had put a lot of effort into refining it, paying particular attention to lubrication and cooling and, by 1940, it had proved itself to be both powerful and reliable.

In virtually every other respect, Willys followed the precedent already established by Bantam, even employing the same Spicer transfer case and axles. Unusually, the Willys prototype had the gearshift on the steering column, and the handbrake lever on the dashboard where, of course, the latter was to remain during the entire production run.

No one could describe the Willys as handsome. The front mudguards were angular in shape with a curious side panel and the whole thing had an ungainly air about it. However, so close were the vehicles in concept that the Chief of (US) Infantry, in describing the comparative tests, wrote in May 1941, 'the Ford and Willys-Overland models are copies of the original Bantam design'.

Testing began on the afternoon of 13 November 1940. The first phase consisted of a 5,000-mile (8,000km) highway run, followed, by the same distance across fields at the camp where ditches, hills and rough country had been constructed in an off-road course. Apparently, the light springs of the Willys prototypes made it easier to remain seated at higher speeds and this encouraged faster driving than with the Bantam. The Willys test driver, Donald Kenower, noted that the Camp

ABOVE: Production Willys MA coming down the steps of the Capitol building. The photograph was apparently also taken in February 1941. *Warehouse Collection*

LEFT: In early 1941, Willys staged a press event in Washington DC, in which the Quad prototype was driven up the steps of the Capitol. The test driver informed a reporter from the Washington Daily News that the vehicle was a 'Jeep' – the name appeared in print and has become permanently associated with the vehicle. *Warehouse Collection*

ABOVE: Nicely restored Willys MA. Although the grille and front-end treatment is unique to this model, other features such as the angled bumper ends and deep body cut-outs had disappeared by the time the standardised MB was developed. *David Doyle*

LEFT: The side cut-outs are deeper and the grille and headlamp treatment remains awkward, the latter being particularly vulnerable to damage from overhanging branches. Nevertheless, the Willys MA is very close to the final form of the Jeep. The photograph is dated 1941. *David Doyle*

Holabird team took advantage of this. However, continuous rain during the cross-country part of the trials had turned areas of the course into a mud bath and the Quad ingested large amounts of mud into the carburettor, ruining the engine. In order that the test could continue, a similar Go-Devil engine was taken from a Willys passenger car and used to replace the faulty unit. Other problems included fractures of the frame, constant overheating, failure of the transfer-case bearings, repeated breakage of the springs, and failure of the axle-mounted steering pin.

However, the Willys offered a far superior performance to both the Bantam and the Ford, which had been delivered later that same month, and Colonel C.C. Duell, Army liaison officer at Holabird, concluded that 'the Willys engine out-classed all the others in power and produced a brilliant performance'. Despite its weight problems, the Willys, too, was approved, subject to a number of amendments, the most noticeable of which changed the shape of the body and radiator grille to more closely match the appearance of the Ford Pygmy.

After considerable indecision regarding quantities, the original plan to split the initial order for 1,500 vehicles between Willys, Bantam and Ford was abandoned. On 3 December 1940, Willys received verbal confirmation of their first production contract, which called for a total of 1,500 'Quad' reconnaissance cars, 49 of which were to be equipped with four-wheel steering. The vehicles, now re-designated 'MA' (Model, or Military A), were priced at $959 each, less 1 per cent for settlement within 10 days.

However, the QMC still considered that the Willys was overweight, and the company was under notice that future contracts would depend on their ability to reduce this to a more acceptable figure.

Ford Pygmy

Although the Ford Motor Company had been invited to bid for the Jeep project in the summer of 1940, they had been reluctant to start manufacturing small cars again, and had declined. It was not until they were approached directly in October of that year that the project was taken seriously.

Ford's engineering department reviewed the QMC specification and, on 16 October, H.M. Cunningham submitted a bid for 500 'light command and reconnaissance cars' at a price of $1,180 each, less $50 per vehicle for settlement within 30 days. The bid was subject to Ford and the QMC being able to reach agreement on variations to the weight and body details. The document suggested that Ford would deliver the prototype within 45 days of the date of 'receipt of the official award'. A second letter, also written on 16 October, stated that should the QMC require a second batch of 500 identical vehicles at the same time, the price for these would reduce to $935 each.

The following day, Ford management authorised the production of two prototype vehicles, one to be constructed at Ford's Rouge River plant at Dearborn, the other by the pressing and engineering works of the Edward Budd Manufacturing Company of Philadelphia, Pennsylvania. One of these prototypes would be put through the standard Ford testing schedule before being delivered to Holabird, while the other would be turned over to the Army as soon as it was completed. Ford was given a full specification for the vehicle, together with copies of the Bantam drawings; the company engineers having already been given the opportunity to examine the Bantam prototype. A team of engineers led by Dale Roeder started work on building the prototypes in October 1940, with Clarence Kramer responsible for the grille and elements of the body.

For the power unit, Ford's engineers specified the Model NNA engine from the company's Ferguson-designed 9N tractor. Essentially half of a Mercury V8 engine, it was a four-cylinder side-valve unit with a capacity of 1,966cc (120in^3), capable of producing 42bhp (31kW) at 3,600rpm from. The engine was coupled to the three-speed transmission from the contemporary Ford Model A car, and used the same two-speed Spicer transfer case as had been specified by both Willys and Bantam, and like the Bantam, the Ford gearshift was in the conventional position, on the floor. Both the front and rear axles included Rzeppa constant-velocity joints, even though the rear axles of these first two vehicles were not designed to steer.

Needless to say, Ford also had their own design ideas, and changes were introduced into the specification by the engineers working on the project, both to simplify production, and to introduce genuine improvements. The Ford Pygmy, as it was dubbed, most closely resembled the vehicle that we would recognise as the Jeep. As regards the body, it was Ford who first came up with the flat bonnet, which was to double as map-reading table, altar, useful storage shelf, and dining table throughout the war. It was also Ford who first used the two-piece opening and folding windscreen, and who devised the protected position for the headlights behind the grille, and the hinge arrangement which allowed the headlights to double as engine compartment inspection lights. And it was

ABOVE: View of the cockpit of the Ford Pygmy. Those bucket seats would have been a lot more effective in restraining the crew than the perches chosen for the standardised Jeep. *Warehouse Collection*

LEFT: View of the Ford Pygmy from above showing the Model NNA engine from the company's Ferguson-designed 9N tractor, the big oil-bath air cleaner and the position of the 6V battery. The design already incorporates the hinged headlights, which could be used to illuminate the engine compartment. *Warehouse Collection*

TOP: Ford-built Pygmy prototype. The vehicle looks to be totally bogged down in the mud; presumably help is on the way because the crew look completely unperturbed. *Warehouse Collection*

ABOVE: The Ford-bodied Pygmy was far more like the final form of the Jeep, lacking the curious bug-eyed headlamps of the Budd version. *Warehouse Collection*

Ford who placed the fuel tank under the driver's seat, which is where it remained on all military Jeeps until the high-mobility multipurpose wheeled vehicle (HMMWV) replaced the Jeep in the 1980s. Changes were also made to the rear seat, and to the spare tyre mounting.

The two prototypes were mounted on identical chassis and were similar in overall shape, but they differed from one another in many small ways. Most noticeably, the Budd version, which looked more like the Bantam BRC-40, did not

LEFT: The Ford-built prototype was the first of the two Pygmys to be delivered to Camp Holabird, arriving on 23 November 1940. It was put through the same trials routine as the Willys and Bantam prototypes. *Warehouse Collection*

share the Ford headlamp arrangements, and presented a taller silhouette around the engine compartment. The front wings, too, were quite different, and small details were changed such as the grab handles and reflector mountings.

The Ford-built prototype was the first of the pair to be delivered to Camp Holabird, where it arrived for testing on 23 November 1940. The vehicle was put through the same 5,000-mile (8,000km) road trial, followed by a further 5,000 miles across country as the Willys had been, with 4 drivers assigned to each vehicle to allow testing to continue 24 hours a day. The tests showed that the Ford was prone to overheating, that the transmission occasionally locked in gear, and that the exposed steering tie rod ahead of the front axle was vulnerable to tree stumps and rocks.

At the end of the test, the vehicles were stripped and inspected for wear and damage, and a test report was completed that included recommendations for remedial or re-design work. The vehicles were re-assembled and returned to Ford. As a matter of record, the chassis of the Ford vehicles was the only one of the three prototypes to survive the test without damage.

However, on 19 November, even before any testing had got underway, Ford had already received a contract for 1,500 pre-production vehicles by now designated 'GP', and nicknamed 'Blitz Buggy'. The contract price was $975 each, less $50 each for settlement within 30 days. Delivery was scheduled to begin with 400 vehicles on 10 March 1941, with completion due by 15 April, and 50 of the vehicles were to be fitted with four-wheel steering.

RIGHT: Head-on view of a preserved Ford GP showing the slightly lower profile of the bonnet, achieved through the use of the Ford NNA tractor engine. *David Doyle*

ABOVE: Official US Army postcard depicting a Ford GP during trials with the American 37mm anti-tank gun. *Warehouse Collection*

THE PRODUCTION JEEP

With the successful completion of the first phase of the project, all three companies had been asked to quote for the construction of a further 500 vehicles. However, it was obvious that this quantity would not allow Spicer, who produced the axles and transfer cases, to tool up for mass production and that this would create a bottleneck. There was some pressure from the Adjutant General's Office and from representatives of the infantry to order 1,500 vehicles from Bantam, and it was pointed out that this would not preclude 'the development of additional productive capabilities' at a later date. The infantry representative was particularly unhappy about buying vehicles from Ford and Willys 'which we have never seen, much less tested', as was the Field Artillery representative. However, while he agreed that there was some degree of urgency, the Quartermaster General, Major General E.B. Gregory, was unhappy about Bantam's ability to produce substantial numbers of vehicles and, in mid-October 1940, just when it seemed that Bantam would get the contract, the QMC decided that it would be better to divide it between the three manufacturers involved, ordering 500 vehicles from each. The Quartermaster General was authorised to negotiate with the three companies for 500 vehicles each at a unit cost of no more than $1,250.

Bantam, which was the only company to have fulfilled the terms of the original bid, was not at all happy about the inclusion of Ford and Willys and protested to the Secretary of War, arguing that they had developed the Jeep without assistance from any other automobile manufacturer. The company made it clear that it could produce 360 vehicles a day and was happy to dedicate its entire factory to producing Jeeps, and that it was more than capable of producing all of the Army's current requirements. If a situation were ever reached where Bantam was not able to produce all of the vehicles required, the company stated that it would be more than happy to turn over all the drawings and specifications and to provide every assistance to whoever else was to be involved. In the end, none of this mattered because, before the orders could be placed, the projected number of vehicles required was increased to 4,500.

By late 1940, contracts had been placed with Bantam and Willys for the supply of 1,500 Jeeps each, based on the prototype or pre-production models already supplied by the two companies, and incorporating the changes and improvements that had arisen during the trials period. The contract with Ford was not signed until early 1941 because the company was unable to agree the specification. The unit prices quoted at that time were $1,123 for Bantam, $1,581.38 from Willys-Overland, and $1,130 from Ford. The four-wheel steer vehicles were priced at about $100 more.

Deliveries of the pre-production vehicles to the US Army began in December 1940 and it was also just a matter of months before Jeeps were put into the hands of the British and Commonwealth forces fighting in North Africa.

Examples of the three machines were put through a comparative trial at Holabird. Nothing new really emerged, but the weight of opinion finally came down in favour of the Willys, due in part to its superior engine and performance, but perhaps also because of its lower price and shorter delivery timescale. However, while the Willys offered the best combination of performance and price, the QMC remained keen to exploit Ford's massive production capacity, and despite the enthusiasm for the Willys, the next contract for 16,000

TOP LEFT: Four Ford GPs, crewed by US Army infantrymen, line up in front of a similar number of White M3 armoured scout cars. *Warehouse Collection*

CENTRE LEFT: Ford GP of 1941 in service with the US Marine Corps. The twin support hoops for the top are interesting because, in theory, this feature was first seen on the standardised Willys MB of 1942 and was never used on the Ford GP. *David Doyle*

BOTTOM LEFT: Like all of the pre-standardised Jeeps, the Ford GP, which was the designation applied to the production version of the Pygmy, remains comparatively rare, especially outside the USA. *Phil Royal*

TOP RIGHT: Contract QM 10651 of 1941 called for 50 examples of the Ford GP to be fitted with four-wheel steering. Note the full-width tie bar connecting the front wheels, which differs considerably from the steering arrangements of the standardised Jeep. *Warehouse Collection*

RIGHT: Application for a patent for the Jeep was made on 8 October 1941 by Byron Q. Jones of the US Army; the application was granted on 7 April 1942. *Warehouse Collection*

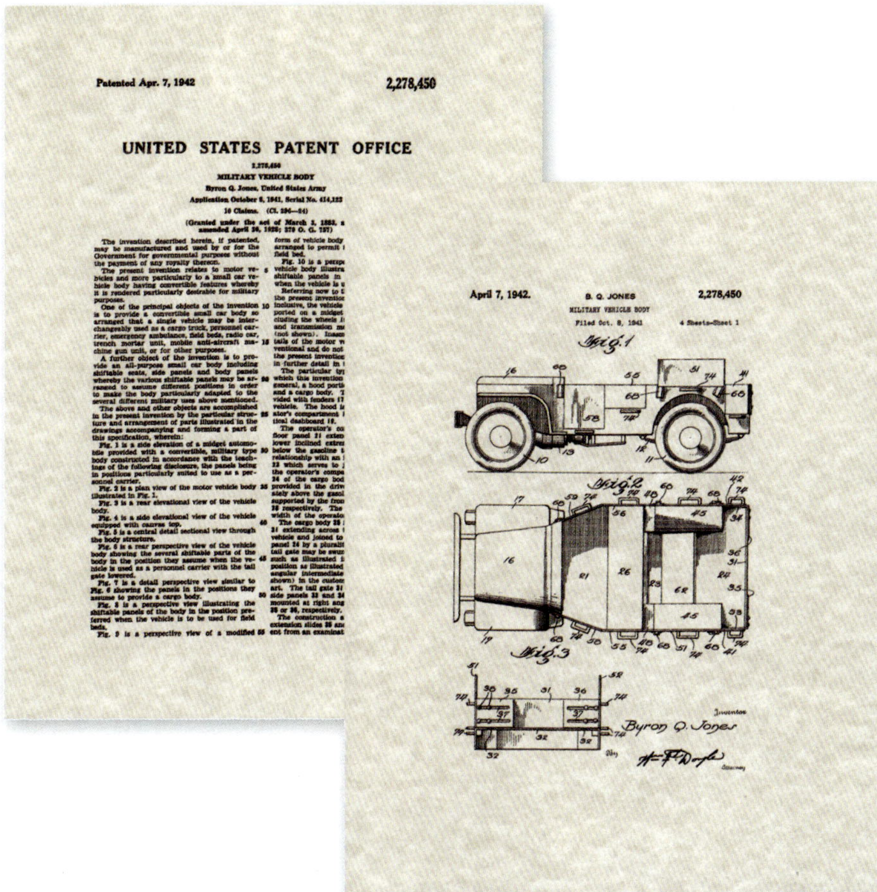
Patented Apr. 7, 1942 2,278,450

UNITED STATES PATENT OFFICE

vehicles was very nearly placed with Ford. It was only intervention from the Office of Production Management that led the QMC to reconsider, and all three manufacturers were invited to submit sealed bids. In the end, the contract went to Willys who, in July 1941, were asked to construct a total of 16,000 MA Jeeps.

The question of excessive weight was now long forgotten – some have even suggested that there was collusion in increasing the weight limit to ensure that the Ford prototype was acceptable. Whatever the truth of the matter, by February 1941, the Quartermaster General's office was openly admitting that a figure of 2,100lb (955kg) was perfectly satisfactory and that this 'provided a balance between performance, stamina and weight'.

The standardised Jeep

With the initial orders out of the way, the QMC seemed satisfied with the specification and performance of the Jeep, and with Willys as a supplier, but was keen to take whatever action might be necessary to 'standardise' the design. Representatives of the user arms and the QMC met at Holabird to discuss what further changes and improvements should be incorporated in order to produce a 'standardised' vehicle, and the QMC began to draw up a definitive specification for the next round of contracts. The revised specification (USA-LP-91-997, subsequently amended to 997A) laid down the following design parameters:

- maximum road speed, 55mph (88km/h)
- minimum speed, no more than 3mph (5km/h) at full engine torque
- approach and departure angles, 45° and 35°, respectively
- fording depth, 18in (450mm) at 3mph (5km/h)
- maximum weight, 2,100lb (953kg), or 2,175lb (989kg) with four-wheel steering
- load capacity, 800lb (363kg)
- towed load, 1,000lb (455kg).

One of the key objectives of the specification was to rationalise the range of components used across all of the standardised US military vehicles. This would reduce stockholding and simplify maintenance and repair procedures, as well as ensuring that only proven and reliable components were used. As part of this process, the QMC specified that the Jeep be fitted with a standard air filter; electrical suppression was introduced into the ignition system; the civilian generator was replaced by a standard 6V 40Ah unit, which was already in use on a number of other military vehicles; and the civilian battery was replaced by a standard 2-H military type. The wiring and lighting equipment were also modified to comply with the then-current military standard, and the civilian instruments were replaced by standard military items. Other changes included the use of split-rim combat-type wheels, and the inclusion of a jerrycan holder and 'pioneer' tools. At the same time as the jerrycan holder was introduced, the practice of allowing the manufacturer to press his name into the back panel was discontinued.

Other changes were made to improve the performance and comfort of the vehicle, or to reduce manufacturing costs. For example, the steering gear was raised as high as possible above the axle to prevent damage. A second hoop was added to the hood frame to provide more headroom; the dash-mounted handbrake was moved to the centre of the vehicle; and the fabricated slatted radiator guard was replaced by a simpler pressed-metal version. Once the vehicle was standardised, further change was more or less ruled out, and only minor revisions were made to the vehicle. The most significant subsequent change came in late 1945, when the engine timing chain was replaced by a gear train, and the handbrake arrangements were modified.

The standardised Jeep, as produced by Willys-Overland, was designated 'MB' (military, model B) to differentiate it from the earlier 'MA' (military, model A).

Production

By October 1941, it was apparent that the demand for Jeeps was such that Willys could not hope to keep up, and there was also a fear that sabotage or accident might halt production at the Willys plant. The QMC started to examine the possibility of involving a second manufacturer and since both Bantam and Ford had already built versions of the pre-standardised vehicle, they would have seemed the obvious choice. For some reason, the QMC seemed to be determined that Bantam should not be further involved in the Jeep project. Quite why

ABOVE: The standardised Jeep appeared in 1941 in the form of the Willys MB. By October that year it was apparent that the demand for Jeeps was such that Willys could not hope to keep up. Willys agreed to turn over copies of their drawings to the Ford Motor Company and Ford became the second supplier, designating their Jeep GPW (GP Willys). This example was photographed in September 1943. *David Doyle*

RIGHT: Press Corps Jeep nicknamed 'Blue Eyes'. *Warehouse Collection*

LEFT: The easiest way to tell the Ford and the Willys apart is by the shape of the radiator cross member: on the Ford it is an inverted U section, while on the Willys and the Hotchkiss it is a circular section. The one-piece wheels suggest that this could be a Hotchkiss M201, dressed as a Second World War American vehicle. *Phil Royal*

this was the case remains something of a mystery, but the company never built a single example of the standardised Jeep.

Negotiations were re-opened with Ford, and a meeting took place between the Quartermaster General, E.B. Gregory, and no less than Edsel Ford himself at which Ford agreed that the company would manufacture Jeeps to the designs prepared by Willys, with every part interchangeable. For their part, Willys agreed to turn over copies of their manufacturing drawings to Ford, without payment, providing Ford Jeeps were sold only to the US Government. On 10 November 1941, the Ford Motor Company was awarded a $14.6 million contract to construct a further 15,000 Jeeps, designated 'GPW' (GP Willys), with the vehicle entering production in February 1942.

Although to all intents and purposes the vehicles produced by Willys and Ford were identical, with all major assemblies interchangeable, in reality, Ford made many minor changes to suit their mass-production methods and the *cognoscenti* have always been able to tell the difference between the products of the two manufacturers.

In August 1942, responsibility for the Jeep, and for all US military vehicles, was transferred from the Quartermaster Corps to the Ordnance Department. Production of the Jeep continued throughout the war and between 1941 and 1945,

ABOVE LEFT: The first 25,808 examples of the Willys MB constructed used this welded slat grille rather than the familiar pressed grille with its distinctive slots. *Phil Royal*

ABOVE RIGHT: Glowing slightly in the evening light this Grey US Navy Jeep shows that Jeeps don't have to be painted in the ubiquitous Olive Green. *Simon Thomson*

LEFT: A still taken from a US Army training aid showing the Jeep's hill-climbing ability. Note the lack of jerrycan holder on this early example. *Warehouse Collection*

BELOW: Replica of a flame-thrower Jeep as used by Popski's Private Army. The flame-thrower was apparently the Allied weapon most feared by German soldiers. *Phil Royal*

RIGHT: Photographed at the British Wheeled Vehicles Experimental Establishment (WVEE), this Jeep is one of 2,000 Ford GPWs supplied under contract SM 2275 in 1941; note the lack of a spare tyre. *IWM, MVEE 9919/1*

Ford's total contribution was believed to be 277,896 GPW Jeeps, with production taking place at five separate plants across the USA, while Willys built a total of 361,349 at their Toledo plant.

There is no doubt that the Jeep was a true original. There had never been anything like it before and the Jeep was largely responsible for the full-scale mechanisation of the Allied armies. Every similar vehicle that has followed has borrowed heavily from the basic design philosophy laid down by the engineers at the American Bantam Company in spring 1940. The truck replaced both the horse and, in many cases, the motorcycle, and provided mobility to the infantryman, which had been impossible a decade earlier. By the end of the Second World War, the vehicle had been used by all of the Allies in every theatre of that worldwide conflict and had proved itself to be reliable, versatile and virtually unstoppable.

No less an authority than General Dwight D. Eisenhower went on record with the view that 'the Jeep, the Dakota and the landing craft were the three tools that won the war'. George C. Marshall, the US Chief of Staff and a man described by Winston Churchill as the 'organiser of victory', clearly shared this view, describing the Jeep as 'America's main contribution to modern war'.

CENTRE RIGHT: British Army Jeep of 21st Army Group, entering the Netherlands as the liberating troops pass through a village on the way to Nijmegen in August 1944. Note the jerrycan carried on the front bumper. *IWM, B10132*

RIGHT: A convoy of Jeeps passes down a flooded road in Cully, Normandy, in July 1944. The two lead Jeeps have jerrycans strapped to the bonnet. *IWM, B7868*

Differences between Ford and Willys Jeeps

Ford	Willys
'F' script on axle shafts	-
'F' script stamped into shock-absorber mounts	-
'F' script on other brackets and small parts	-
11 segments to bonnet hinge	Nine segments to bonnet hinge
Angled ends to rear-seat footrests	Welded saddle clips to rear-seat footrests
'Ford' pressed into rear body panel*	'Willys' pressed into rear body panel*
Pressings in tool box lids	Plain toolbox lids
Rounded toe board gussets with three holes	Angular toe board gussets with five holes
Square impression for toolbox latch	Round impression for toolbox latch
Three holes in bumper	Single hole in front bumper
Use of numerous 'F' script bolts	-
U-shaped radiator cross member	Tubular radiator cross member

*Discontinued from mid-1942

FORD GPA AMPHIBIAN

The story of the Jeep would not be complete without some mention of the amphibious version – sometimes described as a 'Seep', or 'sea Jeep' – which, in the US Army's words, was intended 'to transport personnel on land and water'. It was envisaged that this small amphibian would be useful as a cargo or reconnaissance vehicle in areas where the enemy had destroyed river crossings.

In March 1941, the Motor Transport Board recommended to the National Defense Research Committee (NDRC) that development work be initiated for a ¼-ton amphibious reconnaissance car, based on the engine and running gear of the Jeep. The vehicle was described in specification MCM26, and a research project was opened on 17 April 1941 under the designation QMC-4 'Truck, light, 4 x 4, amphibian'. The design work was undertaken by the naval architects Sparkman & Stephens of New York, who had been responsible for the successful design of the GMC DUKW, with Marmon-Herrington undertaking the prototype work. Jeeps for conversion, together with whatever additional components might be required, were supplied by the Ford Motor Company.

BELOW: Ford GPA photographed after leaving a landing craft, tank (LCT). *The Tank Museum*

ABOVE: Constant immersion in water has inevitably taken its toll on the almost 13,000 Ford GPA amphibians that were constructed during 1942 and 1943, and survivors are rare. *Warehouse Collection*

At the time that the project was initiated, the first Jeeps from each of the suppliers had not been delivered and, based on the performance of the pilot models, the Motor Transport Board felt that the Willys MA might provide the most suitable basis for the amphibian although, in the event, the GPW was used and Ford received the production contract. Three alternative hull designs were proposed by Sparkman & Stephens, and scale models suggested that the vehicle would be able to travel at about 7½mph (12km/h) in the water. In August, a full-size hull was tank-tested at Hoboken, New Jersey. There was some delay in receiving the vehicles from Ford for conversion, and the design work proceeded on the assumption that the net weight of the vehicle would not exceed about 2,640lb (1,200kg). However, this was a considerable underestimate and had a serious effect on the performance of the finished amphibian.

The first of four full-size prototypes was ready for testing in February 1942, and the NDRC arranged a test on the River Huron at Dearborn, Michigan for 18 February. The test was considered to be a success and the various user arms began to express an interest in receiving quantities of the vehicle. Further tests were conducted in the Atlantic at Fort Storey, Virginia, in late March, which indicated that the vehicle would perform well in medium surf.

Meanwhile, under the direction of F.G. Kerby and C.L. Kramer, Ford had set up a manufacturing line and were pressing for a production commitment, indicating that if there was too much delay the available capacity would be reassigned. A verbal order was placed on 10 April 1942 for 5,000 vehicles and the official contract, which followed later, increased this to 7,896 units. Even though the testing phase was not complete, production was expected to start in August. The production vehicles, which were designated GPA (general purpose, amphibian), weighed some 1,100 lb (500kg) more than the standard Jeep and, as a result, the maximum road speed was reduced to 50mph (80km/h), with the speed in water being just 5mph (8km/h).

The engine, transmission and axles were identical to the standard Jeep, although an extra leaf was added to each road spring to help carry the additional weight. A propeller, driven via the transfer case, was provided for propulsion, and steering in the water was by means of a rudder. Unlike the standard Jeeps, which were fitted with a 6V electrical system, the GPA was wired for 12V.

Although the wheelbase had been extended by 4in (100mm), the GPA was very small and, with an effective freeboard of just 9½–17in (240–430mm) front to rear, its uses were very limited.

Production started in September 1942, and the vehicle was standardised on 23 October 1942. The total number produced was 12,778, under three separate contracts. Most of the vehicles had been delivered by the time useful feedback started to come in from users and, although a number of minor changes were put in hand, production was finally terminated on 30 June 1943. The Tank Automotive Center wrote that 'production of further quantities of this vehicle, in addition to the contracts recently completed, is not contemplated, pending review of requirements and reports of field performance'.

ABOVE: The Soviets were enthusiastic users of the amphibious GPW and even constructed their own version in the post-war years. These Red Army GPAs were photographed in 1945. *Warehouse Collection*

LEFT: Photographed in March 1943, these Ford GPA amphibians are undergoing trials on the River Huron at Dearborn, Michigan. *Warehouse Collection*

DESIGN PARENTAGE AND 'THAT' NAME

With so many individuals and organisations involved in the Jeep, it is not easy to allocate credit to the appropriate quarters. While there is little doubt that Karl Probst was a key figure in the design of the vehicle, he was ably assisted by a team at American Bantam. However, one other name is also associated with the project and, although employed by neither Bantam nor Willys, Colonel Byron Q. Jones of the US Army filed an application as 'inventor' with the US Patent Office (No 414.123) in October 1941. The application covered various aspects of the design and construction of the Jeep body and it was stated that 'if granted', the patent would allow the 'invention to be manufactured and used by or for the Government for governmental purposes without the payment of any royalty'. The patent was granted on 7 April 1942.

However, Willys-Overland remained keen to claim much of the honour for itself.

After the QMC had selected the Willys Jeep as the definitive version, Willys began to suggest in advertising that it was they who, in collaboration with the QMC, had designed the vehicle, boasting of the 'engineering skill and creative minds' of the Willys engineers. Wartime advertisements spoke of the pride that Willys bore for the 'engineers who assisted the US Quartermaster Corps in designing the Jeep', and of the 'fine staff of civilian engineers who, in close co-operation with the US Quartermaster Corps, created and perfected this indispensable unit'. As time went on, these claims became increasingly shameless, and when normal advertising resumed after the war, Willys started to market civilian vehicles under the name Jeep in 1945, continuing to claim that they had been the creators and designers of the concept.

At this time, Bantam had not abandoned plans to start marketing motorcars again, and taking exception to Willys' claims, in 1947, Bantam appealed to the US Federal Trade Commission. The Commission agreed with Bantam and filed a complaint against Willys, charging that they did not 'create and perfect' the Jeep, and that, anyway the vehicle was not the product of one manufacturer. In some 3,500 pages of evidence, the Commission stated that 'the idea of creating the Jeep was originated by the American Bantam Car Company of Butler, Pennsylvania, in collaboration with certain officers of the United States Army, and the same was developed by the American Bantam Car Company in collaboration with said officers, and not by the respondent, Willys-Overland Motors Inc'.

Willys was accused of unfair competition and misleading publicity, and was ordered to cease and desist in its claims. On 27 February 1948, the Commission issued a restraining order against Willys, forbidding the company from representing directly, or by implication, that it created or designed the Jeep. With its knuckles firmly rapped, Willys was allowed only to claim that it had participated in, and contributed to the development of the vehicle although the company did register 'Jeep' as a trademark in 1950.

Bantam probably never received proper recognition for its contribution to the development of the Jeep and, within five years, was effectively bankrupt, later being absorbed into American Rolling Mills.

As for the name itself, we may never know its true origins and, despite being initially described as a 'peep', 'bug', and 'Blitz Buggy', it was the name 'Jeep' that stuck.

The first use of the word 'Jeep' for a motor vehicle can be traced back to the First World War, and the name had also been used for a small tractor made by Minneapolis-Moline in the mid-1930s. In his history of the development of the vehicle written for the Army's *Quartermaster Review* in 1941, Major E.P. Hogan claimed that the word 'Jeep' was a military term used by shop mechanics in referring to any new motor vehicle received for a test – and it was certainly applied to various military vehicles during the 1930s. Irving 'Red' Hausmann, who was test driver at Willys-Overland, is also credited with describing the machine as a 'Jeep', similarly in the knowledge that this was not an original name. In fact, it may well be down to Hausmann that the name stuck. In early 1941, Willys staged a press event in Washington DC, in which the Quad prototype was driven up the steps of the Capitol. Hausmann gave a demonstration ride to a group of dignitaries, including Katherine Hillyer, a reporter from the *Washington Daily News*. When Hillyer asked 'what do you call this vehicle?', Hausmann replied that it was 'a Jeep'. Hillyer's article, which appeared on 20 February 1941, included a photograph showing US Senators Meade and Thomas in the Quad mounting the Capitol steps. The caption described the vehicles as 'Jeeps'.

It seems that all of the theories that attach the name to the military ¼-ton 4 x 4 can probably be discounted, including the notion that 'Jeep' was somehow a contraction of 'GP' which, in turn, stood for 'Governmental Purpose' or 'General Purpose' – and even the notion that the vehicle was named after the magical dog 'Eugene the Jeep' in a 1936 *Popeye* cartoon.

In the years that have subsequently passed the name 'Jeep' has come to be associated with just one type of vehicle, and with the Willys company and its successors. As the *Toledo Blade* newspaper once said, 'Jeep is to Toledo what cheese is to Wisconsin, what potatoes are to Idaho... what sunshine is to Florida'. The name is currently the property of Fiat-Chrysler Automobiles (FAC), which owns over 1,100 Jeep trademark registrations throughout the world.

MANUFACTURING PLANTS

The American Bantam plant was located at Hansen Avenue, Butler, Pennsylvania, and all of the Bantam Jeeps were constructed at this location. The factory building still exists and is marked by a commemorative plaque placed there by the Pennsylvania Historical and Museum Commission.

Willys vehicles were assembled at the Parkway Annex of the company's Toledo complex in Ohio. Originally constructed as a cycle factory in 1904, the plant was first used for the construction of motor vehicles when it was purchased by Willys-Overland in 1910. Jeeps continued to be constructed at this site by Willys-Overland, and the company's successors, until it was demolished in 2006.

BELOW: Ford Jeeps were assembled at six of the company's factories. Although the largest number were produced at Louisville, Kentucky, the plant in Richmond, California (seen here) was responsible for building 30,078 vehicles of the total 277,896. *Ford Motor Company*

ABOVE: Jeep production line at one of the Ford plants. The photograph was taken in 1942. *Warehouse Collection*

LEFT: Reassembly of imported US vehicles was originally under the control of the British Ministry of Supply, but in August 1943, the US Army set up their own assembly facilities using military personnel. General Depot 25 (G-25) at Ashchurch, near Cheltenham, was among the largest of these facilities. Here, Jeeps and other vehicles were uncrated, assembled and readied for issue. *Warehouse Collection*

TOP RIGHT: All of the Willys Jeeps were assembled at the Parkway Annex of the company's Toledo complex in Ohio. The plant had originally been constructed as a cycle factory in 1904, and was first used to build motor vehicles when it was purchased by Willys-Overland in 1910. *Warehouse Collection*

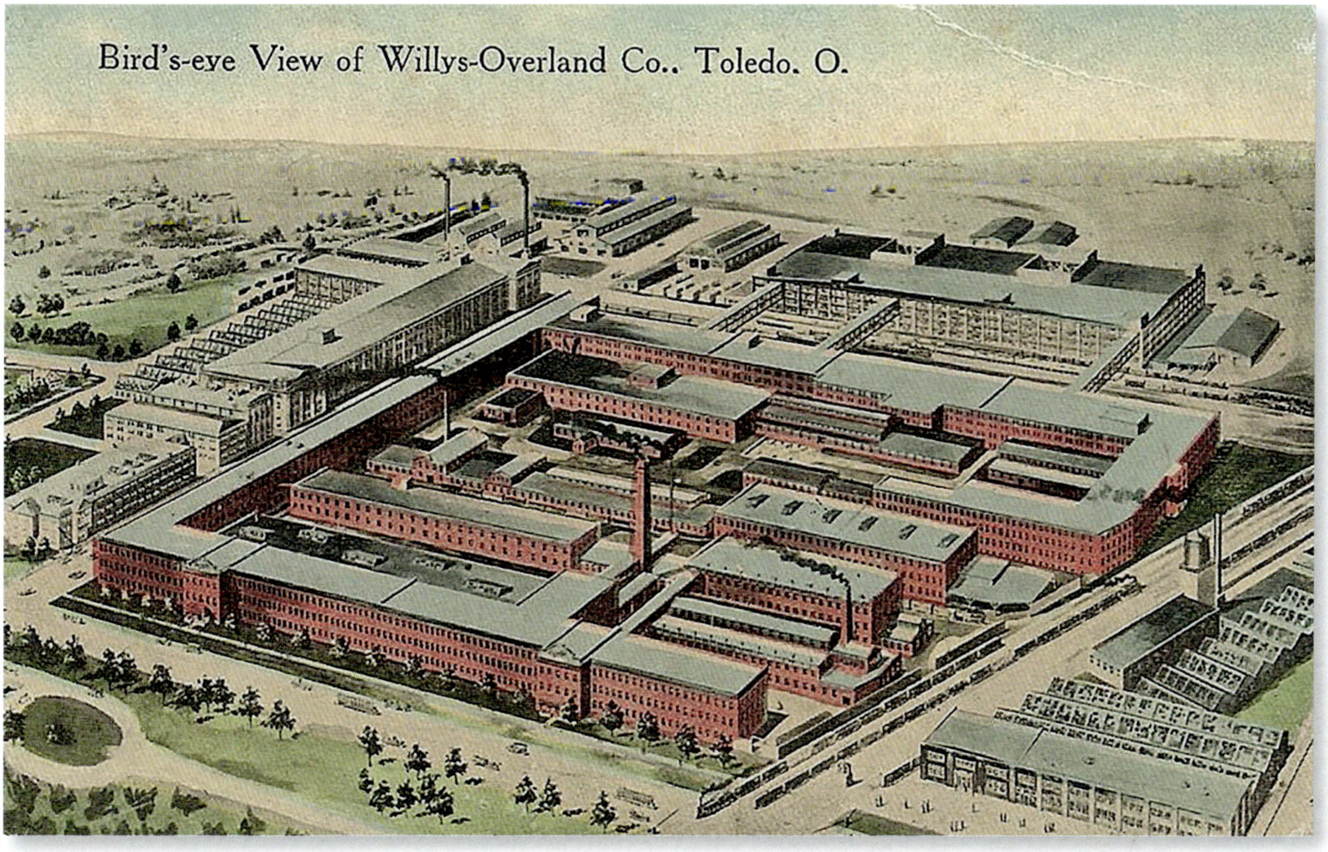

In order to undertake production, Ford was authorised by the US Government to spend up to $5 million for equipment and materials, with retooling costs agreed at a maximum of $2.1 million (although in the end the total for retooling was close to $4 million). The largest number of Ford Jeeps was assembled at Louisville, Kentucky, but production of the GPW was shared between six factories, as listed below:

- Chester, Pennsylvania: 20,573 vehicles, under contracts WM-398-QM-10977, W-398-QM-11424, and W-374-ORD-2798
- Dallas, Texas: 36,474 vehicles, under contracts WM-398-QM-10977, W-398-QM-11424, W-374-ORD-2798 and W-374-ORD-2862
- Dearborn, Michigan: 39,983 vehicles, under contracts WM-398-QM-10977, W-398-QM-11424, and W-374-ORD-2862
- Edgewater, New Jersey: 1338 vehicles, under contracts W-374-ORD-2798 and W-374-ORD-2862
- Louisville, Kentucky: 51,312 vehicles, under contracts WM-398-QM-10977, W-398-QM-11424, W-374-ORD-2798 and W-374-ORD-2862
- Richmond, California: 30,078 vehicles, under contracts WM-398-QM-10977, W-398-QM-11424, W-374-ORD-2798 and W-374-ORD-2862.

Both Ford and Willys chassis frames were made by Midland Steel, albeit with detail differences. Willys bodies were produced by the Auburn Central Manufacturing Corporation of Connersville, Indiana. Willys placed the first contract, for 1,600 bodies, with Auburn on 10 March 1941, and the first body was shipped just 41 days later. In March 1942, Auburn Central changed its name to American Central Manufacturing (ACM) and by the end of June 1943 the company had produced 150,000 Jeep bodies. Ford bodies were originally supplied by Budd until October 1941, when they were produced in-house at the Lincoln plant. From about October 1943, ACM also supplied bodies to Ford. Those bodies supplied by ACM after November 1943 differed in many small ways from the original ACM-built Willys bodies and are generally described as 'composite bodies'.

Production quantities

The generally accepted total number of standardised MB/GPW Jeeps built is 639,245. Of these, the Ford Motor Company produced 277,896, while the most commonly quoted figure for Willys MB production is 361,349. Neither figure can be arrived at by adding the totals of the known contracts, but Ford themselves have stated in archive data that there are other, 'minor' contracts and the same may well have been true for Willys.

Contracts

The American Quartermaster Corps (QMC) initially had responsibility for vehicle procurement and placed contracts directly with the three manufacturers concerned. In late 1941 or early 1942, responsibility passed to the Ordnance Corps. During the same period, the British Ministry of Supply placed ten contracts directly with the manufacturers, and was also supplied with some 4,000 vehicles via two of the American QMC contracts. In addition, there were two British contracts for Ford GPA amphibious vehicles.

List of US Quartermaster and Ordnance contracts

Contract number	Model	Date	Quantity	Registration numbers
American Bantam				
QM 8269	BRC-60	1941	62	USA W 2015324-2015385
QM 8269	BRC-60, 4WS	1941	8	USA W 2015386-2015393
QM 8886	BRC-40	1941	1,350	USA W 2015919-2017268
QM 10263	BRC-40	1941	22	USA W 2030494-2030515
QM 10395	BRC-40, 4WS	1941	50	USA W 2029179-2029228
Ford Motor Company				
QM 8887	GP	1941	1,500	USA W 2017422-2018921
QM 10262	GP	1941	966	USA W 2029494-2030459
QM 10262	GP	1941	33	*for Brazil*
QM 27	GP	1941	1,150	*for China*
QM 10651	GP, 4WS	1941	50	USA W 234075-234124
QM 12937	GPA	1942	10,000	USA 702104-7012103
QM 12937	GPA	1942	2,774	USA 7012105-7014873
ORD 2782	GPA	1943	2,014	USA 7010000-7012013
QM 10977	GPW	1942	15,000	USA 2054778-2069777
QM 11424	GPW	1942	60,823	USA 20100000-20160822
QM 11424	GPW	1942	8	USA 20160824-20160831
QM 11424	GPW	1942	3	USA 20160833-20160835
QM 11424	GPW	1942	3	USA 20160839-20160841
QM 11424	GPW	1942	6	USA 20160846-20160851
QM 11424	GPW	1942	1,641	USA 20161445-20163085
QM 11424	GPW	1942	653	*for US Navy, numbers not known*
QM 11424	GPW	1942	9	*numbers not assigned*
QM 13538	GPW	1942	2,799	USA 20185869-20188667
QM 13538	GPW	1942	18,931	USA 20188669-20207599
QM 13538	GPW	1942	219	USA 20207601-20207819
QM 13538	GPW	1942	49	USA 20207821-20207869
QM 13538	GPW	1942	2	USA 20207871, 2098850
QM 13538	GPW	1942	10	USA 20260783-20260792
QM 13538	GPW	1942	4	USA 20207873-20207876
QM 13538	GPW	1942	2	USA 20207878-20207879
QM 13538	GPW	1942	3	USA 20207881-20207883
QM 13538	GPW	1942	5	USA 20207885-20207889
QM 13538	GPW	1942	100	USA 20207891-20207990
QM 13538	GPW	1942	1,025	USA 20207992-20209016
QM 13538	GPW	1942	2	USA 20160823, 20160832
QM 13538	GPW	1942	3	USA 20160836-20160838
QM 13538	GPW	1942	4	USA 20160842-20160845
ORD W-648	GPW	1943	78,454	USA 20364863-20443316
not known	GPW	1943	1	USA 2097102
not known	GPW	1944	46,447	USA 20512064-20558510
not known	GPW	1944	26,536	USA 20577981-20604516
not known	GPW	1945	17,958	USA 20722020-20739977
not known	GPW	1945	3,304	USA 20741597-20744900
not known	GPW	1945	2,463	USA 20746497-20748959
not known	GPW	1945	1,412	USA 20749897-20751308
Willys-Overland				
QM 8888	MA	1941	1,500	USA W 2018932-2020431
QM 10757	MB	1942	16,000	USA W 2031575-2047574
QM 10757	MB	1942	2,600	USA W 2047614-2050213
QM 11423	MB	1942	5,101	USA 2073506-2078606
QM 11423	MB	1942	5,106	USA 2078697-2083803
QM 11423	MB	1942	47,060	USA 20209017-20256076
QM 11423	MB	1942	4,927	USA 2083804-2088730
QM 11423	MB	1942	4,706	*numbers not assigned*
ORD W-650	MB	1943	66,237	USA 20298626-20364862
ORD W-650	MB	1943	15,650	USA 20443317-20458966
not known	MB	1943	45,000	USA 20467064-20512063
not known	MB	1943	8,812	USA 20561624-20570435
not known	MB	1944	58,684	USA 20604517-20663200

List of British Ministry of Supply contracts

Many of the vehicles supplied under these contracts were also covered by US QMC contracts

Contract number	Model	Date	Quantity	Registration numbers
American Bantam				
SM 2262	BRC-40	1941	1	M4589425
SM 2262	BRC-40	1941	1,000	M4611718-4612717
SM 2099	BRC-40	1943	150	originally for Yugoslavia, numbers not known
Ford Motor Company				
SM 2324	GP	1941	270	numbers not known
SM 2275	GPW	1941	2,855	M5473073-5475927
SM 2275	GPW	1941	654	M5557518-5558171
SM 2275	GPW	1941	1,798	M5571048-5572845
SM 2275	GPW	1941	1,000	M5583414-5584413
SM 2275	GPW	1941	1,500	M5825890-5827389
SM 2275	GPW	1941	1,614	M5844127-5845740
SM 2275	GPW	1941	2,000	M6181796-6183795
SM 2275	GPW	1941	1,000	M6269725-6270724
SM 2275	GPW reconditioned	1941	5,000	M6133340-6138339
SM 2621	GPA	1942	4	numbers not known
SM 2820	GPA	1943	185	P5219692-5219876
SM 2820	GPA	1943	101	P5219881-5219981
SM 2820	GPA	1943	100	P5587101-5587200
BM 5485	GPW	1944	93	M5558376-5559875*
Willys-Overland				
SM 2275	MB	1941	3,110	M4768471-4771580
SM 2275	MB	1941	1,200	M5220001-5221200
SM 2275	MB	1941	5,560	M5534138-5539697
SM 2275	MB reconditioned	1941	5,000	M6128340-6133339
SM 2275	MB	1942	2,000	M4921997-4923996
SM 2402	MB	1943	270	numbers not known
BM 5485	MB	1944	1,407	M5558376-5559875*

Note: *Allocation of these numbers between the Ford and Willys vehicles is not available.

CRATING FOR EXPORT

During the early years of the Second World War, Jeeps were shipped to Britain on their wheels, sometimes stacked in pairs, and sometimes packed in wooden cases. Losses on the Atlantic convoys began to put pressure on shipping space and, by 1943, most vehicles coming from the USA were broken down after production, and packed in crates.

Considerable research went into devising the most effective ways of packing and eventually a four-tier system evolved, with packs described as alpha, or 'single unit packs' (SUPs); beta, 'twin unit packs' (TUPs); gama, and delta, both of which were described as 'multi-unit packs' (MUPs). Being relatively compact, Jeeps were carried in alpha packs, with one vehicle per case; the gross weight of the complete pack was about 3,300lb (1,500kg). The windscreen and wheels were removed and packed inside the body, with the spare wheel carried ahead of the radiator. Small fittings such as the body handles, spare wheel bracket, bumpers etc, were packed under the body; the hood frame was strapped to the front bumper and stowed under the front wheel arches; and the steering wheel, top and upholstery were carried inside the body.

Once the crated vehicles arrived in Britain, they needed to be reassembled. Prior to July 1942, this work was carried out by

ABOVE: Hundreds of newly-built Jeeps parked on the roof of the Willys-Overland plant. The spare wheels are stowed inside the body to save space. *Warehouse Collection*

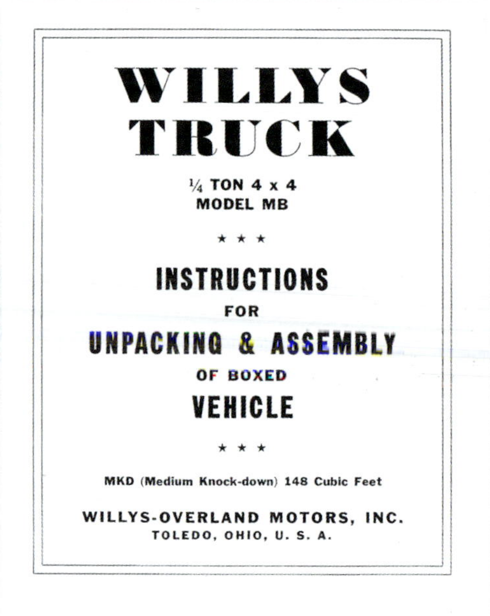

WILLYS TRUCK

¼ TON 4 x 4
MODEL MB

* * *

INSTRUCTIONS
FOR
UNPACKING & ASSEMBLY
OF BOXED
VEHICLE

* * *

MKD (Medium Knock-down) 148 Cubic Feet

WILLYS-OVERLAND MOTORS, INC.
TOLEDO, OHIO, U. S. A.

ABOVE LEFT: Jeeps were crated for export using so-called alpha, or single unit packs (SUPs), each crate containing a complete vehicle in medium knocked-down condition, with the wheels and windscreen removed and packed inside the body. The spare wheel was carried ahead of the radiator and many of the smaller components were packed inside the body. *David Doyle*

ABOVE RIGHT: Assembly instructions for the Willys MB; a similar document was produced by the Ford Motor Company. *Warehouse Collection*

civilian contractors engaged by the Ministry of Supply on behalf of the British and Canadian Armies. Early in 1942, Section TT2 (Tanks and Transport) of the Ministry of Supply was requested by the US Army to expand the assembly facilities to also cover their requirements. Under the codename 'Tilefer', the number of assembly plants was increased from 12 to 26 but, later that year, when the numbers of vehicles arriving failed to meet the original estimates, the number of plants was reduced to 14. However, by May 1943, the number of British assembly plants had increased to 39, with some 10,000 operatives assembling vehicles as diverse as Jeeps, DUKWs and tank transporters.

It was not always easy to find suitable facilities, and the Ministry began contracting the work to all kinds of organisations, often requisitioning premises and contracting the work to companies who had no previous experience, but who were able to offer the right combination of manpower and accommodation. Among others, assembly was undertaken by a football pools company, a soap manufacturer, a corrugated-iron producer, a tube company, and an iron and steel producer. As regards Jeeps, much of the reassembly work for vehicles supplied under contract SM 2275 was undertaken by N.W. Nash & Company of Cardiff, while the Bantams supplied under contract SM 2262 were reassembled by Pearsons Garage of Liverpool, and Alexanders of Edinburgh (based in Glasgow!).

Despite the fact that 436,170 vehicles of all types were assembled between 1940 and the end of 1944, the Americans felt that the productivity was not adequate for the numbers of vehicles required in the build-up to the invasion. In August 1943, the US Army set up their own assembly facilities, using military personnel to do the work. The largest US assembly site in Britain was General Depot 25 (G-25) at Ashchurch, near Cheltenham, where Jeeps and other vehicles were uncrated, assembled and readied for distribution to storage depots. Other depots were based around the country, always close to the ports where the vehicles arrived.

The assembly of a Jeep consisted of little more than unpacking the components and bolting them together, adding vital fluids, running the engine up for a short test, and touching-up the paintwork, before inspecting for damage and leakages. All timber packing was carefully salvaged.

RECONDITIONING

Like most military activities, the maintenance procedures for motor vehicles are well documented. In the US Army, for example, maintenance tasks are categorised at five levels, or 'echelons'. As a matter of course, all Jeeps were subject to this organised system of maintenance.

First echelon maintenance covers the simple daily and weekly tasks carried out by the driver to keep a vehicle in good working order. Second echelon work is also preventive maintenance, but requires a vehicle mechanic and often involves slightly more complex equipment. Third echelon maintenance includes major repairs and the rebuilding or replacement of unit assemblies; while at the fourth echelon, a badly-damaged vehicle might be dismantled to provide donor parts to keep other vehicles running. Finally, fifth echelon maintenance covers the total disassembly of a truck down to its basic components, followed by rebuilding using new or reconditioned parts as appropriate.

During the Second World War, the US Army rebuilt Jeeps at Army workshops, both at home and in the overseas theatres, as well as subcontracting the work to civilian companies. During any rebuilding process, no regard was paid to the source of the components used and, inevitably, Jeeps were rebuilt with a mix of Ford and Willys components, as well as sometimes using parts of British or French origin. After the war, many US Army Jeeps were rebuilt in the US Army facility at Esslingen in Germany. From about 1951, many rebuilt Jeeps were fitted with a modified version of the CJ3A Universal Jeep engine, which was developed by Willys as a replacement for the original.

Similar maintenance and rebuilding systems existed in other European armies. For example, fifth echelon maintenance in the British Army is described as a 'base overhaul' and, as they aged, Jeeps in service with the British Army were rebuilt either by the workshops of the Royal Electrical and Mechanical Engineers (REME) or, between 1939 and 1945, often by a civilian contract workshop. These civilian workshops, which were under contract to the Ministry of Supply, were known as Army Auxiliary Workshops and many had been commercial garages during the pre-war period.

Any rebuilt Jeep will generally be identified by a data plate that states where the work was carried out and when.

EXPERIMENTS AND FURTHER DEVELOPMENTS

Armoured Jeeps

To suit its intended role as a reconnaissance vehicle, it would have been natural to provide the Jeep with some form of armoured protection against small-arms fire and the first experiments in this direction came from the Smart Safety Engineering Corporation of Detroit, Michigan, who specialised in armoured bullion vans and armoured limousines. In November 1941, Smart demonstrated an armoured Willys MA to the US Armored Board at Aberdeen Proving Ground, Maryland. The vehicle had 6mm armoured steel replacing the bonnet, radiator grille, and windscreen, and was fitted with armoured doors but, unfortunately, the weight proved to be too much for the standard chassis and suspension.

Although the vehicle was not a success, the British still believed that it had possibilities, and placed an order for armoured Jeeps

RIGHT: Produced in late 1942 by the Smart Safety Engineering Corporation of Detroit, the T5E1 armoured Jeep incorporated a full-height armoured body sloping towards the rear. *Warehouse Collection*

BELOW: Later versions of the armoured Jeep were designated T25E2 and T25E3. The T5E3, seen here in mid-1943, had an extended wheelbase which, together with the weight of the armoured body, added some 1,200lb (545kg) to the weight of the vehicle. *Warehouse Collection*

ABOVE: This standard Jeep has been fitted with a makeshift armoured body and a protective plate for the radiator. *The Tank Museum*

in the very same month that the trials were initiated. The order was later cancelled when it became obvious that it was not possible to produce an armoured version without compromising production of the standard vehicle.

Smart took the vehicle away and reduced the weight, returning with a second prototype, officially designated T25, in June 1942. Later that same year, a third version, known as T25E1, was produced with a full-height armoured body sloping towards the rear. Fourth and fifth versions, designated T25E2 and T25E3, were produced on an MB chassis, which had a complete armoured body, intended to protect the crew of three. None was successful simply because the chassis and power train were unable to cope with the increased weight, which by the fourth and fifth versions, weighed an additional 1,200lb (545kg) or more.

There were no more official armoured Jeeps, but many attempts were made to fit appliqué armour in the field.

ABOVE: The Willys MT-Tug was an attempt to produce a ¾-ton 6 x 6 vehicle using as many Jeep components as possible; this example was subsequently upgraded to give a 1-ton capacity. Several examples of the chassis were constructed, but the vehicle never went into series production. *Warehouse Collection*

Willys MT-Tug

In 1942, Willy-Overland constructed a ¾-ton 6 x 6 vehicle, which was designed to use as many components of the Jeep as possible. Designated as the MT-Tug, at least 24 examples were built, including an ambulance, and it was comprehensively tested before being rejected as impractical. Six examples were tested with the 37mm anti-tank gun mounted in the rear bed, and the same chassis was also used as the basis for the T24 armoured scout car with bodywork by the Smart Safety Engineering Corporation.

ABOVE: Although at least one genuine MT-Tug has survived and has been restored, this replica equipped as an ambulance looks the part, but lacks the additional width of the genuine article beyond the scuttle. *Simon Thomson*

Long-wheelbase Jeeps

Other experimental models included the MLW-4, a 4 x 4 chassis with a 92in (2,337mm) wheelbase and oversize tyres, and with larger load-carrying area designed to carry a 1,100lb (500kg) load; two versions were produced with different axle and wheel configurations. One of these was supplied to Britain.

During the Second World War, several examples of standard Jeeps were produced that had been increased in length by letting an additional section into the chassis and body between the front and rear seats, with the average wheelbase stretch something like 30–39in (750–1,000mm). The best known is probably that produced by, or for, the US Coast Guard for shore patrol work, but others were used by the US 9th Army, the 5th Armored Division, the 15th Air Force and others. The Coast Guard version had seating for 10 men, others used different seating configurations, carrying a total of 6, 8, or even 11 passengers.

Half-tracked Jeeps

Experimental half-track Jeeps were produced in several versions during 1942–43. The first was the T28, a lengthened Jeep fitted with a Bombardier or Chase flexible track drive at the rear, and designed to carry two stretchers as well as providing accommodation for walking wounded. There was no steering assistance from the tracks, which made handling very difficult. This led to the Willys-built T29, and the subsequent T29E1, which was constructed by International Harvester. The design used the lengthened frame of the Willys MT-Tug, to which was attached a lightweight walking-beam bogie assembly shod with a steel track system. The front axle was a simple, non-driven tubular affair, and the front wheels could be replaced by skis for use in snow.

Photographs taken at Fort Hood, Texas, which, during the Second World War was used as the Tank Destroyer Tactical and Firing Center, show a third half-track experiment. In this case, the Jeep is a Ford GPW, and the track system is supported on both front and rear sprockets and a pair of bogie wheels. The track is of a similar type to that fitted to the M3/M5 half-track vehicles, consisting of a continuous rubber belt with moulded pads on the outer face, and metal cleats forming lugs at the edges; these cleats fit into teeth in the drive sprockets.

LEFT: The T28 stretcher carrier was one of a series of half-tracked experiments built by Willys and International Harvester for over-snow use. One problem with the whole series was that the lack of track braking made the vehicles difficult to steer. *Warehouse Collection*

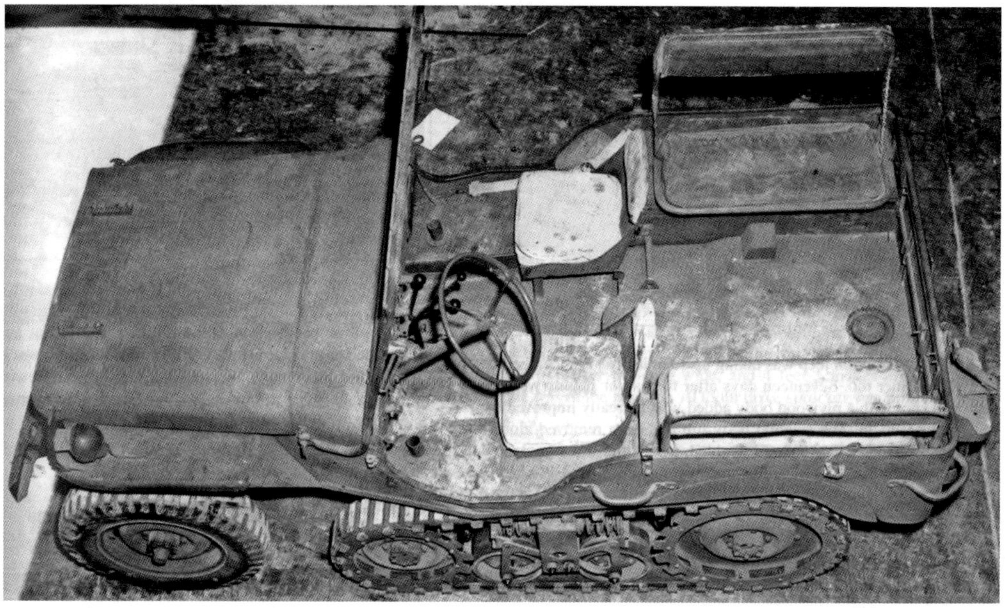

RIGHT: Mystery half-tracked Jeep based on a Ford GPW using a track bogie with the horizontal volute spring suspension. This vehicle was possibly photographed at Fort Knox, Kentucky, where the Armor Engineer Board was based, but nothing is known of its origins or purpose. Other photographs in the series show the Jeep with a version of the standard bodywork fitted with seating for six – two in the front and four in the rear on inward-facing seats. The fuel tank was relocated under the rear floor. *Warehouse Collection*

The tracks are driven by the rear sprockets, which are attached to the standard rear axle in place of the normal road wheels which, in this case, have had a ring of teeth welded to the rim to enable the wheel to be used as a drive sprocket. The front sprocket that follows the same pattern is reduced in diameter and presumably serves to keep the tracks in place. The track suspension uses the principle of the horizontal volute system as fitted to late-model Sherman tanks. The two bogie wheels are pivoted in such a way that they act against a pair of horizontal coil springs, while the rear axle retains its original semi-elliptical leaf spring.

Film also exists showing that at least one Jeep was modified as a fully-tracked vehicle using the track and suspension system of the Studebaker M29 Weasel.

Jeep 'tank'

In 1943, at the request of the Canadian Army, and in conjunction with Marmon-Herrington, Willys constructed a light armoured, tracked Jeep for airborne use, which was occasionally called a 'Jeep tank'. Five, open-topped 'TJ Mk 1' examples were produced with a transverse rear engine and Cletrac steering, and six of the Mk 2, which had the engine mounted longitudinally and featured a raised hull.

Lightweight Jeeps

During the Second World War, many attempts were made to produce a 'better' Jeep, although the truth is that it was not easy to improve on the original. Many of the experiments were in the field of lightweight vehicles intended for airborne operations, and for use in difficult terrain where the weight of the standard Jeep often made progress difficult.

In 1943, Chevrolet produced two examples of a lightweight, two-seat Jeep for airborne operations, weighing just 1,558lb (708kg). The vehicles were powered by an Indian 20bhp (15kW) V-twin motorcycle engine, and the transmission had three forward gears and one reverse, with a two-speed transfer case. There was a tubular chassis, and the suspension was independent at all four wheels.

The American firm of Crosley had been founded by Powell Crosley Jr in 1922, growing to become one of America's largest manufacturers of radios and, in 1939, the company moved into automobile production, producing a tiny two-seat motorcar powered by a 580cc (35in^3) flat-twin engine at a factory in Richmond, Indiana. This vehicle had undercut the rival Bantam by $62, and there was considerable rivalry between the two firms. Representatives of Crosley had been present at Camp Holabird when Bantam and Willys had presented their bids in 1940 and it seems that Crosley was also keen to become involved in the Jeep project. The company manufactured its first lightweight Jeep prototype in February 1942, demonstrating it to the US Army at Fort Benning in Georgia. The vehicle was fitted with a two-cylinder air-cooled Waukesha engine, boasting a power output of just 13bhp (10kW), and was equipped with permanent four-wheel drive; the kerbside weight was just 1,624lb (738kg).

Some 36 examples of this miniature Jeep were produced, originally known as the CT 13 Pup, but renamed Scout, and six were despatched to the European Theatre, there being some suggestion that the vehicle might be suitable for air-dropping.

In 1943, Ford also submitted their version of the ultra-lightweight Jeep using the same tractor engine that had been used in the original Pygmy prototype. The vehicle was effectively a scaled-down Jeep but, like all of the lightweights, nothing came of it.

The Kaiser Corporation, who were later to take over Willys, built a number of lightweight Jeep-type vehicles powered by a 30bhp (22kW) air-cooled Continental HO four-cylinder engine, but using the standard Warner gearbox and Spicer transfer case and axles of the standard Jeep. The smallest of these, the so-called ultra-light Midget Jeep, weighed 1,598lb (726kg) fully laden, and there was also a standard lightweight version known as the Type 1160; two examples of the Midget were constructed, and four of the Type 1160.

RIGHT: In April 1943, the US Army ordered 12 lightweight Jeeps – 6 from Henry J. Kaiser, 2 from General Motors Chevrolet, 2 from Willys-Overland, and 2 from Ford. This is the Chevrolet, which used a tubular frame and had all-round independent suspension. Power came from a V-twin Indian motorcycle engine. *Warehouse Collection*

LEFT: Dating from 1942, the Crosley Pup was one of several attempts at producing a lightweight Jeep-like vehicle suitable for airborne use. It weighed around 1,100lb (500kg) and 36 examples were constructed for evaluation. *Warehouse Collection*

Alongside the various experiments produced by other manufacturers, Willys themselves produced a number of development vehicles, but nothing really came of these simply because Willys lacked spare production capacity. In the lightweight category, the company produced two models. The first, produced in 1943–44, was a semi-forward control design known as the Willys air-cooled (WAC), fitted with the engine from a Harley-Davidson WLA motorcycle. The second, known as the Willys MB-L Special (MB, light), and for some reason nicknamed 'Gipsy Rose Lee', was a stripped down, two-seat version of the standard MB. By fitting only skeleton bodywork aft of the scuttle, removing the lighting equipment and rear-wheel brakes, and installing undersize wheels and tyres, the total weight was reduced to 1,483lb (674kg). There was no series production, but there is some evidence that four were supplied to the British under contract SM 6047.

The lightweight programme was abandoned when transport aircraft improved sufficiently to render the vehicles obsolete.

Rotabuggy flying Jeep

During 1940, work was being carried out at the British Airborne Forces Experimental Establishment at Ringway, Manchester, on a device described as the Rotachute, which used an air-driven rotor rather than a parachute as a means of accurately landing troops in enemy territory. In 1942, the designer of the Rotachute, Raoul Hafner, suggested that similar principles could be applied to loads larger than men, including vehicles, and work was started on the Jeep-based Rotabuggy.

A development contract was placed with the ML Aviation Company at White Waltham in 1942. A Jeep was adapted by fitting a streamlined tail fairing with twin rudderless fins, Perspex door panels, and a 'hanging' rotor control next to the steering wheel, together with a rotor tachometer and navigational instruments. A twin-bladed rotor of 46ft 9in (12.4m) diameter was fitted and the vehicle was tow-tested behind a Bentley motorcar, achieving gliding speeds of up to 65mph (105km/h). The first proper flight was made on 16 November 1943, but the development of larger, vehicle-carrying gliders, such as the Horsa II and Hamilcar brought the project to a premature conclusion.

Similar work was also carried out in Australia.

LEFT: The Rotabuggy, constructed by the ML Aviation Company at White Waltham, Berkshire, was – literally – an attempt at making the Jeep fly. The development of larger gliders, combined with the frightening experience of actually flying the thing, brought the project to a conclusion at the end of 1943. *Warehouse Collection*

Snow tractors

The Canadian Bombardier company used the Jeep as the basis for a small over-snow vehicle intended for rescuing aircrew in Northern Canada and Alaska where deep, soft snow was frequently encountered. Designated 'Snow tractor, half-track, T28 (Willys MB modified)', the vehicle featured a lengthened chassis and was fitted with steerable rubber tracks at the rear; skis could be fitted to replace the front wheels. There was a larger load-carrying compartment, with a full-length canvas top covering both the driving and load-carrying areas. Dubbed 'Penguin', the vehicle was driven by either the tracks, or by a combination of the tracks and the front wheels. The standard Go-Devil engine was retained, but the power output was increased to 63bhp (47kW) at 3,900rpm.

The first prototype snow tractor was not entirely suitable, and two further examples were produced. Now described as 'Snow tractor, half-track, T29/T29E1', both had their weight reduced by simplifying the rear bodywork. The vehicles were extensively tested in Alaska, but the project was eventually abandoned.

Wooden bodywork

In 1942, shortages of steel gave rise to experiments with constructing Jeep bodies of timber. During spring 1943, the Alma Trailer Company and the Canadian-American Truck Company both built complete Jeep bodies of timber that could be mounted on the standard chassis with minimal modification. The heavier of these, constructed of kiln-dried oak, weighed 420lb (191kg) – 150lb (68kg) more than the standard steel body. A lighter design used plywood to reduce the weight to almost the same figure, at 268lb (122kg). A third body design was subsequently produced by Canadian-American, Alma Trailer and the Covered Wagon Company, which used a mixture of steel, solid timber and plywood.

The experiments were eventually abandoned since plywood was as critical to the war effort as sheet steel.

BRITISH MODIFICATIONS AND EXPERIMENTS

The British demand for Jeeps was substantial at all stages of the war, with the total requirement amounting to more than 100,000 units. Unfortunately, the US authorities were unwilling to meet this requirement in full, often questioning the need for the projected numbers of vehicles. For example, Ministry of Supply (MoS) contract SM 2275 originally called for 80,000 vehicles and yet less than 23,000 were actually supplied. In all, Britain and the Commonwealth (excluding Canadian) forces received a little over 40,000 Jeeps out of a total production of more than 600,000 units.

By 1943, the MoS was becoming extremely frustrated with the difficulties of procuring the numbers of Jeeps required for the British and Commonwealth forces and began to examine the possibility of producing the vehicle in Britain with a domestic engine and transmission. After all, they reasoned,

Willys had turned over their drawings to Ford, so why not to a British company. In June 1943, the MoS asked Willys to supply copies of all of the manufacturing drawings and, at about the same time, placed a contract with Austin (294/23/3685, 24 June 1943) for the design and production of a 60bhp (43kW) four-cylinder engine, which was to be installed in a 'Willys car, 5cwt, 4 x 4'. The contract required the vehicle to be delivered to the Mechanical Warfare Experimental Establishment (MWEE) for trials by the end of the year. Although no photographs have emerged, the vehicle was definitely constructed and trials almost certainly took place at the Royal Artillery Eskmeals depot in Cumbria, and the MWEE report of these trials is numbered 1796.

The same contract also asked Austin to design and produce one prototype 'car, 5cwt, 4 x 4 – similar to the Willys vehicle of this type but incorporating engine and other components of British manufacture and design'. There is no evidence that this work was ever done and for their part, it seems that Willys was reluctant to release the drawings to yet another manufacturer. Eventually, the request was withdrawn.

Nuffield Mechanizations

In 1943, Nuffield Mechanizations produced a lightweight version of the standard Jeep, again intended for airborne operations. Described as 'Morris, 4 x 4, light airborne tractor', one of its intended roles was to tow the 20mm anti-aircraft gun.

The vehicle was mounted on a cut-down Willys chassis on which the main chassis rails had been removed ahead of the front spring hangers and behind the rear hangers. The standard motor was retained but was fitted with a British Solex carburettor,

ABOVE: Nuffield Mechanizations modified a standard Willys MB in 1943 to produce this lightweight airborne vehicle. Although it retained all of the Willys automotive components, it was designated 'Morris, 4 x 4, light airborne tractor'. *Warehouse Collection*

ABOVE: One of the intended roles of the Nuffield Jeep was to tow light guns, such as this 75mm M8 airborne howitzer, or a 20mm anti-aircraft cannon. The markings on the body sides indicate that the vehicle was under test at the Wheeled Vehicles Experimental Establishment. *Warehouse Collection*

RIGHT: Replica of the Nuffield airborne Jeep. *Simon Thomson*

and a lot of the under-bonnet components were relocated to save space. A special lightweight, two-seat body was fitted, which followed the general lines of the original although, apart from the inner windscreen and the front wings, none of the panels was identical. The bonnet, for example, was shorter and lower, the front grille was much simplified and was moved back by some 6in (150mm), and there was no body aft of the rear wheels. The lower panel on the outer frame of the windscreen was deeper to compensate for the shallower bonnet. To reduce the overall height in airborne operations, the steering wheel and column were removable.

Although the prototype performed well, the project was subsequently abandoned.

Standard Motor Company

Despite having had no previous experience of such a vehicle, in 1943, with shortages of Jeeps at crisis levels, the Standard Motor Company was asked to produce a prototype Jeep. The vehicle, described as 'car, 5cwt, 4 x 2', closely resembled the Jeep in overall layout, although the wheelbase was reduced to 75in (1,905mm), and it featured only rear-wheel drive, combined with independent front suspension. Power came from a side-valve Standard 12 engine producing 44bhp (33kW), coupled to a Standard four-speed transmission. The whole vehicle weighed 1,900lb (865kg), which was a lot closer to the QMC's original 1,300lb (590kg) figure than Bantam or Willys ever got.

Nothing came of this project either, and soon after there was some improvement in the supply position of Jeeps.

BELOW: Nothing is known of the story behind this Ford GPW Jeep other than the fact that it is a post-war Australian right-hand drive conversion. Apparently, conversion kits were produced by the Australian Army to permit the Jeep to be used in states that had rules about the use of left-hand drive vehicles. *Warehouse Collection*

Chapter 2

The Hotchkiss M201

'La Jeep M201 modèle militaire... une production Hotchkiss licence Willys.'

HOTCHKISS-BRANDT SALES LEAFLET, 1957

Even if you disregard the literally hundreds of Hotchkiss Jeeps that are currently being passed off as American, it can be argued that the French-built M201 Jeep has ensured the survival of many more Second World War Jeeps than would otherwise have been the case, simply because of the interchangeability of parts.

While building some 30,000 Jeeps during the period 1955 to 1966, Hotchkiss also supplied the French Army with the thousands of parts required to keep these vehicles running over more than 25 years. Obviously, many of these parts were equally at home on a Jeep that had been constructed during the Second World War as they were on the postwar French-built equivalent – leading to the inevitable soubriquet of 'Hotchpotch'.

JEEPS IN FRANCE

Production of the Ford GPW ended in July 1945, while that of the Willys MB continued for another month or so, with the last example rolling out of the Toledo factory on 20 August. By this time, Willys-Overland had already started to concentrate on the post-war CJ2A Universal Jeep – but, this was not to be the end of the MB, and the story now moves to France.

At the end of the war, the US Army had supplied 8,000 Willys and Ford Jeeps to the French Army as part of the post-war programme for re-equipping the liberated European nations. Many were in poor condition and work on refurbishment was put in hand at ERGM (*Etablissement de Réserve Générale du Material Automobile*) in the Paris suburb of La Maltournée.

Some of the parts that were required to carry out this work were obtained by dismantling the worst of the American Jeeps; other parts were already being manufactured in France under licence by SOFIA (*Société de Fabrication Industrielles et Automobiles*), a subsidiary of Hotchkiss, using the brand name WOF, or Willys-Overland France. However, there were still difficulties finding enough dollars to buy from the US those parts that were not available domestically. Partly for this reason, the French military authorities believed it would be sensible to construct a French Jeep, and set to work developing a specification for a home-built replacement.

The French motor industry was invited to bid for the work but, ironically, only two companies, Delahaye and Peugeot, showed any interest. Ultimately, Peugeot was too late in

RIGHT: Although the sidelights on the tops of the mudguards are more generally seen on British Army Jeeps of the Second World War period, in all other respects, the M201 is picture perfect. *Warehouse Collection*

LEFT: Now owned by The Tank Museum at Bovington in Dorset, this unrestored Hotchkiss M201 is still in its original military condition. *Roland Groom, The Tank Museum*

responding, and although they possibly had a better vehicle, the contract went to Delahaye. The first examples of their VLR-D light 4 x 4 vehicle were produced in 1951 and, over a five-year period Delahaye produced a total of almost 10,000 vehicles. However, anxious to 'improve' on the American original, the French Army and Delahaye had introduced all kinds of technical innovations, which eventually proved to be the vehicle's downfall (see page 156).

By 1954, the French Army was once again trying to decide how to replace not only its still-ageing Second World War Jeeps, but also the unreliable Delahayes.

WILLYS-OVERLAND FRANCE

Back in 1952, SOFIA had been licenced by Willys-Overland to produce Jeep parts in France to enable the French Army's MB and GPW Jeeps to be maintained in running condition. At the same time, Willys had granted the French Hotchkiss company a licence to build civilian Jeeps in France, initially using knock-down kits, but ultimately with domestic content. The first French Jeeps, designated JH101, appeared in 1954 and were based on the American CJ3A and CJ3B Jeeps.

The JH101 was a curious hybrid model consisting of the post-war American CJ3B Jeep body, with the high bonnet that was normally required to clear the height of the Hurricane engine, combined with running gear that came from the same source. But, under the bonnet was the Go-Devil Type 442 side-valve engine, a design that had first appeared towards the end of the war years.

From 1960, the JH101 was replaced by an entirely French machine designated JH102, still powered by the trusty Go-Devil Type 442 engine. This was followed by the Indénor diesel-powered JH102D and the reinforced JH102R, the latter designed for fire-fighting. In 1962, the long-wheelbase HWL appeared, based on a stretched CJ3B chassis and powered by a choice of petrol or diesel engines, the latter designated HWLD.

Looking at the simplicity and reliability of these early civilian Jeeps, the French military authorities must have realised that here was a possible home-grown product, with all of the advantages of the original and well-proven MB/GPW, which might allow them to continue to use their huge inventory of parts. However, there was just one small problem – these parts were for the original Jeep and therefore the Army had no interest in buying something that was even slightly different.

By the time that it was obvious that the Delahaye VLR-D was never going to be reliable, Hotchkiss had been building civilian Jeeps under licence for three years and was in the perfect position to effectively build more wartime Jeeps. In 1955, Hotchkiss (who by now, coincidentally, had taken over Delahaye) was contracted to do just that, building more 'Second World War' Jeeps under licence to Willys, using French components wherever possible.

THE HOTCHKISS M201

The first French military Jeep to be produced in France was described as the *licence MB 6V*, with just 465 examples constructed during 1955. Equipped with a 6V electrical system, the *licence MB* resembled the original in almost every respect. The following year, it was superseded by the definitive M201, which had a 24V electrical system as well as incorporating other detail changes.

In general appearance, the Hotchkiss was identical to the Second World War original and such differences as existed were relatively minor. The chassis was fabricated from thicker steel, and there were additional reinforcements behind the bumper. Under the bonnet, the most obvious change was the use of two 12V batteries giving a 24V electrical system. Because of the batteries, the air cleaner was moved from its normal position back by the right-hand side of the firewall to the front left, behind the headlight. The distributor and coil were enclosed in a waterproof housing, while the spark plugs,

ABOVE: Although it should never be considered as anything other than a licence-built version of the original Second World War Jeep, the Hotchkiss M201 has some unique features. Aside from the 24V electrical system, the radial tyres tend to give the vehicle a slightly more purposeful look, perhaps because the width across the wheels is increased slightly. *Christophe Muller*

RIGHT: Driving a Jeep in wet weather is not fun. Even the electrically-operated windscreen wipers are scarcely adequate and passing vehicles throw spray onto the inside of the windscreen. This can be avoided by investing in a complete winter enclosure, but some say this is akin to driving a motorised tent. *Simon Thomson*

starter, generator and generator control box were all unique to the Hotchkiss. The engine was the Go-Devil Type 442, in which the camshaft was driven by a fibre gear rather than a chain – this unit was also used on late-Second World War production and on post-war CJ3A civilian Jeeps. The carburettor was a French Solex 32PBIC downdraught unit rather than the Carter fitted to the original, giving slightly improved fuel consumption.

Other modifications when compared to the Second World War machine included one-piece wheels, eventually shod with radial tyres, thicker seat cushions, which both made the M201 more comfortable to ride in and at the same time more difficult to get into due to the seat cushions being closer to the steering wheel. The rests provided for the windscreen in its folded position were now placed on the 'screen itself rather than the bonnet, and there were tandem electric windscreen wipers, as opposed to the original manual, or vacuum, units. The body itself was scarcely altered.

The French Army made these changes to improve reliability and longevity. Many believe that this also made the Hotchkiss a better vehicle without detracting from its essential Jeep character.

Variants

All M201s were constructed to the specification of the basic *Véhicule de Liaison Tout-Terrain* (VLTT). Subsequently, individual vehicles were selected for conversion to one of a number of specialised roles, including the following:

- Sahara desert kit, comprising heavier springs, sand tyres, high-efficiency air filter, dual fuel tanks, and electric fuel pump. Both 6V and 24V vehicles
- Mount for 106mm M40 recoilless rifle. Both 6V and 24V vehicles
- Mount for Nord Aviation SS10 anti-tank missile
- Mount for ENTAC (Engin Téléguidé, Anti-Char) anti-tank missile
- Mount for MILAN (Missile d'Infanterie, Légère, Anti-Char) anti-tank missile.

A number of fully-enclosed steel station wagon bodies were also designed and constructed for the French Air Force.

LEFT: The US Army started to equip Jeeps with the 106mm M40 anti-tank gun during Second world war and the French Army continued to do this into the late 1950s. In order to accommodate the barrel during transit, this split windscreen was devised based on the windscreen fitted to the post-war M38A1 Jeep. *Warehouse Collection*

BELOW: A Jeep is not strong on safety features, but some vehicles serving with the French Army towards the end of the vehicle's career were fitted with a substantial roll cage that also provides a secure attachment point for seat belts. The hoops prevent the hood supports from being stowed away around the rear of the body. *Warehouse Collection*

RIGHT: Armed and accessorised Hotchkiss M201, all gussied up for display. Note the spots of colour on the suspension grease nipples. *Christophe Muller*

BELOW: Well-used ex-French Army M201 awaiting final disposal. *Warehouse Collection*

Je ne regrette rien!
211 0767
GAS 562

ABOVE: Unusual high-level view showing the roll cage and radio sets, and the rear-mounted rack for a camouflage net. *Warehouse Collection*

ABOVE LEFT: Perfectly restored M201 equipped with radios, a side-mount for the AA52 machine-gun, and unusual infra-red driving lights on the bumper and in front of the passenger seat. *Christophe Muller*

BOTTOM LEFT: Although it wears Second World War-style bar-grip tyres, this is perfectly legitimate for an early- or mid-production example of the breed, and this Hotchkiss M201 is nicely turned out as the personal transport of a three-star Divisional General of the French Army. *Phil Royal*

Production

Hotchkiss Jeeps were assembled by Hotchkiss and Hotchkiss-Delahaye at the Boulevard Ornano in the Paris suburb of St Denis. From about 1958/59, when Hotchkiss merged with Brandt to form Hotchkiss-Brandt, the production line was moved to the Brandt site at Stains, a few miles north of St Denis.

The total number of Hotchkiss Jeeps assembled is believed to be 465 examples (although some sources suggest that the figure was 882) of the original *licence MB*, all of which were constructed in 1956, and 27,628 examples of the definitive M201 built between 1957 and 1966.

Many remained in service or storage until the end of the 1990s, despite the decision, finally taken in 1981, to replace the M201 with licence-built Peugeot P4 Mercedes. It has even been suggested that the last M201 was not taken out of French service until the year 2000.

LEFT: Many M201 Jeeps remained with the French Army, in storage, until about 1990. In many cases, a fresh coat of paint was all that was required to make them an attractive proposition to collectors. *Warehouse Collection*

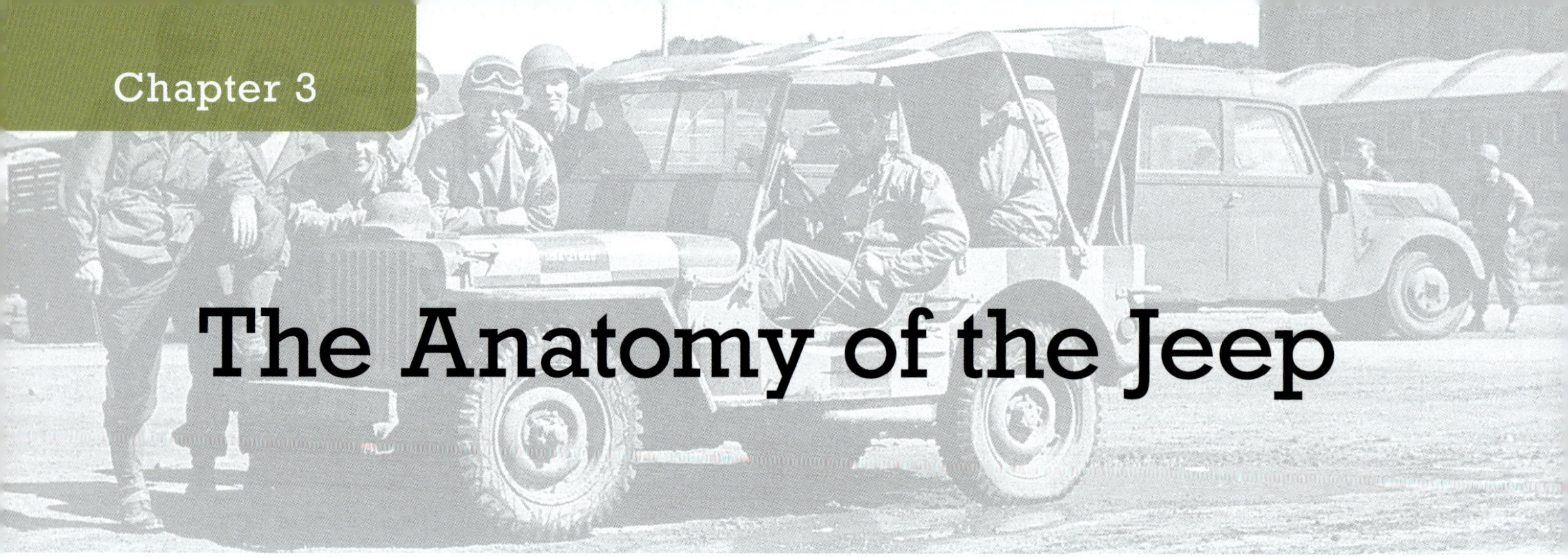

Chapter 3

The Anatomy of the Jeep

'The Jeep... is a four-wheel vehicle with four-wheel drive... the engine is a four-cylinder gasoline unit located in the conventional place... a conventional three-speed transmission equipped with a transfer case provides additional speeds for traversing difficult terrain.'

TM9-803, FEBRUARY 1944

Although the concept was innovatory, the Jeep was a very basic and straightforward vehicle, with any real engineering innovation confined to the overall package and the use of four-wheel drive.

In truth, the vehicle was not much more than an assembly of proprietary parts, packaged together to satisfy the military specification for a light reconnaissance field car. The engine was a much-improved version of the well-proven Willys Go-Devil that had first appeared in 1933, while the transmission and axles were proprietary units that could be found on other vehicles of the period. However, the Jeep certainly formed the benchmark by which all subsequent 4 x 4 utilities were – and to a certain extent, still are – judged. And such admirably simple and durable engineering, combined with an impeccable supply of parts, means that almost any Jeep can be brought back from the dead, regardless of its current condition.

ABOVE: Bill Padden's superb ghost drawing of the Jeep shows exactly how the main components of the vehicle are arranged; to buy a copy of this drawing, visit www.williampadden.com. *Bill Padden*

THE DESIGN OF THE JEEP

Nomenclature

The US Army described the Jeep as 'Truck, ¼ ton, 4 x 4; Willys-Overland Model MB and Ford GPW; SNL G-503'.

Early French Jeeps were designated '*Voiture de liaison, tout-terrain; Hotchkiss licence Willys Type MB, 4 x 4*', while the definitive Hotchkiss M201 was '*Voiture de liaison, tout-terrain; Hotchkiss Type M201, 4 x 4*'.

The description that follows applies only to the standardised Jeeps produced by Ford (GPW), Willys-Overland (MB) and Hotchkiss (*licence MB 6V*, and M201 24V). Unless otherwise described, it can be assumed that details of the M201 are identical to the MB/GPW.

Chassis frame

The heart of the Jeep is a rigid steel frame, of ladder design, parallel-sided and upswept over the axles. This provides attachment points for the suspension, the engine and transmission, and the steel body tub. On both the Willys and Ford Jeeps, the chassis was manufactured by Midland Steel, and was formed from two channel-section side members, 4.186in x 1.75in (106.5mm x 44.5mm) in section, and rolled from 0.083–0.093in (2.1–2.36mm) thick carbon steel to specification SAE 1025. The chassis of the Hotchkiss M201 is more substantial, with 0.157in (4mm) thick side members. Aside from its increased thickness, the M201 chassis can be identified by the inclusion of vertical U-shaped reinforcements welded into the open channel section of the main side members, ahead of the radiator cross member.

Five cross members are used to provide reinforcement and structural rigidity to the frame, while a substantial, full-width removable bumper at the front acts as an additional cross member. Ford-built chassis can be identified by the use of a channel section cross member to support the radiator, while Willys and Hotchkiss chassis can be recognised by their use of a tubular cross member ahead of the radiator. Note, however, that Ford used the Willys frame on very early production vehicles. Small spring-steel loop-shaped bumpers are mounted on the rear cross member, together with a K-shaped, triangular braced mount for a towing pintle. The third cross member includes a circular platform that provides a reinforced support for a machine-gun pedestal mount.

The battery – or batteries in the case of the 24V Hotchkiss M201 – is carried behind the right-hand front wheel on a small steel shelf welded to the chassis, and the fuel tank is supported by flanges on the edges of a fabricated well beneath the driver's seat.

LEFT: 'X-ray' photograph of the M201 showing what goes on under the skin. The side-mounted machine gun is the French 7.7mm AA52. *Christophe Muller*

LEFT: The chassis (M201 shown) is a simple ladder affair, upswept over the axles; note the circular reinforcement above the rear axle for the machine-gun mount. *Christophe Muller*

Engine

The original engine, which was fitted until 1945 by both Ford and Willys, was the Willys Go-Devil Type 441, a four-cylinder, water-cooled side-valve unit of 2,199cc (134.2in^3), producing a maximum of 60bhp (45kW) at 4,000rpm. In late 1945 (engine numbers above 175402), and in all Hotchkiss Jeeps, this unit was replaced by the Go-Devil Type 442 engine which, at the time, was being developed for the civilian CJ2A Universal Jeep launched in July 1945. The design was similar to the original, but included a redesigned oil pump, together with a gear train to drive the camshaft in place of the previous gear and timing chain setup.

Engines were constructed by both Ford and Willys to the same basic design with only detail differences one to another; the Ford blocks are said to be more prone to frost damage around the distributor drive adapter due to the nature of the castings. The Hotchkiss-built engines are similar to the Willys units.

BELOW: Overhead view of the engine compartment showing the positions of the major components; battery and voltage regulator on the left of the photograph, oil filter and distributor on the side of the block, and air cleaner on the bulkhead. *Warehouse Collection*

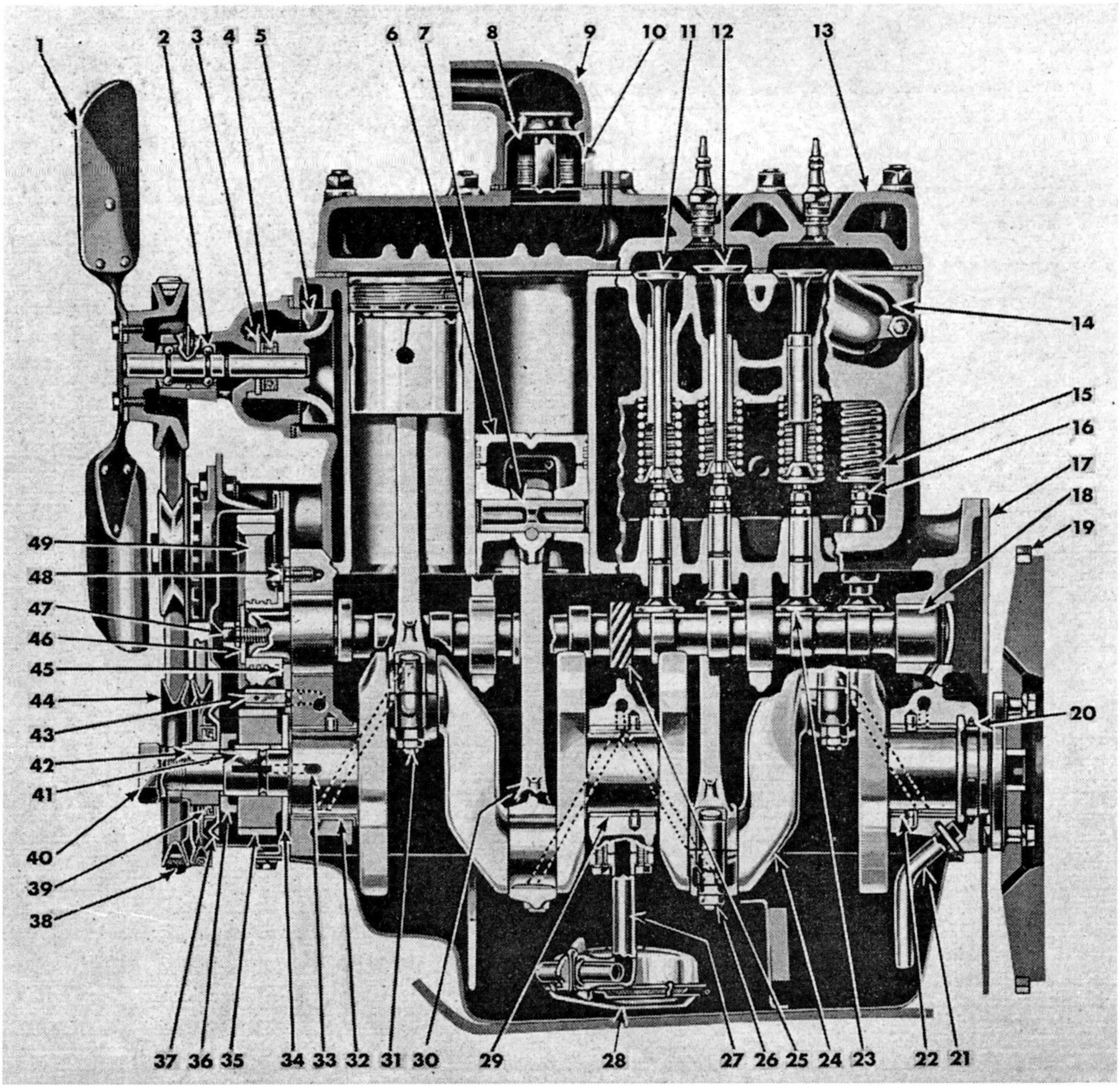

ABOVE: Sectional view of the Type 442 Go-Devil engine. *Warehouse Collection*

1 Fan assembly
2 Water pump, bearing and shaft assembly
3 Water pump seal washer
4 Water pump seal assembly
5 Water pump impeller
6 Piston
7 Gudgeon (wrist) pin
8 Thermostat assembly
9 Water outlet elbow
10 Thermostat retainer
11 Exhaust valve
12 Inlet valve
13 Cylinder head
14 Exhaust manifold
15 Valve spring
16 Tappet adjustment and lock nut
17 Rear engine plate
18 Camshaft
19 Flywheel and starter ring gear
20 Rear crankshaft seal
21 Rear main bearing drain tube
22 Rear main bearing cap
23 Tappet
24 Crankshaft
25 Oil pump and distributor drive gear
26 Bolt for connecting rod cap
27 Support for oil strainer pick-up
28 Floating oil strainer assembly
29 Centre main bearing cap
30 Connecting rod assembly
31 Lock nut for connecting rod bolt
32 Front main bearing
33 Crankshaft oil passages
34 Crankshaft thrust washer
35 Crankshaft timing gear (Type 441 engine used a timing chain)
36 Crankshaft gear spacer
37 Timing gear cover
38 Drive belt for fan and generator
39 Crankshaft nose seal
40 Starter crank nut
41 Crankshaft gear Woodruff key
42 Fan pulley Woodruff key
43 Timing gear lubrication jet
44 Fan and generator drive pulley
45 Camshaft thrust plate
46 Camshaft gear retaining washer
47 Camshaft gear retaining screw
48 Camshaft gear thrust plate retaining screw
49 Camshaft gear (Type 441 engine used a sprocket to drive a timing chain)

Engine specification

Designation: Willys Go-Devil, Type 441 or Type 442
Type: in-line, water-cooled, four cylinders, L head (side valve)
Capacity: 2,199cc (134.2in3)
Bore and stroke: 3.125 x 4.375in (70.4 x 111.13mm)
Power output: 52–54bhp (39–40kW) net at 4,000rpm; 60bhp (45kW) gross
Maximum torque: 105–110 lbf/ft (156-164kgm) at 2,000rpm
Compression ratio: 6.48:1
Compression: 110lbf/in^2 (7.7kgf/cm^2) at 185rpm
Firing order: 1-3-4-2
Static ignition timing: spark occurs, 5° BTDC
Maximum spark advance: 11–12° at 1,500rpm
Valve timing: inlet opens, 9° BTDC; inlet closes, 50° ABDC; exhaust opens, 47° BTDC; exhaust closes, 12° ATDC
Valve clearance (cold): inlet and exhaust, 0.014in (0.35mm)
Contact-breaker gap: MB/GPW, 0.02in (0.51mm); M201, 0.015–0.018in (0.35–0.45mm)
Spark-plug gap: MB/GPW, 0.03in (0.75mm); M201, 0.018–0.02in (0.45-0.55mm)
Dwell angle: 47°
Engine oil capacity: 0.875gal (3.97 litre).

Crankcase and cylinder block

The crankcase and cylinder block is a one-piece casting of graphited iron, with the cylinder bores machined directly into the block. Older engines may have been over-bored and sleeved back to standard size by the use of pressed-in dry liners. A removable tappet chest cover on the exhaust side of the block provides access to the valve gear.

An integral water jacket allows the cooling water to circulate around the cylinder walls, and the valve guides and seats. The water jacket is closed off by means of pressed-in core plugs.

Cylinder head

The cylinder head is of cast-iron, with integral, recessed combustion chambers; the spark-plug tappings are threaded directly into the casting. On Willys and Hotchkiss engines, the cylinder head is secured with studs; Ford engines use a combination of nine bolts and six studs. Hotchkiss cylinder heads, and some of the post-war engines fitted during US Army rebuilds, have additional longitudinal cast reinforcing ribs between the clearance holes for the securing studs.

The head is jacketed, with cored-in passages for the circulation of cooling water around the combustion chambers and the spark plug seats. A thick copper-asbestos-copper gasket provides a seal at the cylinder head joint. Later, replacement gaskets are of a composition construction, and are prone to failure at the narrowest point between the pairs of cylinders if the head is even slightly warped.

ABOVE: The engine on Ford Jeeps was originally painted in this Medium Grey. *Warehouse Collection*

LEFT: Willys engines were painted in Olive Drab to match the body, but the engines of the M201 were finished in this glossy Blue-Green colour. *Christophe Muller*

BELOW: Like that used on the post-war Jeep CJ2A engine, the cylinder head of the Hotchkiss M201 includes longitudinal reinforcing ribs. *Christophe Muller*

Crankshaft
The crankshaft is a fully-machined heat-treated forging of nickel-chrome steel, with large-surface main bearing and crank pin journals, and integral crank counterweights; some later crankshafts for the Type 442 engine, possibly intended for the CJ2A Universal Jeep, have separate, bolted, crank counterweights. The main journals are cross-drilled for lubrication in the conventional manner, with diagonal drillings providing a feed through the webs of the crankshaft to the big ends. The crankshaft is supported in three thin-wall steel-backed bearings, with a lining of Babbitt white metal alloy. Crankshaft end thrust is accommodated by means of a thrust washer and shims fitted between the timing sprocket and the front main bearing; the washer is flanged both sides. A woven asbestos-rope type oil seal is fitted into the timing gear housing at the nose end; on the later, Type 442 engines this was replaced by a rubber lip-type seal. Similarly, at the flywheel end, an asbestos-rope type seal is located in a groove in the rear main bearing cap and crankcase.

Pistons and connecting rods
Pistons are of the Lo-Ex Lynite type, made from light aluminium-alloy and tin-plated, with a T slot opposite the thrust face; the pistons are oval-machined, with the greater diameter being across the thrust face. There are three ring grooves, all above the gudgeon pin, intended for two compression rings, the lower with a tapered face, and one oil-control ring. Pistons are available in oversizes of 0.010, 0.020, 0.030 and 0.040in for use in re-bored units, although these may no longer be easy to find.

The gudgeon pin, which is of hollow heat-treated steel, is a light press-fit into the piston and is clamped into the rod by a pinch bolt at the small end.

The connecting rods are I-section steel forgings, with each rod drilled through from big end to small end for lubrication; a small bleed hole cross-drilled through the bearing shoulder directs oil onto the cylinder wall. Ford-produced rods have integral studs and bolts for the bearing cap, whilst those of Willys and Hotchkiss manufacture use loose nuts and bolts.

Camshaft
The camshaft is of nickel-steel and is supported in four plain bearings. The front bearing is a steel-backed, Babbitt metal-lined type, press-fitted into the crankcase and staked in place; the other three bearings are formed directly within the crankcase itself. There are two camshaft designs, intended for use with the Type 441 and Type 442 engines, respectively. The two types of camshaft are not interchangeable: that intended for use with the Type 441 engine is provided with a driving sprocket for the timing chain; while the Type 442 is fitted with a helical driving gear, which meshes directly with the crankshaft timing gear.

On Type 441 engines, camshaft end float is controlled by a plunger and spring at the front of the shaft. In both types of engine, a thrust plate is installed between the camshaft drive gear and the cylinder block.

In addition to the valve cams, the camshaft includes a skew gear for driving the oil pump, which in turn provides a dog gear for driving the distributor.

Valve gear
The exhaust and inlet valves are installed directly into the block, with two large-headed poppet valves per cylinder. The valves, which operate in cast-iron guides, press-fitted into the block, are not interchangeable. Although there are no separate valve seats, the engine is sufficiently low-revving to avoid damage from the use of unleaded fuels.

The valves are fitted with single return springs, retained by split, conical cotters, and are operated by mushroom-headed tappets bearing directly onto the camshaft, and sliding in guides formed in the block itself. The tappets are fitted with self-locking adjusting screws that are used to set the correct clearances.

Timing gears
For most of the production life of the MB/GPW, the camshaft was driven by an endless chain, running on toothed sprockets keyed onto the camshaft and crankshaft nose. There was no timing chain tensioner. Engines with serial numbers above 175402, and all Hotchkiss engines, use a geared drive, with a fibre-reinforced composite gear wheel attached to the camshaft, meshing with a steel gear on the crankshaft nose. The two systems are not interchangeable.

Flywheel
The flywheel is a heavy steel casting, balanced during manufacture, and machined on one surface to provide a clutch facing. A steel ring gear is shrunk onto the outer edge to mesh with the drive pinion of the starter motor.

RIGHT: View of the flywheel and clutch assembly showing how a spare gearbox shaft is used to centre the friction plate before the gearbox and bell housing is refitted. *Christophe Muller*

LEFT: The oil filter is of the by-pass type, with the inlet connected to the oil distribution gallery by an adaptor at the front of the engine, and the return made via the timing gear housing. The replaceable element is described as a 'military junior', produced by either Fram or Purolator. *Christophe Muller*

Lubrication system

The engine uses a standard wet-sump lubrication system, with oil taken from the sump, via a floating strainer and pick-up, and delivered by pump directly to the high-pressure side of an adjustable relief valve mounted on the pump cover. The oil pump is a planetary-gear unit, driven by a spiral gear on the camshaft. Two different types of pump are employed: the later high-capacity type used with the Type 442 engine is not interchangeable with the earlier model. The pump supplies oil to an integral gallery in the crankcase, and then to the main bearings, camshaft bushes, and timing gear. From the main bearings, drillings conduct the oil to the big ends, the small ends, and, through a spray jet, to the cylinder walls. Oil returns to the sump via a drain tube on the rear main bearing cap.

The relief valve consists of a cylindrical plunger held against its seat by means of spring pressure, and can be adjusted by adding or removing shims inside the cap nut to control the pressure in the lubrication system at about 40lbf/in^2 (2.8kgf/cm^2). For the MB/GPW and *licence MB 6V*, oil pressure is indicated to the driver by means of a capillary-tube Bourdon gauge on the dashboard; the M201 24V uses an electric sender unit in the engine block and a pressure gauge on the dash.

A standard, external pattern, 'military junior' by-pass type oil filter is fitted, employing a replaceable element produced by either Fram or Purolator. The inlet to the filter is connected to the oil distribution gallery by an adaptor at the front of the engine, with the return made via the timing gear housing.

The engine has a simple closed-circuit system for crankcase fumes in which the oil filler riser is vented into the air intake cross tube, and fumes from the tappet chest cover are piped into the inlet manifold beneath the carburettor.

Cooling system

The engine is water-cooled in the conventional manner with coolant designed to circulate by pump-assisted thermo-siphon action through passages formed in the castings around the cylinder bores, the valve guides and seats, and the combustion chambers. Normal operating temperature is 165–175°F (75–80°C), and the cooling system is pressurised to effectively raise the boiling point of the coolant to 221°F (105°C). A conventional bellows-type thermostat unit is fitted, employing a mushroom valve to restrict the water supply. As the valve opens, over the temperature range 145–155°F (63–78°C), it progressively closes the by-pass aperture, and is fully open at 170°F (77°C).

The water pump is mounted on the front of the cylinder block, and is fitted with a centrifugal, vane-type impeller and a spring-loaded seal that prevents water from seeping into the bearings. A four-bladed fan is bolted to the pump nose. The pump and fan are driven by a substantial single V belt, or, for the M201, narrower twin belts. Correct belt tension is adjusted by moving the generator position in a sliding bracket; the correct tension is obtained when the upper run of the belt can be deflected no more than 1in (25mm) for the heavy single belt used on the MB/GPW and ⅜in (10mm) on the twin belts of the M201. A de-tensioning device integral with the generator brace on the MB/GPW allows the fan drive to be disconnected before fording to prevent drowning the engine.

RIGHT: The cooling system consists of a belt-driven fan and water pump together with a large-capacity pressurised radiator; a bellows-type thermostat is fitted into the elbow bolted to the top of the cylinder head. *Christophe Muller*

Fuel system

The engine is normally aspirated and is designed to burn leaded or unleaded petrol of 68–70 (RON) minimum octane rating. Fuel is drawn from the tank using a standard AC Type AF, or similar, mechanical diaphragm pump mounted on the engine block, and driven directly by an eccentric on the camshaft. For most Second World War Jeeps and all Hotchkiss vehicles, a separate brass-foil filter unit assembly is mounted on the bulkhead between the pump and the float chamber of the carburettor.

On the MB/GPW, the standard carburettor is a down-draught Carter Type WO-198S, 539S, or 698S, with a throttle-operated accelerator pump and economising device, produced by the Carter Carbureter Corporation of St Louis, Missouri. It may be of passing interest to know that the company spelled 'carbureter' in this eccentric manner because it enabled the word 'Carter' to be made for their branding from the first three and last three letters.

The Hotchkiss *licence MB 6V* and M201 24V were both fitted with a Solex Type 32PBIC down-draught carburettor,

ABOVE: The fuel pump is of the mechanical diaphragm type, produced by AC, and mounted low down on the engine block on the left-hand side where it is driven directly off a camshaft lobe. *Christophe Muller*

ABOVE: A brass foil fuel filter unit is fitted to the engine bulkhead. Leaks at the joint of the bowl of this unit are a common source of fuel starvation problems. *Christophe Muller*

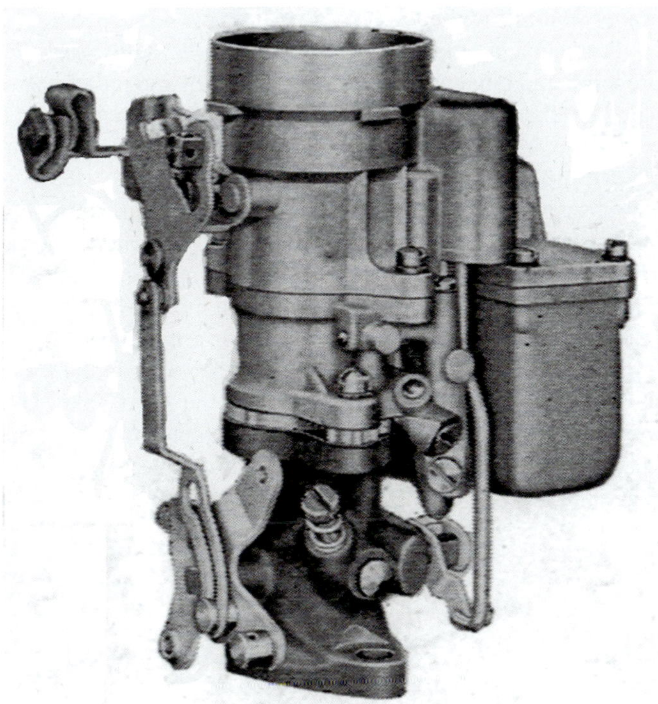

ABOVE: Both the MB and GPW employed a down-draught Carter Type WO-198S, 539S, or 698S carburettor, with a throttle-operated accelerator pump and economising device. *Warehouse Collection*

ABOVE: The Hotchkiss licence MB 6V and the M201 24V were fitted with a Solex Type 32PBIC down-draught carburettor, which also included a throttle-operated accelerator pump. Similar carburettors, of British origin, were also used on Jeeps rebuilt by the British Army. *Christophe Muller*

which also included a throttle-operated accelerator pump and economiser device. Similar units were also used as a replacement on US Army Jeeps rebuilt in France during 1944–45 and on British Army Jeeps during the 1960s.

The Carter and Solex carburettors are interchangeable.

The carburettor breathes through a large oil-bath air cleaner mounted either on the engine bulkhead on the MB/GPW and *licence MB 6V*, or on the inside of the left-hand wheel arch on the M201. A cross tube, of which there are several patterns differing in detail, connects the air cleaner to a horn on the carburettor inlet. The cross tube fitted to the M201 includes a small capillary pipe, which allows the distributor body to be vented into the inlet system.

Exhaust system

The exhaust system consists of just three parts – a down-pipe, which connects to the manifold and includes a flexible section, the silencer, and a tailpipe, the latter sometimes welded directly to the silencer on replacement exhaust systems. The silencer is fitted longitudinally under the passenger's foot well, and the outlet of the short tailpipe exits just ahead of the right-hand rear wheel. From mid-1945, many Jeeps were fitted with a deep-mud exhaust system in which the silencer was relocated further to the rear, parallel to the axle.

The exhaust system was originally manufactured from mild steel, but stainless-steel replacements are available, which will greatly increase the life of the system.

Transmission

Drive from the engine is conveyed to a unit-constructed Warner T84J three-speed and reverse gearbox, with synchronised second- and third-speed gears. The design of the gearbox was improved from late 1944, with the oil capacity increased, and these gearboxes are identified by a cast letter 'H' beneath the oil filler plug. The gearbox in the M201 is a Hotchkiss-built unit patterned on the original Warner 'box. The gear selector operates through a conventional H pattern, with reverse at top left, and without any detent to prevent accidental selection of reverse. Gearbox ratios are 2.665:1 in first, 1.564:1 in second, and 1:1 for top; reverse is 3.554:1.

The clutch is a standard 7in (180mm) Borg & Beck (MB/GPW) or Ferodo (M201) single dry-plate unit, with a pressure plate and cover assembly supplied by Atwood (MB/GPW), Auburn (M201) or Ferodo (M201). The clutch-release mechanism is mechanically operated via a system of levers and an adjustable steel cable. Correct clutch pedal clearance is ¾in (19mm).

Like the gearbox, the transfer case is also a proprietary item, this time a Spicer Type 18 (some early vehicles used a Brown-Lipe transfer case), unit-mounted at the rear of the transmission. The transfer 'box provides a 1:1 ratio in top, and 1.97:1 in low, with the two gears selectable from interlocked, floor-mounted levers that allow the low ratios to be engaged only in conjunction with four-wheel drive. The high gears of the transfer case are of the helical type, while the low gears are straight cut. A sliding dog on the output shaft is used to engage or disengage drive to the front axle. The speedometer drive gear and transmission handbrake are mounted on the rear-drive output shaft of the transfer case. An angle drive adapter is fitted to the M201 to compensate for the larger rolling radius of the tyres; a similar adapter was used on Second World War Jeeps when 7.50-16 tyres were fitted.

Drive is taken to the front and rear wheels by means of open Spicer Series 1200 propeller shafts with needle-roller universal joints at the yokes.

Provision is made on the amphibious GPA for the propeller and bilge pump to be driven by belt and pulley from a power take-off on the rear end of the transfer box.

Steering gear

The steering is controlled by a Ross Type T12 cam and twin-pin steering box with a variable ratio: 12:1 at straight ahead, and 14:1 at full lock. The backlash between the cam and the pins is adjustable via a nut on the steering box cover. A short drag link is attached to one end of the drop arm of the steering box and, at the other end, to a steering relay unit, in the form of a bell crank mounted on the top of the front axle. The forward extension of the bell crank is connected to each front hub by means of a track rod with an adjustable ball joint at each end.

LEFT: All Jeeps, regardless of origin, used this Warner T84J three-speed gearbox (M201 shown) bolted directly to the clutch bell housing and coupled directly to a two-speed Spicer transfer box, interlocked with the front-axle drive. From late 1944, Second World War Jeeps were fitted with a gearbox having an increased oil capacity; these gearboxes are identified by a cast letter 'H' beneath the oil filler plug. *Christophe Muller*

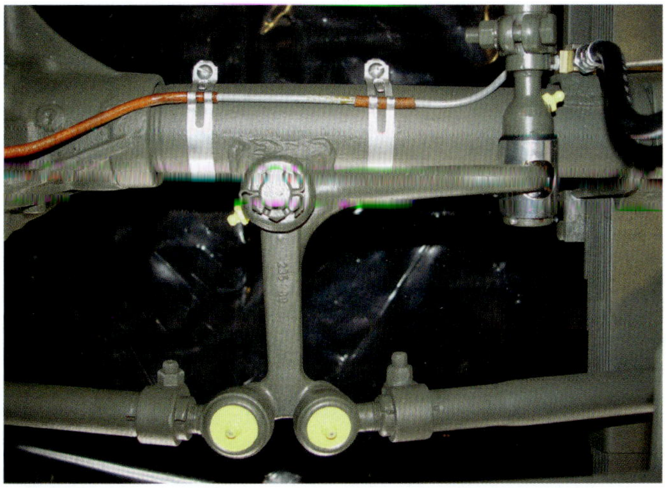

ABOVE: Overhead view of the steering bell crank fitted to the front axle (M201 shown); the drag link at the top right of the photograph is connected to the drop arm of the steering box, while the tie rods at the bottom of the picture are attached to the hubs. *Christophe Muller*

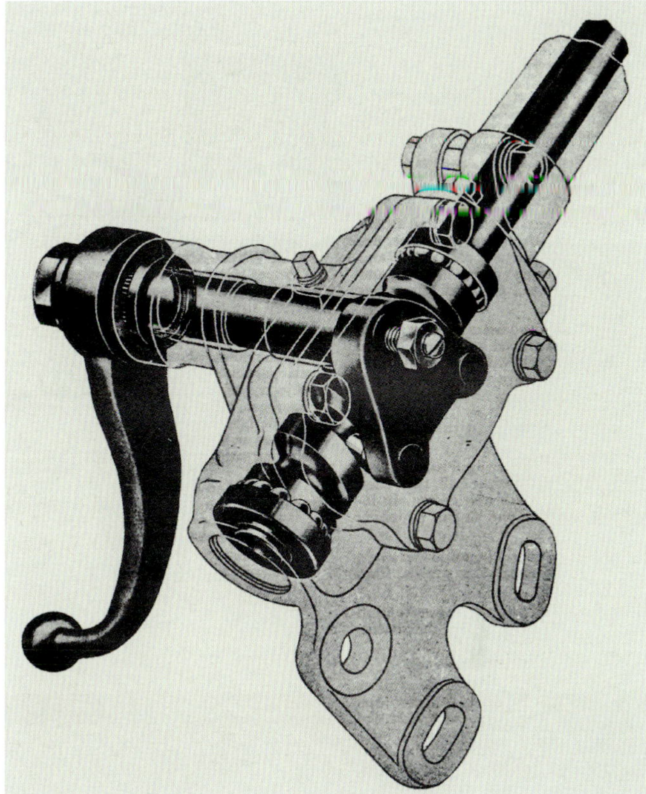

RIGHT: Ghost view of the Ross T12 cam and twin-lever steering box. *Warehouse Collection*

Three types of steering wheel were used on the Second World War Jeep, all 17in (430mm) in diameter, and with three spokes: early models had a wheel made from black composite material, but this was later replaced by a wheel of green composite, and then, from late 1942, by a steel-spoked wheel with a thinner rim, also of green composite. The M201 has a black composite steering wheel of 18in (457mm) diameter, the increased diameter presumably being provided to overcome the additional resistance of the radial tyres that were fitted.

The steering column is mounted at about 45° to the vertical position, with the steering box bolted directly to the inside face of the left-hand chassis main member and with the column braced to the underside of the dash. The lack of any adjustment in the front seat tends to put the steering wheel, particularly the larger wheel of the M201, uncomfortably close to the driver, forcing him to adopt a distinctive splayed-leg position.

From new, backlash at the steering wheel rim was stated as 'zero', and when properly set-up, this gives a nicely balanced steering system. Unfortunately, there are rather too many possible wearing points, which means that older Jeeps that have not been well maintained tend to wander slightly on the road. In addition, the system suffers from one unpleasant defect. Under heavy braking, the front axle would naturally 'roll' forward in reaction to the weight transfer of the vehicle, and this could cause the drag link to be pulled with it, which in turn would result in the steering wheel being pulled to the left. The torque-reaction spring fitted under the left-hand front spring was supposed to prevent this happening, but users would still often report the vehicle pulling to the left under heavy braking.

Steering specification

Backlash at steering wheel: zero
Castor angle: 3°
Camber: 1.5°
King-pin inclination: 7.5°
Toe in: 0.045–0.09in (1.15–2.3mm)
Toe out on full lock: inside wheel, 20°; outside wheel, 19.45°.

Axles and suspension

The front and rear axles are of hypoid bevel design, with a gear ratio of 4.88:1 and, with the obvious exception of the steering arrangements and the inclusion of constant-velocity joints at the front, the two axles are virtually identical. Those fitted to the MB/GPW were produced by Spicer, while the axles on the M201 were produced by Hotchkiss to the same design. The rear axle has fully-floating half-shafts splined at the inner ends, and bolted to the hubs at the outer. At the front, there are fully-floating shafts fitted with fully-enclosed constant-velocity joints, of either Bendix-Weiss, Rzeppa, Spicer or Tracta design; Spicer and Rzeppa joints were not generally used on the M201. Tapered roller bearings are fitted to the kingpin, above and below the steering knuckle.

The suspension is extremely basic, consisting of a multi-leaf semi-elliptical (parabolic) spring at each corner, with a non-adjustable telescopic hydraulic damper fitted vertically above each wheel, attached by rubber bushes to the pins welded to the chassis and the spring anchor plate, at roughly the centre point of the spring. The axles are mounted above the springs, located on welded saddles, with a rubber bump stop on the chassis to limit movement.

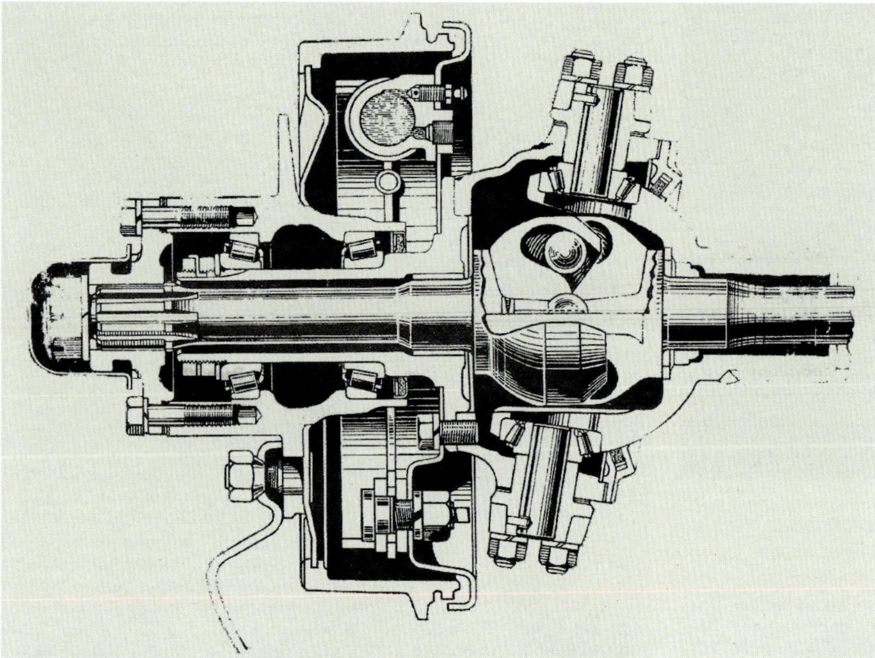

LEFT: Sectional drawing of the front axle drive shaft, constant-velocity joint and steering swivel. The CV joints were fully enclosed and were supplied by either Bendix-Weiss, Rzeppa, Spicer or Tracta; Spicer and Rzeppa joints were not used on the M201. *Warehouse Collection*

BELOW LEFT: The left-hand front spring on Willys vehicles with a chassis number above 146774, and all Ford GPWs and M201s, carries an additional torque-reaction spring fitted between the axle and the rear shackle. This is intended better to support the off-centre weight of the engine, and to stabilise the torque imparted to the axle during braking. *Christophe Muller*

BELOW RIGHT: Rear suspension showing the springs and the double-acting hydraulic telescopic shock absorbers (dampers). *Christophe Muller*

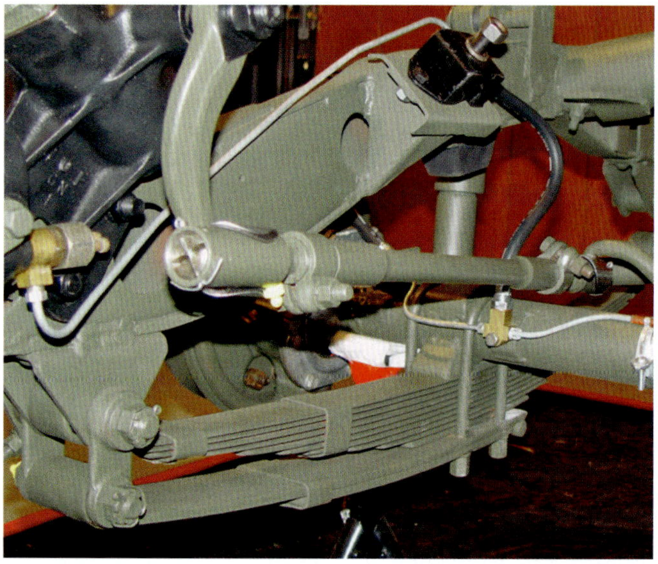

The springs are anchored to the chassis by means of plain or screwed bushes fitted into the spring eye, with a U-shaped pin fitted through both the bush and the chassis spring anchorage to provide a swinging shackle at the forward end of each front spring, and at the rear of each rear spring. At the other ends the springs are attached directly to the chassis spring anchorage by means of a plain pin.

On most vehicles, the front springs have eight leaves, 36¼ x 1¾in (922 x 44mm) in size, while those at the rear, which are longer at 42in (1,066mm), have nine leaves; the springs on the MB/GPW were originally supplied by the Mather Spring Company of Toledo, Ohio. The two front springs are not interchangeable since the side-to-side loadings of the vehicle are unequal. On Willys vehicles with a chassis number above 146774, and all Ford GPWs and M201s, the front left-hand spring also carries an additional torque-reaction spring fitted between the axle and the rear shackle; this is intended better to support the off-centre weight of the engine, and to stabilise the torque imparted to the axle during braking and thus prevent adverse effects on the steering.

The rear springs of the Hotchkiss M201 'Sahara' and ATGW variants have 13 leaves, while the ATGW and recoilless-rifle equipped variants have additional coil springs fitted outboard of the leaf spring.

Braking system

Bendix hydraulic brakes are fitted at all four wheels with the hand (parking) brake acting mechanically on a drum attached to the output shaft of the transfer case. The shoes are of the leading and trailing pattern; eccentric anchor pins on the trailing ends of the shoes are used to centre the shoe on the drum. The brake drums are 9in (225mm) diameter x 1¾in (44mm) width, giving a total area of friction lining material of 118in^2 (0.076m^2).

There are two types of hand-brake assembly. On most MB/GPW Jeeps the brake is of the external contracting type, with a single, 18in (470mm) long, lining operating on a 6in (150mm) diameter x 2in (50mm) width drum; late production vehicles from the Second World War and all M201s use an internally expanding brake with twin shoes acting on the drum.

The handbrake lever is mounted centrally on the dash, angled slightly towards the driver. It is not particularly easy to pull out and requires a rotating action to secure and release the ratchet. During the post-war years some British Army Jeeps were apparently fitted with a conventional ratchet lever-type handbrake on the floor.

BELOW: Rear brake assembly with the drum and drive shaft removed. Note the eccentric adjusters at the bottom, which are used to position the shoes correctly in relation to the drum. *Christophe Muller*

BOTTOM: On most wartime MB/GPW Jeeps, the brake is of the external contracting type, with a single lining operating on the drum. Late production vehicles from the Second World War and all M201s use an internally expanding brake, as shown here, with twin shoes acting on the drum. Leaks from the transfer case rear seal play havoc with the linings of this unit. *Christophe Muller*

Electrical equipment

The engine electrical equipment consists of the battery, ignition system, starter, and generator, and is wired with the negative pole as the earth return. This is the area where there are the greatest differences between the original MB/GPW, with its simple 6V electrical system, and the post-war M201, which has a fully-screened 24V system, employing a pair of 12V batteries.

A total of 26 earthing bond straps are fitted between the body and the chassis, and between various body panels, in an attempt to reduce electrical 'noise'. Second World War vehicles with a registration number which included an 'S' suffix are also equipped with radio filters in the ignition, generator and regulator circuits. The filters are fitted to the inside face of the bulkhead, under the dash. Several styles of these so-called 'filterette' units were employed, produced by Sprague or Tobe-Deutschmann.

A radio connection box was fitted on the inner face of the right-hand side of the body, beside the passenger seat, from about mid-1943; a similar unit is fitted to the Hotchkiss M201.

Battery

Willys and Ford vehicles were originally fitted with a Willard SW-2-119 or Autolite TS-2-15 battery with a case of black composite material, providing a maximum output of 116Ah from a nominal 6V rating. The Hotchkiss *licence MB 6V* variant is fitted with a USL battery with a capacity of 90Ah, while the M201 uses a pair of standard NATO 2HN 12V batteries, connected in series, with a maximum capacity of 45Ah from a nominal 24V.

The battery or, in the case of the M201, the batteries, are carried on a bracket welded to the chassis on the inside of the right-hand wheel arch.

Ignition system

The ignition system consists of a conventional contact-breaker distributor and a high-tension coil. Although early Jeeps have an ignition key, their use was discontinued from mid-1942 – which makes it pretty easy to steal a Jeep. In an attempt at preventing casual theft, most French Jeeps will have been retro-fitted with a master cut-out switch with a removable key, bolted through the engine bulkhead up by the passenger's feet.

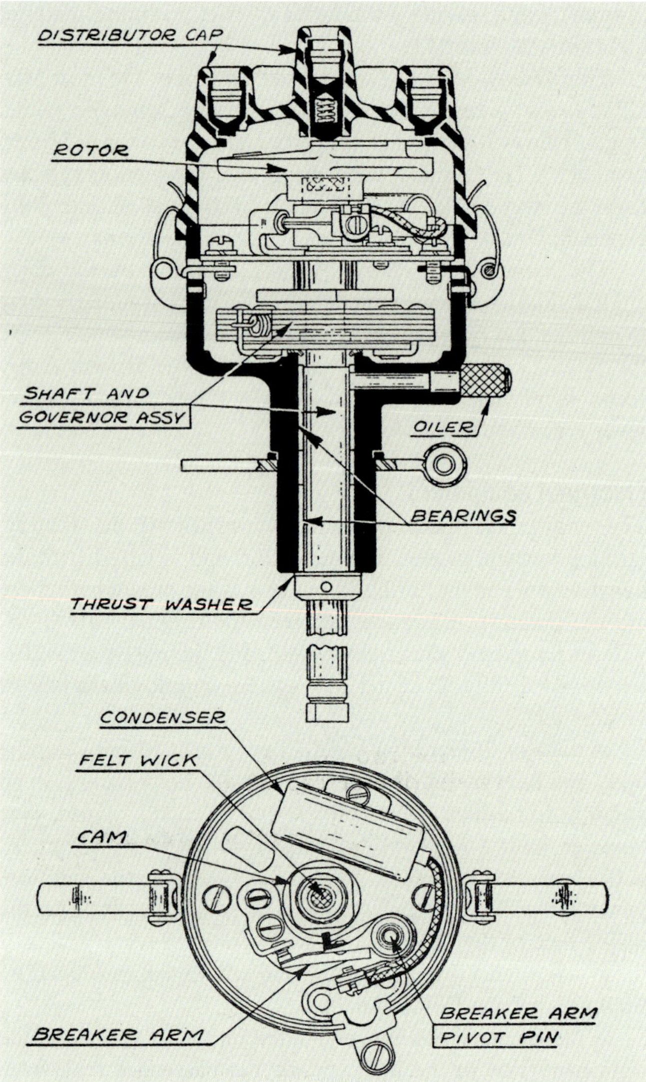

LEFT: Sectional view of the standard distributor as fitted to Second World War and early Hotchkiss licence MB Jeeps. *Warehouse Collection*

ABOVE: The 24V Hotchkiss M201 was fitted with a radio-screened and waterproofed housing, which included both the distributor and the coil. The plug leads were also waterproofed and radio-screened. *Christophe Muller*

The standard ignition set-up for the MB/GPW consists of an Autolite IGC-4705 or IAD-4008 distributor, in conjunction with an Autolite Type IG-4070L 6V coil or a Ford-built equivalent. In some cases, the distributor will have been fitted with an internal dustproof cover. The standard spark plugs are short-reach, 14mm thread, Autolite AN-7 or Champion QM2, or similar, connected to the distributor cap via ¼in (7mm) high-tension rubber-covered cable; inverted cone-shaped water deflectors of Bakelite were installed over each spark plug at the connector until mid-1943.

The French *licence MB 6V* is fitted with a Ducellier Type 2159A distributor, not dissimilar to the Autolite units used during the Second World War, and is fitted with AC number 44 plugs, which are no longer manufactured.

For the M201, the coil and distributor are contained in a single, radio-screened housing, either an ABG AL4D1 unit or an SEV AB4X S24. The spark plugs are also radio-screened items, either ABG 708SR4 or Brois BDP1-4, with screw-in connectors to suit the rubber-covered screened ignition leads. Although similar in design to the spark plugs and leads used on post-war M38 and M38A1 Jeeps, the items are not interchangeable.

In all cases, the distributor rotates anti-clockwise, and is driven by the camshaft through a dog gear, which engages with a shaft extension on the oil pump drive. Automatic advance and retard of the spark is handled by a simple centrifugal rolling-weight mechanism giving a maximum 11–12° spark advance at 1,500rpm; none of the units employ a vacuum return device. The dwell angle is 47°.

Starter motor

The MB is fitted with an Autolite MZ-4113 6V four-brush standard US military starter motor employing a spring-loaded pinion and Bendix sleeve drive; maximum current draw is 420A for a cranking speed of 185rpm. The GPW generally uses a Ford-built equivalent, almost identical to the Autolite machine. There is no solenoid and the motor is engaged via a foot-operated Autolite SW-4015 starter switch mounted on the floor to the right of the accelerator pedal.

On the French *licence MB 6V* the starter arrangements are similar, using a Ducellier Type 438A starter motor, which is also operated by a foot switch.

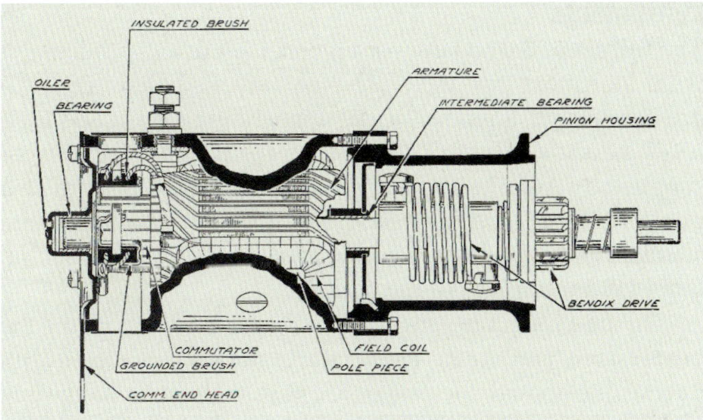

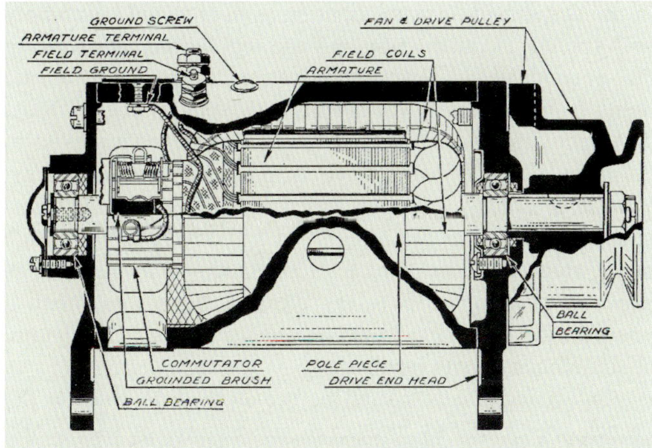

ABOVE LEFT: Sectional view of the four-brush 6V starter motor. *Warehouse Collection*

ABOVE RIGHT: Sectional view of the 6V generator; 24V Hotchkiss M201s are fitted with a larger, radio-screened and waterproofed unit driven by twin belts. *Warehouse Collection*

On the 24V M201, the engine is started by operating a rubber-covered push-button on the centre of the dash, which actuates the motor via a solenoid and pre-engaged Bendix drive. The motor is a 24V Ducellier Type 6090A unit with two brushes.

Generator

A military standard Autolite GEG-5002D generator is fitted to the MB, with a maximum rated output of 40A at 6-8V for a pulley speed of 1,460rpm; the GPW uses a Ford-built equivalent. The generator is mounted on sliding brackets on the inlet side of the engine, and the driving belt tension is adjusted by pivoting the generator outwards, and sliding it along the top bracket. The bracket also has a spring-loaded quick-release device, intended to disconnect the fan and generator drive during wading operations. Certain radio-equipped vehicles were fitted with a 12V 55A generator in place of the standard 6V unit, or alternatively, an auxiliary 12V generator with a higher output was positioned between the front seats and belt-driven from the transmission power take-off. In both cases, a second 6V battery was installed in series to give 12V for the radio circuits.

The charging circuit is controlled by an Autolite VRY4203A or VRY-4203G current-voltage regulator, the latter fitted from early 1945, installed on the inner face of the right-hand mudguard.

Equipped in the same way as the Second World War Jeeps, the *licence MB 6V* variant uses a Ducellier Type 7077A generator with a maximum output of 40A at 6-8V for a pulley speed of 1,465rpm. The generator output is controlled by a Ducellier Type 8162A current-voltage regulator.

The 24V M201 is equipped with either a Paris-Rhône Type G15R39, G15R48 or G15R51 generator, or with a Marchal Type BPG24 unit, all of them providing a maximum rated output of 22A (at 28.5V) for a pulley speed of 1,800rpm. Twin belts drive the generator rather than the single belt used on the Second World War Jeeps and there is no provision for disengaging the generator drive since the ignition system is waterproofed. A huge rubber-covered, screened lead connects the generator to the current-voltage regulator, the latter consisting of either a Paris-Rhône Type ZT3115A or ZT3118A unit, or a Marchal Type BPR24. The batteries of the M201 are carried on the chassis against the inner face of the right-hand wheel arch, which means that the regulator is fitted to the engine bulkhead.

Lighting equipment

Lighting equipment includes headlamps, front blackout marker lights, a blackout driving light installed on the left-hand front mudguard, tail and brake lights, and a single blackout rear lamp. By changing their appearance according to the distance from which they are viewed, the blackout lights are specifically designed to make it easy for individual vehicles to maintain station in a convoy at night. The M201 is also fitted with a blackout brake light at the rear and in many cases will have been retro-fitted with flashing indicators by the French Army.

A pair of large red reflectors is also fitted to the rear, adjacent to the rear lamps, with a similar red reflector mounted on each side of the body behind the rear wheel arch, acting as a marker.

BELOW: At the rear, there are standard rear running lights, brake lights, blackout lights and reflectors; the circular cap above the lights conceals the trailer socket. *Christophe Muller*

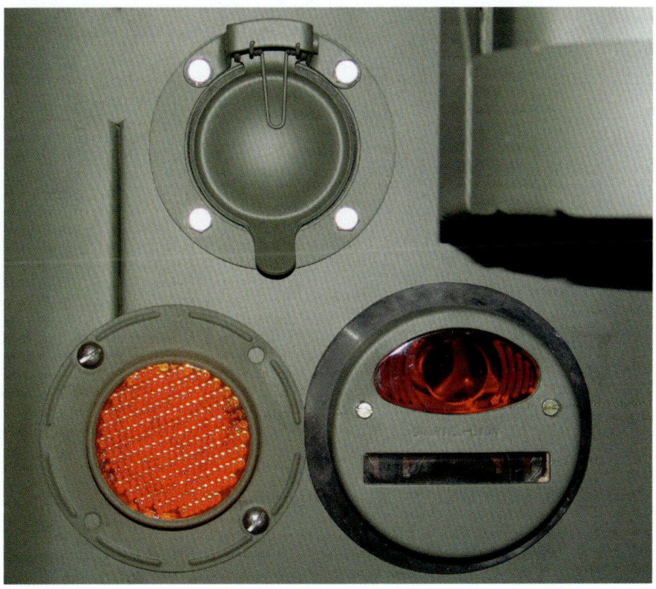

In its standard form, the lighting equipment did not comply with the UK 'Construction and use regulations' and, during the Second World War, modifications were made to the lighting system during re-assembly of Jeeps in Britain. Most noticeably, the front blackout marker lights were moved to the front mudguards and rewired to also act as side lamps; additional lamps were often added at the rear, and the right-hand headlamp was often removed and covered by a bridge plate. Many of those vehicles that remained in the UK, as opposed to going to overseas theatres, were fitted with a hooded and louvred blackout mask on the left-hand headlamp, or sometimes to both headlamps.

On all Jeeps constructed before June 1944, and on the French *licence MB 6V*, the lamps are operated by means of a push-pull switch mounted on the dashboard; the switch is locked by a thumb-operated button to prevent inadvertent operation of the main lighting during blackout driving conditions. Later vehicles, and all M201s, are fitted with a rotary switch, which is also locked to prevent the main lighting system being actuated in error. A 30A thermal-trip is incorporated in the lighting circuit at the main switch.

All vehicles are fitted with a standard four-blade Wagner-type socket at the rear, providing lighting connections for the trailer. On French Jeeps, the socket does not allow for any wiring connections to retro-fitted indicator lights.

Instruments

The full set of dashboard instruments includes a speedometer with indicators for total distance travelled and trip, oil-pressure gauge, ammeter, water temperature gauge, and fuel-level indicator. Most of the gauges for the MB/GPW were supplied by Autolite and Stewart-Warner, although Ford also used Waltham speedometers, and all of the gauges are standard military items, interchangeable with those used on other US-built trucks of the period.

On the M201, the gauges came from OS or Jaeger and the oil-pressure and water temperature gauges are electrically operated. Although the gauges are physically interchangeable with the Second World War equivalents they are, of course, marked in metric units.

BELOW: M201 dashboard showing the standard switchgear and gauges; on the extreme left of the photograph is the windscreen wiper switch and indicator switch (neither fitted to wartime Jeeps), to the right of this is the service/blackout lighting switch and a push-button switch for the headlights (not fitted to wartime Jeeps). The choke and hand throttle controls flank the ignition switch (partially hidden by the steering column); a panel light switch is fitted to the right of the hand throttle. Gauges include oil pressure, charge indicator, water temperature, fuel load and speedometer. *Christophe Muller*

LEFT: Hand-operated windscreen wipers were standard on the wartime Jeep. On early examples, there was just a single wiper. *Warehouse Collection*

BELOW: Many wartime Jeeps were subsequently fitted with vacuum-operated windscreen wipers; the M201 uses electric wipers as standard. *Warehouse Collection*

Windscreen wipers

Early Jeeps were fitted with a single, hand-operated windscreen wiper system operated from inside the vehicle by a small cranked handle attached to each pivot; this was eventually superseded by a twin wiper system, but the two wipers were not interconnected. From May 1944, a tandem system was fitted with interconnected wiper arms that allow the wipers to be operated by either the driver or the passenger. From about 1942/43, a vacuum-operated wiper kit was made available, with alternative types of vacuum motor, which gave automatic operation of the wipers by means of manifold depression, but this was not a standard installation.

All French-built Jeeps are fitted with electrically-operated tandem windscreen wipers, actuated by a switch to the lower left of the dash. A spring-loaded plunger inside the dash is used to transfer current to the wiper motor, which is fitted to the folding windscreen. A distinctive protector plate is fitted above the motor and the wiper linkage.

Wheels and tyres

Although initially fitted with conventional one-piece drop-centre (well base) 4.00in x 16in wheels (Kelsey-Hayes Type 24562), almost all standardised Second World War Jeeps employed steel, divided-rim road wheels, size 4.50 x 16in,

FAR LEFT: The standardised wartime Jeep was fitted with split-rim combat wheels generally shod with simple bar-grip non-directional mud and snow (NDMS) tyres. The ring of bolts around the outside of the rim holds the two parts together. A hinged bead lock was fitted to ensure that the tyre stayed on the rim in the event of a puncture. *Simon Thomson*

LEFT: Early M201s also used NDMS tyres, fitted to one-piece well-base rims, but the vehicle was subsequently fitted with a wider-profile radial tyre, which gives a more compliant ride. *Christophe Muller*

also of Kelsey-Hayes manufacture. Enthusiasts tend to call these 'combat rims'. The use of bolted two-piece rims allowed hinged metal beadlocks to be fitted, which press the beads of the tyre outwards against the rim and prevent a deflated tyre from slipping or becoming detached from the rim if it was not convenient for the driver to stop. The valve stem was often fitted with a cone-shaped protector to prevent damage to the valve or to prevent the valve from being pulled inside the tyre following a puncture.

Second World War Jeeps were shod with 6.00-16 cross-ply (bias) tyres with squared shoulders and a simple bar-grip pattern non-directional mud and snow (NDMS) or 'cross-country' tread. This was the US Army's standard tactical tread pattern as specified in OCM 17926. Oversize, 7.50-16 six-ply tyres were occasionally specified for particular conditions. There was also a round-shouldered military desert (MD) tread pattern developed specifically to provide optimum traction in soft terrain, for example in the loose sand of the Middle East. Tyres were supplied by, among others, Firestone, Goodyear, BFGoodrich or, until the Ford tyre plant was shipped to the Soviet Union in early 1943, Ford themselves. Ford-marked tyres have become much prized by collectors.

Shortages of rubber following the Japanese invasion of the Far East meant that Jeeps were often seen fitted with standard commercial (road) tyres and even 'seconds'. Synthetic rubber tyres were also developed during this period and can be identified by either the presence of a red dot or the letter 'S', 'S1', 'S2' etc on the sidewall. The correct pressure for the standard tyre is 35lbf/in^2 (2.5kgf/cm^2 or 2.4 Bar).

The M201 reverted to one-piece 4.50 x 16in steel wheels and, although early vehicles used 6.00-16 bar-grip tyres, many being shod with these well into the 1960s, they were eventually replaced in production by larger-section 6.50-16in radial tyres manufactured by Kleber-Colombes or Goodyear. The correct pressure for these tyres is 30lbf/in^2 (2.1kgf/cm^2 or 2.1 Bar).

A single spare wheel is carried, mounted at the rear of the vehicle, although there is evidence that some Ford vehicles were supplied without a spare tyre. For some roles, the wheel was carried between the chassis rails at the front, strapped back to the radiator grille.

TOP: The body tub is a simple one-piece welded structure, which incorporates the firewall, dash panel, floor, inner rear wheel arches and tool lockers, scuttle top, steps, and side and rear panels. Reproduction bodies are easily available for vehicles that are rusted beyond repair. *Christophe Muller*

ABOVE: The front wheel arches and radiator grille are separate from the body and can be attached to the chassis without the body being in place. Once the body is fitted, the wheel arches are attached to the side panels (three bolts either side) and the step (two bolts). *Christophe Muller*

Body

The open-sided body consists of a one-piece welded steel tub, which includes the floor and scuttle/dashboard assembly, and onto which the windscreen, front mudguards, bonnet (hood) and grille are bolted. The body construction is extremely simple, using mostly flat panels that can be easily replaced or repaired in the field and the body is bolted to the chassis frame via six rubber-insulated mounts. Drain points are provided in the floor, one on either side, normally closed-off by means of a brass plug.

Lacking the massive pressing tools of the mighty Ford Company, the bodies used by Willys differed in many small ways because of the simpler production techniques adopted by the company. For example, the front mudguards were fabricated from smaller pressings spot-welded together rather than from one piece.

The first 25,808 Willys-built Jeeps were fitted with a fabricated slatted grille but, on the standardised vehicles, this was replaced by the familiar nine-slot pressed-steel grille.

A typical military two-piece windscreen is fitted, with two separately-glazed flat glass lights. The 'screen can be hinged open from the top, or the complete assembly can be folded flat onto the bonnet, and secured with spring latches. The folded windscreen rests on green composite rubber or canvas-padded wooden blocks fitted to the bonnet; on French-built Jeeps the 'screen rests are fitted to the upper rail of the windscreen itself rather than to the bonnet.

On the left-hand side of the body, there is provision for mounting pioneer tools, consisting of a shovel and axe. The tools are held in place by a curious complex system of canvas straps. At the rear, the standardised vehicles are fitted with a jerrycan holder; this is not fitted to the so-called 'script body' Jeeps built prior to January 1943, which had the maker's name pressed into the rear panel in the position normally occupied by the jerrycan holder. Small stowage compartments are provided in the rear wheel arches, and most vehicles (Willys MB serial numbers above 120698, all Ford GPWs and all Hotchkiss vehicles) also have a lidded locker in the dashboard, positioned in front of the passenger.

Various, relatively minor features distinguish Ford, Willys and Hotchkiss-built bodies and their dates of origin. The major differences between the Second World War bodies and those used by Hotchkiss lie in the shape of the toe-board gussets, the radiator grille, and the body side reinforcements.

Weather equipment

Standard weather equipment is minimal, consisting of a one-piece lightweight top and rear curtain with a small, open rear window. The top was produced from olive drab-coloured waterproofed canvas for the MB/GPW, the French *licence MB 6V* and the early M201. Late model M201s were supplied with a similar-shaped top, fabricated from green plastic-coated nylon with a pair of larger plastic-glazed lights in the rear panel. The top is supported on a pair of tubular hoops fitted into brackets in the body sides, with the fabric clipped and/or strapped to the windscreen top rail, and secured by straps and buckles on the rear panel and to the tubular supports.

In order to convert to an open vehicle, the canvas is simply removed altogether and stowed under the passenger's seat where footman loops are provided for straps that will hold the folded top in place. With the top removed, the hoops are lowered and stowed around the top of the rear body where

ABOVE: Well-laden Military Police Jeep with the standard summer top. The photograph was taken in Tinchbray during the advance on Flers in August 1944; note the additional jerrycans carried on the front bumper. *IWM, B9289*

BELOW: Jeeps were generally only supplied with what was described as a 'summer top', but there were several patterns of canvas side curtain and door available, which provided a fully-weatherproofed enclosure. The most successful was apparently produced by Humber. *Phil Royal*

RIGHT: Although Willys did supply a number of hardtop enclosures after the war, there never really was an official hardtop for the Jeep. However, there were plenty of locally-produced examples and this restored US Navy Jeep is fitted with a very professional and attractive aluminium enclosure. *Simon Thomson*

they are strapped into place. It is also possible to leave the hoops in place and to simply roll the hood down to the first hoop or to the rear of the vehicle, or to roll the rear of the hood up to the rearmost support hoop.

Clip-on half-height canvas doorway curtains were supplied with the pre-production Jeeps and with the early Ford GPW and Willys MB, but they can have done little to keep out rain and snow and were soon deleted even though the holes for the press studs continued to be punched into the bodies. Similar curtains were supplied with the early M201. Various experiments were carried out during the Second World War with a view to providing a more satisfactory weather enclosure, including a full-length tonneau, which was produced experimentally in the USA. An official US Army 'body enclosure kit' was produced in late 1944, but the best enclosure was probably that produced in Britain by Humber, which included full-height canvas doors and glazed side curtains.

A set of purpose-designed weather equipment was produced for the M201, consisting of metal-framed plastic-coated doors, attached to pin-type hinges, which need to be welded to the windscreen pillars. Plastic-coated glazed quarter panels and side curtains were provided to complete the enclosure.

Upholstery

Seating is scarcely one of the Jeep's strong points, consisting of two separate non-adjustable front seats, the right-hand being front-hinged, together with a small bench seat with a folding squab, fitted in the rear. The seats, on which the cushions are barely 2in (50mm) thick, are upholstered in heavyweight drab-coloured waterproofed canvas (22oz/yd^2, 550g/m^2) with a zip fastening at the front of the cushion, which allows it to also double as a handy waterproof storage container for documents. Early Second World War seat cushions were padded but without springs; the springs did not become standard until mid-1943. The front seat cushions of late production M201s were thicker and were upholstered in a coated plastic cloth, in a mid to dark green colour.

Small triangular crash pads are fitted alongside each of the front seats to protect the occupants' hips from injury as the Jeep bucks and pitches during cross-country work. Canvas safety straps are also available, which can be latched across the door openings, giving the passenger something to hang on to when the going gets rough.

LEFT: The standard upholstery on wartime Jeeps and early Hotchkiss vehicles consists of thin seat cushions with a heavy-duty canvas covering. The cushions are simply screwed to the sheet metal seat pans using self-tapping screws and cup washers (M201 shown). There is provision for stowing the folded top under the passenger seat. *Christophe Muller*

Tools

Second World War Jeeps were generally issued with the following items, stowed in a canvas tool roll in the rear lockers, or as described below:

- Air-pressure gauge
- Axe (strapped to the left-hand body side)
- Camouflage net
- Grease gun (clipped to a bracket on the inside of the bonnet on the left-hand side)
- Hand tools (including screwdriver, spanners, adjustable spanner, hammer and pliers)
- Hub puller
- Jack
- Shovel (strapped to the left-hand body side)
- Sparkplug box spanner and tommy bar
- Standard First Echelon spare parts kit, containing lamps, wire, fan belt, split pins, insulating tape, and a spark plug
- Starting handle (clipped to the inner face of the rear body panel behind the seat)
- Technical manuals (stowed in the glovebox)
- Tow rope (often wrapped around the front bumper ready for immediate use)
- Tyre chains
- Tyre pump (stowed under the rear seat)
- Wheel brace (lug wrench).

PAINTWORK AND MARKINGS

The subject of the correct colour for a wartime Jeep remains extremely contentious and the choice made during restoration will depend on factors such as the date of manufacture of the vehicle, and whether it is being presented in factory-fresh or in-service condition. In the latter case a decision will also have to be made regarding the army, branch of service and period being represented.

The US military description for the paint used originally was QM Specification ES-474 'Enamel, synthetic, olive drab, lustreless', and there is strong evidence that the standard factory finish for the MB/GPW was matt Olive Green (US Federal Standard 595, shade FS 34087), although early Ford-built Jeeps had a somewhat greener cast to the finish. The final coat of paint was uniformly applied to every visible part of the vehicle after assembly, and there was usually considerable over-spray on the radiator, engine and engine accessories. Over time, the matt finish would become faded and degraded by grease marking and handling.

Small numbers of Jeeps in US Army service were camouflaged using the three-colour system laid down in US Army Field Manual FM 5-21. Others were painted matt Sand in service, or in other colours to suit a particular theatre of operation.

Vehicles intended for the US Navy were generally, though not always, painted all-over Grey. Jeeps were frequently used on US Army Air Force airfields to direct aircraft to dispersal points and taxi-ways, and on airfields that were not too close to the frontline, these so-called 'follow me' Jeeps were often brightly painted so that they could be easily seen by the

LEFT: Stone or Sand colour was used to camouflage vehicles used in the North African desert. Note the twin blackout masks and canvas half doors. *IWM, E17900*

ABOVE: Complex multi-colour camouflage pattern as used by SAS in North Africa. As with any such pattern, the idea is to break up the vehicle's outline. *Simon Thomson*

RIGHT: The standard factory finish during the Second World War was a completely matt Olive Green (US Federal Standard 595, shade FS 34087), applied to every visible part of the vehicle. Despite the US Army markings, the vehicle shown is almost certainly an M201. *Phil Royal*

ABOVE: Jeeps used by the US Navy were generally painted in matt Grey. *Simon Thomson*

RIGHT: So-called 'follow me' Jeeps were used to guide aircraft to dispersal and storage points and were generally painted in a chequer-board pattern, either in Red and White or, as here on this US Army Air Force-marked Jeep, in Yellow and Black. *Simon Thomson*

pilots. Common colour schemes included overall Yellow, or a chequerboard pattern of Black and Yellow, Black and White or Red and White. The squares themselves were about 8–10in (200–250mm) on each side, or sometimes as large as 12in (305mm), and were usually applied to all of the external surfaces of the Jeep.

It is extremely unlikely that new Jeeps entering British service were repainted but, when it came to time for a rebuild, the standard colour for British Second World War vehicles was matt Dark Earth or Dark Brown, often with an overlaying circular camouflage pattern of Black or Dark Green. This is frequently described as 'Mickey Mouse ears' camouflage. A Sand or Stone colour was used on vehicles in the Middle East and North Africa. Royal Air Force vehicles were painted in RAF Blue and Royal Navy vehicles were Battleship Grey.

ABOVE LEFT: Sand or Stone colour was often used for Jeeps used in North Africa. *Simon Thomson*

ABOVE RIGHT: US Air Force personnel pose with a typical chequer-board 'follow me' Jeep. *Warehouse Collection*

LEFT: Genuine Second World War colour photograph showing a Yellow-finished US Army Jeep used on an airfield, probably as an aid to taxiing aircraft. Note the unusual black-painted star and huge 'USA number' on the bonnet. *David Doyle*

French Jeeps were originally finished in a semi-gloss Green, which weathers to a distinctive chalky Grey-Green colour. From the mid-1980s, many of the Jeeps remaining in military service were repainted in a new three-colour camouflage finish, consisting of a base colour of mid-Green with disruptive patches of Black and mid-Brown; the finish was often applied across the canvas top as well as the body.

Engine and transmission

Under the bonnet, Willys painted the engine and transmission matt Olive Drab, while Ford used a glossy Medium Grey colour, changing to a slightly lighter colour during the production run. Hotchkiss engines are painted a glossy Blue-Green. The gearbox of both a Hotchkiss and Ford Jeep should match the engine, while the transfer case was Olive Drab. Axles, of course, were painted to match the body.

Lubrication points

Both the US and French Armies used coloured circles to identify grease nipples and other locations on the Jeep that needed regular attention. In the case of the US Army, after about 1943, Signal Red circles, about ¾in (20mm) in diameter were painted over all grease nipples; the oil filler cap, axle filler plugs, gearbox and transfer case fillers and radiator cap were also painted Red. The French Army used Chrome Yellow paint, applied in the same way.

ABOVE: Unless they were serving in action, during their post-war service British Army Jeeps were repainted in gloss Deep Bronze Green; the bonnet star, which was the air recognition symbol used on all Allied vehicles after June 1944, was not generally retained on post-war British vehicles. Note the slat grille and tandem towing attachment. *Simon Thomson*

Markings

The whole subject of the correct and historically accurate marking of military vehicles is fraught with difficulty and is way beyond the scope of this volume. Both the British and US Armies have published *diktats,* which lay down how vehicles should be marked, but there is plenty of photographic evidence to indicate that these regulations were not necessarily followed by the man wielding the stencil brush. It should also be remembered that the rules were changed from time to time and what might have been correct in, say, 1941, is not necessarily correct for 1945. The same is equally true of French Army Jeeps.

For the US Army, the position and content of vehicle markings was laid down in Army Regulations AR850-5 and AR850-10. To summarise, it would be true to say that during the Second World War, all US Army Jeeps carried the 'USA number' – the registration number – stencilled onto the bonnet sides in 2in (50mm) high letters of blue, and later white, matt paint. In addition, a 15in (380mm) diameter white star, sometimes in a three-segment circle, was painted onto the bonnet top overlapping the scuttle to enable it to be seen from the air when the screen was folded. Smaller stars were applied to the upper rearmost corners of the body and on the front bumper. It was permissible to cover these stars if tactical conditions demanded concealment.

Unit markings were generally carried on the front and rear bumpers. These numbers consisted of four groups of figures indicating the unit, regiment or brigade, and company to which the vehicle was assigned, with the fourth group used to denote the serial number of the specific vehicle in the normal order of march in the organisation to which it was assigned. The windscreen panel was also occasionally used, either to identify a Military Police Jeep or for soldiers' personal markings. 'Star' markings to indicate that the Jeep was the property of a high-ranking officer were generally carried on plates attached to the front bumper. This does not mean that there were not other markings applied to the vehicle for specific reasons. Post-war markings for American Jeeps were similar but often more detailed or elaborate, and for example, tended to include the tyre pressures and other specific data.

US Navy and US Army Air Force vehicles were differently marked.

In Britain, Jeeps similarly carried the registration, or census, number on the bonnet sides, although for British vehicles it was applied in 3in (75mm) high lettering; Canadian Army vehicles were identified in the same way but the number included a 'C' prefix. During, and after, the build-up to D-Day, all Allied vehicles carried the white invasion star on the bonnet although, prior to this, and during the North African and Italian campaigns, the red, white and blue RAF roundel had been used as an air recognition symbol on British vehicles. Unit markings were either applied to the front and rear bumper, or to plates that were attached to the bumpers. The invasion star was generally removed from British military vehicles after 1945 and, from 1949, British military registration numbers were carried on the front and rear of the vehicle rather than on the bonnet sides.

French Army Jeeps carried the registration number, and a small national tricolour recognition mark, on the front bumper. The registration number was also applied to a metal plate fitted to the body above the left-hand rear bumper and the tricolour was painted onto the rearmost chassis cross member to the left of the towing hook. In the 1990s, a sword and tricolour marking in a grey self-adhesive circle was also applied to the curve of the scuttle, with a similar rectangular marking applied to the bumpers. Coded unit markings were applied to the front and rear bumpers. French Jeeps also usually carried a black rectangle on the bonnet sides, which was divided into three separate areas; this area was used to chalk numbers to indicate, for example, the position of a vehicle in a convoy.

During the 1950s, most French Jeeps were also marked with a figure '1' in a white 'flame'-topped circle low down on the scuttle panel on either side. This indicated the weight of the vehicle ('1' being assigned to the lightest of four classes) and was used to determine how many vehicles could be loaded onto a standard French railway wagon. During the 1960s and 1970s the 'flames' were omitted and the '1' was replaced by a '0' (zero), with vehicle weights now being assigned to five classes.

ADAPTATIONS FOR SPECIALISED ROLES

Airborne Jeeps

With a fair bit of persuasion, a Jeep could just about be coaxed into the hold of a C-47 Dakota transport aircraft, and Jeeps were also delivered by Airspeed Horsa and Waco Hadrian gliders, notably for the landings in Normandy and at Arnhem.

The vehicles were modified in various minor ways, to reduce weight and to make it easier to load and unload into the relatively narrow bodies of the transport aircraft and gliders. For example, to help reduce the height of the vehicle,

ABOVE: The box of explosives tied to the front bumper is a nice touch. The vehicle is also equipped with a radio and machine-gun, which would have been an unusual combination during the Second World War. *Warehouse Collection*

BELOW: British 6th Airborne Division loading a Jeep into an Airspeed Horsa glider in preparation for the Rhine crossing in March 1945. *IWM, H41547*

ABOVE: The Jeep nearest the camera carries a radio set, machine-gun mount, a siren (on the right-hand chassis member), a decontaminator (on the front mudguard), canvas half-doors, a radiator expansion tank, and the usual items of personal kit in musette bags. *Simon Thomson*

RIGHT: British Jeep adapted for use as a high-speed signals line layer by the Royal Corps of Signals. The official caption, dating from February 1944, states that the cables can be laid at up to 40mph (65kmh) and each drum holds 1 mile (1.62km) of cable. *IWM, H35776*

the nut securing the steering wheel was often adapted to allow rapid removal of the wheel; occasionally the wheel itself was cut through to form just two-thirds of a circle. The front bumper was cut back to the chassis rails, and the spare wheel and jerrycan holder were often removed, to allow the Jeep to turn through 90º after entering the side-loading door of a Horsa or Dakota. These airborne Jeeps were also often fitted with large rear stowage baskets, or stretcher frames, which necessitated mounting the spare wheel at the front between the chassis rails.

Experiments were also conducted with air-dropping Jeeps on purpose-designed platforms or 'Jeep-dropping crates', slung under, for example, the bomb bay of an RAF Handley Page Halifax aircraft. Some 2,000 of these special airborne crates, complete with crutching support sets, were ordered by the Ministry of Supply in 1944.

Cable laying

In 1941, the US Signals Corps issued a technical bulletin (TM 11-362) showing how the standard RL-31 cable reel unit could be installed in the back of a Jeep to produce a line-laying vehicle. In the first version of this application, the back panel of the Jeep was cut away and the reel unit installed on the rear floor, braced onto the rear cross member of the chassis. This method of installation was subsequently revised so that the Jeep body did not need to be modified and the cable reel was mounted outside the vehicle.

This idea was also adopted by the British Royal Corps of Signals and, in 1944, a Jeep was modified to allow cable laying across country at speeds of up to 40mph (65km/h). With a crew of four, consisting of a driver and three linesmen, the vehicles carried up to ten or a dozen reels of signal cable, each with a cable capacity of 5,000ft (1,600m), mounted on special brackets at the front and rear. It was possible to lay 10 miles (16km) of cable between two points, in little more time than would be taken to complete the journey in the Jeep. The Jeep was also adapted to carry the various tools and pieces of equipment for the job, together with poles and ladders that might be required for making road crossings. The hood and windscreen were removed, and the spare wheel was carried flat on the bonnet.

LEFT: Keep it simple – the Australian flag goes very nicely with the driver's Australian slouch hat, while the radiator expansion tank suggests that the vehicle is equipped for the sunnier climes found in the Antipodes. *Simon Thomson*

Sahara Jeep

The French Army had a version of the M201 equipped to withstand the punishing conditions encountered in the Sahara Desert. Modifications included heavier rear suspension, repositioned shock absorbers (dampers), sand tyres, a high-efficiency wing-mounted air cleaner, dual fuel tanks with an auxiliary electric fuel pump, and a sealed cooling system. Both *licence MB 6V*, and M201 24V Jeeps were converted in this way.

Field ambulance

During the First World War, the motorcycle had frequently been used as a means of evacuating wounded men from the front line but, in the Second World War this role was generally taken over by the Jeep. Rather than being produced as ambulances during original manufacture, the Jeeps were modified in either a base or unit workshop, and there were several different variants, all of which followed a similar theme.

The simplest version, originally used by the American Medical Corps, and referred to as the 'Janes', carried a tubular frame fitted over the bonnet, intended to carry two stretchers. The windscreen was removed and an extended hood was sometimes fitted to protect the occupants from sun and rain. A variation of this allowed the vehicle to carry three, or even four stretchers – two positioned over the bonnet, and two over the rear compartment.

The US Marine Corps (USMC) used a three-stretcher version in the Pacific theatre, with a full canvas enclosure. These vehicles were converted by the Australian GM Holden Company, and were sometimes described as the 'Australian' system. Modifications included the addition of lifting rings and tow hooks, the inclusion of a side stowage compartment in place of the passenger seat, a change to the rake of the windscreen to a more upright angle, and the use of a top extension to the screen to increase the internal headroom.

The British 'Carter' system also carried two stretchers over the rear of the vehicle on a folding tubular framework fitted with runners to carry the stretchers. The hood was also extended over the stretchers at the rear, to provide some weather protection. Other variations were described as the 'Edwards' system, and the 'airborne' – and, *in extremis*, casualties were even carried in Jeep trailers.

BELOW: British Army Jeep fitted with the Carter stretcher carrier. The patients were protected from the weather by a rear extension to the hood and side curtains. *The Tank Museum*

RIGHT: A pair of Royal Army Medical Corps (RAMC) 3rd Army Jeeps fitted with the Edwards – or the airborne stretcher – conversion. Photographed in the Caen area in July 1944 *IWM, B6826*

LEFT: This army medical officer apparently acted as GP to the residents – and animals – of Bénouville during the times that he was off duty. The medical officer is from Pietermaritzberg, South Africa, and is photographed with his interpreter (Mlle Dervis) loading medical supplies into the Jeep in July 1944. *IWM, B8625*

None of these conversions improved the vehicle's handling, nor did they offer much comfort to the wounded men. The Americans tried to get around the problems of instability by fitting racks, which allowed the stretchers to be carried above the driver's head rather than behind or in front of him – one variation of this allowed the Jeep to carry four wounded in two tiers. However, those designs that placed the stretchers above the windscreen must have made the Jeep far more inclined to roll on side slopes because of the way the centre of gravity was raised.

ABOVE: Janes Jeep ambulance showing the removable canvas top designed to shelter the hapless patients. There are two stretchers across the bonnet and one at the rear. *IWM, MH1004*

BELOW: Jeeps intended to be delivered by air were modified in various ways – both to reduce the weight, for example by removing the top, windscreen and spare wheel – and to simplify the loading operation, for example by removing the front bumper ends and the steps. *Phil Royal*

ABOVE: The simplest, if not the most comfortable, way of carrying stretchers on a Jeep was to lay them across the bonnet and the rear of the body. *Simon Thomson*

RIGHT: One of the more unusual weapons of the period, at least as regards Jeep mounts, was the 0.303in water-cooled Vickers. Note the Bren gun with its standard bi-pod carried in the passenger compartment. *Phil Royal*

Gun mount

Although the relatively light construction of the Jeep meant that it was difficult to find the structural strength necessary for a machine-gun mount, experiments into arming the vehicle were being carried out as early as the spring of 1941. The first such attempt, somewhat unsuccessfully, mounted a .50-calibre machine cannon on the standard US Army ground tripod, bolted to the rear floor of the vehicle. A .30-calibre machine-gun was also tried, mounted on a low column.

The standardised Jeeps included a reinforced area on the third chassis cross member, just behind the front seats, and the first successful attempt at arming the vehicle used a T47 monopost, or pedestal mount, bolted through the floor to this point on the chassis, braced with a single leg to the rear. Proving itself to be unstable during test firing, the T47 mount was subsequently modified and standardised as the triple-braced M31 from 1942, with some 31,653 examples constructed by James Cunningham & Sons before it was replaced in service by the M31C in March 1945. The mount consisted of a tubular column with a socket at the top into which was clamped a gun pintle and ammunition tray. Various types of pintle were available according to the weapon in use; the most common types were the D3857 pintle and D38571 ammunition tray, and the E10014, which included both tray and pintle.

The M31 became the standard method of equipping a Jeep with either a .30-calibre M1919A4 Browning machine-gun, or the larger .50-calibre M2 Browning heavy machine-gun. However, there was also a scuttle-mounted support for the .30-calibre weapon, designated M48, which could also be used as a mount for the .30-calibre M1918A2 BAR (Browning automatic rifle). Less successful than the M31, the M48 mount suffered from having a restricted field of fire, and was also unable properly to withstand the recoil forces generated by the .50-calibre weapon.

During the early years of the Second World War, British Jeeps were occasionally fitted with a spring-balanced mount that allowed a Bren gun to be used in the anti-aircraft role. The mount was fitted to the right-hand body side. There are also photographs of Jeeps with all kinds of other weapons, including those designed for the anti-tank and anti-aircraft role. Examples include twin Vickers K machine-guns, Boys anti-tank rifle, Bren guns, the water-cooled M1917A1 machine-gun, and a 4.2in mortar on a standard bipod mounting in the rear.

During the 1950s and later, the French Army also used an external mono-post mount on both the M201 and the wartime Jeep, bolted down to the right-hand step and to the body side. The mount, which was designed to carry the AA52 (*Arme Automatique Transformable, Modèle 1952*) 7.7mm general-purpose machine-gun, included a long swivelling arm, which curved back sufficiently to allow the passenger to fire the gun with the windscreen erected.

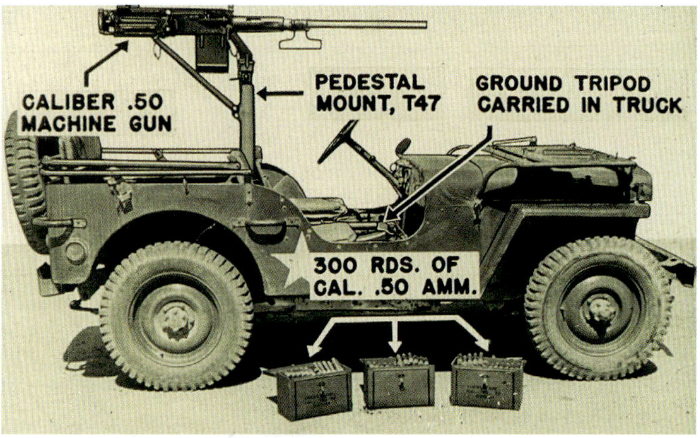

ABOVE: US Army training aid shows a Jeep fitted with a mono-post pedestal mount and .50-calibre Browning M2HB heavy-barrel machine-gun, as well as indicating that there is stowage space for 300 rounds of ammunition and a ground tripod. *Warehouse Collection*

LEFT: The M48 scuttle mount was designed for the .30-calibre Browning machine-gun, but the field of fire was restricted. *Phil Royal*

LEFT: Heavily-armed SAS Jeep fitted with single and twin Vickers K machine-guns and a .50-calibre Browning. Each of these patrol vehicles carried at least 20 jerrycans of fuel, together with sufficient ammunition, food and water for a month. January 1943. *IWM, NA675*

ABOVE: Photographed in Cyrenaica during a pause in the advance into Syria in December 1942, this well-loaded Jeep belongs to the SAS. *IWM, E20084*

ABOVE: The .50-calibre Browning M2HB heavy machine-gun fitted onto a mono-post pedestal mount in the rear of this US Army Jeep was a formidable weapon with a rate of fire of 500 rounds per minute. There is also a .30-calibre machine-gun on a scuttle mount. *Warehouse Collection*

BELOW: The French Army fitted a scuttle, or side-mount for the 7.7mm AA52 (*Armée Automatique Transformable, Modèle 1952*) general-purpose machine-gun, which was deployed between 1952 and 2008. *Christophe Muller*

ABOVE: In the last few months of the Second World War the US Army started to deploy the 106mm M27 and M40 recoilless rifles against enemy armour, both of which could be carried in a Jeep using the M79 tripod mount. The weapon remained in use into the post-war years and was also fitted into the M201. *Warehouse Collection*

BELOW: Introduced in 1964, the Franco-German gas-launched MILAN (*Missile, d'linfanterie, Légère, Anti-Char*) anti-tank missile made the M201 into a highly mobile tank killer. With no distinctive thermal signature, the MILAN missile was designed not to betray the firing position of the launch vehicle; spare missiles were carried across the back of the Jeep, necessitating the relocation of the spare wheel to the side panel. *Simon Thomson*

ABOVE: French Army M201 Jeeps mounting the ENTAC (*ENgin, Téléguidé Anti-Char*) anti-tank missile, developed by the Franco-German Saint Louis Research Institute and manufactured by Nord Aviation. ENTAC replaced the earlier SS11 missile in 1958. *The Tank Museum*

Anti-tank role

The low-silhouette and cross-country mobility of the Jeep made it eminently suitable for use in the anti-tank role. Although there was no armoured protection for the crew, beyond any afforded by the gun shield, the agility of the vehicle allowed it to exploit the 'shoot and scoot' capability that remains a useful tactic to this day. The first experiments took place in August 1941, when two Bantam BRC-40s were modified at Aberdeen Proving Ground to provide a mount for the American 37mm anti-tank

gun. The resulting vehicle was designated '37mm gun motor carriage, T2'. A revised model, designated T2E1, incorporated serious modifications that included the removal of all of the rear body in order to provide sufficient space to allow the gun to traverse through 360º, as well as repositioning the steering column at a more upright angle. There was no series production.

In the last few months of the Second World War the US Army started to deploy the 75mm M20 recoilless rifle against enemy armour. The weapon fired a shaped charge, which was effective against 100mm of armour and it could be mounted in a Jeep using the standard M31C pedestal. This was subsequently replaced by the 106mm M27 and M40 weapons, both of which could be carried in a Jeep using the M79 tripod mount. The French Army continued to use the M40 until the mid- to late-1950s, mounting it on both *licence MB*, and M201 Jeeps, when it started to be replaced by wire-guided ATGW (anti-tank guided weapon) missiles.

The first anti-tank missile to be used by the French Army in the M201 was the Nord Aviation SS10, three of which were carried in a hydraulically-operated launcher. The missiles were carried in the launch position and were fired over the rear of the vehicle. In 1953, the SS10 was replaced by the SS11, but by 1958 both had been rendered obsolete by the introduction of the ENTAC (*Engin Téléguidé Anti-Char*) missile, developed by the Franco-German Saint Louis Research Institute and manufactured by Nord Aviation. In 1966, an M201 anti-tank variant was introduced, which was equipped with four ENTAC missiles that could be fired from inside the vehicle or remotely using a separation sight.

Within little more than a decade, ENTAC had itself had been superseded by the Franco-German MILAN (*Missile, d'Infanterie, Légère, Anti-Char*), which was introduced in 1964. MILAN missiles started to enter service in 1972 and, by 1976, the ENTAC-equipped M201s were being replaced by Jeeps equipped with MILAN launchers. The gas-launched MILAN, in its MILAN 3 configuration, remained in widespread use across Europe until it started to be replaced by the Javelin system in 2005, by which time the French Army had disposed of all of its M201s.

Rocket launcher

The US Seventh Army in Alsace fitted a number of Jeeps with 4.5in rocket launchers. A mount/launch rail at the rear carried 12 rockets that could be fired at two-second intervals. A steel roof was fitted over the front seat area to protect the crew.

Odograph

One of the more unusual applications for the Jeep was as a mount for the electro-magnetic odograph. Designed by a team at the Monroe Calculating Machine Company led by the company President, E.F. Britten Jr, the 'Land odograph, Model M1' consisted of four major components – an electronic magnetic compass, a valve-driven power supply, a calculator, and a plotter – which, together, could measure the direction and distance of the vehicle as it travelled. The equipment was manufactured in such a way that it was unaffected by the metal mass of the vehicle itself.

ABOVE: The odograph consisted of an electronic magnetic compass, a valve-driven power supply, a calculator, and a plotter, designed to measure the direction and distance of the vehicle as it travelled. The data was processed through a mechanical calculator, and could be used to draw a map of where the vehicle had travelled, or to plot the position of objectives relative to a given base. The scale of the map could be adjusted to any scale between 1:20,000 and 1:500,000. A total of just 1,500 were constructed. *David Doyle*

The data relating to distance and direction was processed through a mechanical calculator, and could be used to draw a map of where the vehicle had travelled, via a plotting pencil, or to plot the position of objectives relative to a given base, with a margin of error of around two to three per cent. The map could be adjusted by the user to any scale between 1:20,000 and 1:500,000, which meant a scale could be selected that would allow the resulting map to be overlaid on a standard topographic map, to give a complete picture of the terrain. Counters on the plotter indicated the number of miles travelled north, south, east and west, as well as the total distance travelled and an azimuth dial showed the direction in which the vehicle was heading at any given moment.

A patent application (No 2,533,029) was made in June 1944 for the odograph by Alvin McNish and Bryant Tuckerman on behalf of the US Secretary of War. The patent was granted in December 1950. A total of 1,500 of these units were manufactured both by Monroe and IBM during 1943 and something like a dozen are believed to have survived.

Radio communications

Although radio – or wireless – communications had played a small part in the First World War, the equipment involved was generally large and cumbersome and did not lend itself to rapid deployment. The Second World War was different, and radio equipment had become both sufficiently portable and reliable to be installed in a range of military vehicles, including Jeeps. However, there was certainly no question of radios becoming a universal fitment and, it should also be pointed out, that most required a 12V supply rather than the standard 6V system found in the Jeep. Nevertheless, large numbers of Jeeps were adapted for radio communications.

Earthing bond straps and a capacitor filter unit were fitted to all Jeeps as standard equipment, but this was not always sufficient to prevent interference from the vehicle's electrical system and, in 1943, the US Signal Corps produced a shielding system for the coil, distributor, ignition leads and spark plugs. An 'S' was generally appended to the vehicle census, or registration, number to indicate that the vehicle had been fitted with the radio suppression equipment. The lesson was obviously well learned because the 24V Hotchkiss M201 was fitted as standard with a fully-screened ignition system, as were post-war US-built Jeeps.

The radio installation kit consisted of a connecting box – although this became a standard fitment in the vehicles after December 1943 – mounting hardware for the radio set, aerial brackets, and connecting leads. The radio sets themselves were normally mounted on the inner rear wings, or on a table fitted across the back of the vehicle in place of the rear seat.

Typical US Signal Corps radio stations included the SCR-510 or SCR-610 sets, which were designed to operate on either 6V or 12V systems, and the SCR-193, SCR-193-K, SCR-506A, SCR-508, SCR-528, SCR-608, SCR-628, SCR-808, and SCR-828 sets, which were suitable only for 12V operation. As regards the provision of a 12V supply, there were two possible methods. For the smaller equipment, a 12V 55A generator was installed in place of the standard 6V unit, together with a special regulator and a second 6V battery, the latter connected in series to provide a 12V supply for the radio. Alternatively, the larger equipment was powered by a 12V auxiliary generator, belt-driven from the transfer case power take-off, again using two 6V batteries.

In British service during the war years, the vehicle would have been used with equipment such as the No 19, No 22 or No 37 W/T sets. Those vehicles that were converted to the so-called 'fitted for wireless' or 'fitted for radio' (FFW/FFR) role by the British in the post-war years, carried a pair of additional 12V batteries in the rear compartment to power the radio equipment; these batteries were not connected to the electrical system of the vehicle and were recharged either by a 'charge horse' generator or a workshop battery-charger system.

Towards the end of the Jeep's service life with the British Army, it would have been fitted with Larkspur equipment using the installation kit that had been designed for use with the FV1801 Austin Champ. The Larkspur sets were installed on a rail-mounted carrier, fitted across the rear body in place of the rear seat, with the batteries installed beneath. The aerial tuner unit was installed on a simple bracket fitted to the top of the left- or right-hand front mudguard according to the application, with the aerial bases fitted on top of the tuner

TOP RIGHT: As long as the back-seat passenger was happy to sit alone, there was sufficient space in the back of the Jeep for radio sets on either side of the body. *Warehouse Collection*

RIGHT: This Jeep is carrying three radio sets: an SCR-608 in the rear; an SCR-609 or SCR-610 (including the plate power supply) on the left-hand side; and an AN/GRC9 (in vehicular AN/VRC-34 form) on the right-hand side. The AN/GRC-9 (the so-called 'angry nine') was a low-power transportable radio set operating on 2–11.7MHz, which first appeared in the late-1940s to replace the SCR-284, SCR-288 and SCR-694. *Warehouse Collection*

ABOVE: A Jeep loaded with the US Army SCR-399A radio set, which was normally carried in a Studebaker 2½-ton truck but which, in this form, could not be loaded into a glider. The Jeep is carrying the antenna, frequency meter and tuning unit; other parts of the set were carried in other vehicles. *IWM, NA18769*

RIGHT: Bearing a slight resemblance to the ubiquitous No 22 set, which it replaced in 1945, the British No 62 radio set was intended for vehicle and ground stations and transmitted on the range 1.6–10MHz. *The Tank Museum*

unit. The front sidelights were moved onto the bracket, ahead of the tuner. The headset adapter was fitted to the fascia, to the right of the handbrake and immediately in front of the co-driver. The most common Larkspur installation in a Jeep was a single C45HF set, but it is possible that combinations of both high-frequency and very high-frequency sets may also have been installed. Examples would have included C13/C42; or the C42/B47, C45/C45 and C42/BE201 VHF sets; hybrid combinations such as 19HP/C45 were also being installed in the late 1950s.

The French Army continued to use radio sets that were identical to the American equipment of the Second World War during the 1950s and 1960s. Typical installations might have included SCR-506, SCR-528, SCR-608, SCR-628, SCR-808, SCR-826, SCR-193K, and the waterproofed version, SCR-193KW. The French also used the post-war US Signal Corps AN/VRC-1 or AN/GRC-9 sets, made under licence in France.

ABOVE: The French Army also used a version of the 'angry nine' in the M201, in this case in AN/GRC9F form. Note also the LS-7 loudspeaker unit, and the DY-88 Dynamotor power supply unit. *Christophe Muller*

ABOVE: In the immediate post-war years, the French Army used either domestic versions of US Army radios of the Second World War era or surplus/reconditioned US sets. This is the SCR-609 or SCR-610 with its plate power supply unit. *Warehouse Collection*

BELOW: By carrying two sets of wheels, this Jeep can be readily converted from railway to road operation. During the conversion the vehicle is suspended on a jack that allows it to be rotated onto the railway lines. *IWM, E27538*

ABOVE: Jeep train on the vital supply route between Myitykina and Mogaung, Burma, where Japanese action had destroyed the road. December 1944. *IWM, SE2870*

Railway Jeep

With railway wheels fitted in place of the standard wheel and tyre combination, a Jeep could form a useful locomotive, shunting engine (switcher), or railway patrol vehicle, travelling ahead of a regular train. Surprisingly, a rail-equipped Jeep was able to handle gross train weights up to 250 tonnes – representing 10 British-style freight wagons.

The British Army ran feasibility trials on such a modification in March 1943, with at least one vehicle mounting brackets to allow whichever set of wheels was not in use to be carried on board, thus facilitating a quick changeover from one mode to the other. The steering gear was locked in the straight-ahead position to prevent the driver derailing the 'locomotive' by attempting to steer into a curve. For performance, much depended on the diameter of the railway wheels, and thus the overall gearing, but the absence of friction between the wheels and rails allowed the vehicle to attain quite considerable speeds. The modification was used in France during the latter part of the war, particularly on the Isigny–Saint-Lô route, and was also seen in Burma and Australia where the railway routes were better developed than the roads.

In the USA, the Evans Autorailer Company produced a standard conversion kit for Jeeps, and other vehicles, which mounted railway wheels on a hydraulically-operated frame, allowing rapid conversion from road to rail. Seven Jeeps are said to have been equipped with this conversion in 1945.

Recovery Jeep

In 1943, during the Italian campaign, the REME were quick to realise that the Jeep was about the only practicable vehicle for use on the unimproved Italian mountain roads, and set about devising a light recovery variant. The vehicle was fitted with a simple A-frame jib in the rear compartment, together with a hand-operated winch

In India, similar light-recovery vehicles were constructed using a frame of angle iron attached to the rear of the Jeep to allow a second vehicle to be carried on suspended tow.

Waterproofing for wading

In the standard ex-factory condition, Jeeps were not suitable for deep-water wading. Prior to the D-Day landings REME developed reliable techniques, equipment and materials for waterproofing vehicles that would enable them to wade ashore from landing craft that could be 40 or 50ft (12–15m) from the beach.

The problems of waterproofing vehicles had first been considered as early as 1941 and a small staff of Royal Army Ordnance Corps (RAOC) personnel attached to 110 Force – the invasion troops, later to be known as 2nd Expeditionary Force, then 1st Army – started to select and test suitable materials. In July 1943, a new department was established under the Director of Mechanical Engineering (DME) to take responsibility for wading trials and techniques. For the D-Day invasion, 21 Army Group laid down a basic specification for wading, which stated that soft-skin vehicles must be able to wade to a depth of 4ft (1,220mm) as well as being able to withstand 18in (450mm) waves for a period of six minutes. For the average soft-skin vehicle this meant that the engine would need to be sealed to

ABOVE: Successful waterproofing involved sealing all possible apertures in the engine and transmission with large quantities of an asbestos fibre-filled grease. A raised snorkel attached to the windscreen pillar and an extension to the exhaust allowed the engine to breathe underwater. *IWM, H37983*

allow it to continue to operate under water, and some means had to be devised to provide air to the carburettor, to allow the crankcase to breathe, and to keep water out of the vital electrical and fuel systems.

Kits were developed for most vehicles, including Jeeps and, by March 1943, illustrated instruction books had been prepared to clarify the procedures involved, breaking the process down into a series of separate tasks. Generally, these were carried out at different locations prior to the actual amphibious landing – the last of these tasks, for example, which was the sealing of breathers, was actually carried out after embarkation since the vehicle was only able to travel less than a mile before the sealing materials had to be removed. Proper application of the waterproofing kit, which involved large amounts of asbestos fibre-based grease or rubber solution, was time consuming, with the average time required to waterproof a soft-skin vehicle at around 55 hours.

During the lead-up to D-Day, thousands of vehicles were waterproofed and put into store. Unfortunately, it was found that the materials deteriorated in storage and when a test wade was made with a selection of vehicles in early 1943, all of them failed. This showed that it was necessary to waterproof the vehicles no more than six or eight weeks before undertaking wading and thousands of vehicles had to be waterproofed again. REME employed 1,200 men on waterproofing soft-skin vehicles between May and June 1944, and a further 1,300 men working on armoured vehicles during the same period.

However, despite the somewhat makeshift nature of the waterproofing techniques, the process was surprisingly successful. Of the total number of vehicles landed across the beaches from D-Day to 17 June (D+11), it was estimated that just 4.2 per cent of soft-skin and 0.5 per cent of armoured vehicles were 'drowned'. A large proportion of the drownings were due to the vehicles being offloaded into deeper water than was intended (1.5 per cent of losses), or through becoming bogged down or lost due to enemy action (1.3 per cent), with the remainder due to inefficient waterproofing or bad driving.

BELOW: There's nothing wrong with keeping your Jeep absolutely devoid of unnecessary clutter. *Simon Thomson*

ABOVE: A pair of Jeeps, at least one of which is clearly a Hotchkiss M201, restored as vehicles of Popski's Private Army (No 1 Demolition Squadron, PPA). Note the big, .50-calibre machine-guns and extra fuel and ammunition stowage. *Phil Royal*

ABOVE: Accessories on this Jeep include the obligatory tow rope wrapped around the front bumper, leather rifle scabbard, scrim camouflage net, and bits and pieces of personal kit. *Simon Thomson*

LEFT: This well-armed SAS Jeep carries German, British and US jerrycans as well as three Vickers K machine-guns, with their distinctive round magazines, and a Browning .50-calibre. *Simon Thomson*

ABOVE: A nice shot of a Browning 1919A4 .30-calibre machine-gun on the standard mono-post pedestal mount. Although the rear gunner Is seated way too high for it to be effective, this view clearly shows the front-mounted wire cutter. The Jeep is also carrying a radio on the inside rear wheel arch, an additional jerrycan on the front step, and the windscreen has been put into the canvas cover. *Phil Royal*

RIGHT: Marked as a Military Police vehicle, this Ford GPW proudly flies the Stars and Stripes, as well as being fitted with a leather scabbard, a siren and more than its fair share of musette bags. *Warehouse Collection*

ABOVE: Radio, side-mounted jerrycan, ammo box on the bumper for stowage, and a canvas windscreen cover to reduce tell-tale reflections. Note how the aerial is tied down using the correct insulated cords. *Phil Royal*

LEFT: The etiquette of correctly flying a national flag, particularly the 'Stars and Stripes', is fraught with difficulty. This flag has the correct 48 stars for the period, and looks good, but it is almost certainly oversized for the vehicle. *Phil Royal*

FIELD KITS AND ACCESSORIES

There are those who claim that 'Jeep' stands for 'just enough essential parts' and while this is almost certainly not the case, there is a grain of truth in the sentiment and a Jeep was a very basic machine when it left the factory. However, soldiers are a pretty down-to-earth bunch, often regarding a vehicle simply as a tool to get a job done and, aside from the equipment that was used to adapt the vehicle to a specific role, Jeeps in the field were fitted with all kinds of bits and pieces intended to enhance their utility in whatever way they were being used. However, many restorers make the mistake of trying to fit too many of these accessories to their Jeep. It is very rare to see a Jeep in service with what might be described as 'multiple' accessories.

Air compressor

One of the rarest of all Jeep accessories, and one which can easily fetch more than $1,500 on the collectors' market, is the T1 tyre-inflation air compressor manufactured by the Westinghouse Air Brake Company Industrial Division of Wilmerding, Pennsylvania, and made available from October 1944. The compressor unit itself is carried on an extension to the left-hand engine mount and is driven by a V belt running on a twin pulley that replaces the standard crankshaft pulley. A large stowage bin, attached to the step and the rear face of the right-hand front mudguard, was used to carry the airline and fittings.

Jeeps that were equipped with the compressor unit were also shod with oversized 7.50-16 tyres. This necessitated the removal of the lower support for the spare wheel since the overall diameter of the wheel and tyre was larger.

TOP: When the Jeep has been completely restored, many owners choose to buy a trailer. The ¼-ton cargo trailer is the most commonly encountered type, but this 10cwt British water purifier trailer will provide a real talking point, particularly since it was built by SS Cars, now better known as Jaguar. *Phil Royal*

ABOVE: It's an interesting way of carrying extra ammunition, but would be unlikely to survive a jaunt in the rough stuff. *Phil Royal*

RIGHT: The component parts of the T1 tyre inflation air compressor manufactured by the Westinghouse Air Brake Company Industrial Division, including one of the larger 7.50-16 tyres worn by vehicles that were equipped with the compressor. *Eagle Jeep*

Antenna mounts

When you are restoring a Jeep don't make the mistake of fitting a radio aerial regardless, no matter how cool it looks. Generally, only those Jeeps that were fitted with radio sets were also fitted with antenna mounts. The complete antenna consists of a bracket or mount, an insulating base unit, and up to five standard aerial sections, the actual number and type of these depending on the radio set in use.

The standard mount for the antenna base unit was the American MP50, a box-shaped bracket, which is bolted to the side panels at the rear corners of the Jeep; the M201 generally uses the same bracket (sometimes marked MP50-FR to indicate its French origin), bolted to a separate right-angled bracket which, itself, is attached to the side and rear panels.

Second World War American antenna base units include the MP37, the spring-loaded MP48 or MP48A – generally described as the Ohio Brass – or the MP57. The French Army also used versions of these base units as well as the post-war MP65. Jeeps in British service were usually fitted with the No 10 aerial base bolted to the MP50.

Other arrangements also exist for non-standard radio sets.

BELOW: A beautifully-restored M201 showing a pair of post-war MP65 antenna mounts, a canvas water bucket held under the jerrycan strap, and a French decontaminator on the front mudguard. Note, also, the distinctive rear window shape of the French plastic-coated hood. *Christophe Muller*

TOP LEFT: British No 10 aerial base bolted to a simple right-angled bracket on the side of the Jeep. *Warehouse Collection*

TOP RIGHT: Polished Ohio Brass MP48 or MP48A antenna mount fitted to the MP50 bracket, which has been attached to the rear of the Jeep. *Warehouse Collection*

ABOVE LEFT: French MP57-Fr spring-loaded antenna mount showing the distinctive right-angled brackets used to carry the MP50 on the rear body corners of the M201. *Warehouse Collection*

ABOVE RIGHT: Another Ohio Brass-style antenna mount, this time the French-made MP48-Fr, bolted to the MP50 bracket on the side of the Jeep. *Warehouse Collection*

ABOVE: Vehicles used by units such as the SAS and the LRDG were generally fitted with the desert cooling kit to reduce the loss of vital water. This example packed to the nines with weapons, spare fuel and water, ammunition and personal kit, and mounts twin Vickers K machine-guns at the front, with a single example of the same weapon at the rear. The jerrycans are a mix of US and British designs. *Simon Thomson*

Carbine holder

After 1943, most Jeeps were fitted with a metal holder described as the 'universal rifle bracket'. Attached to right-angled brackets on the inside of the lower windscreen panel, the carbine holder incorporated springs that allowed it to accept any one of five US standard rifles without modification, including the M1 Garand, the Springfield, the Thompson sub-machine gun, and the Browning automatic (BAR). Vehicles in British service tend not to have been fitted with the carbine holder since, presumably, it would not accept the standard Lee Enfield rifle. Some British Jeeps will be seen with U-shaped rifle clips bolted directly to the windscreen panel or to the scuttle top.

The French Army devised brackets that could be attached to the windscreen panel to allow the standard FAMAS (*Fusil Automatique, Manufacture d'Armes de Sainte Etienne*) F1 assault rifle to be carried in the Jeep.

Cold-starting kit

With a 6V electrical system it is hardly surprising that Jeeps operating in cold climates were not always easy to start. A cold-starting stove kit (Willys part number WOA-7156) was devised in an attempt to minimise the problem by keeping the engine cooling water well above ambient temperature. The kit consisted of a Superfex paraffin (kerosene) burning heater, made by the Perfection Heater Company, together with a fuel tank and connecting pipes. The heater was installed under the bonnet in the space under the voltage regulator and behind the generator, while the fuel reservoir was positioned on the body side above the right-hand step. Connections to the cooling system were made at the rear of the cylinder head and at the water pump. It was necessary to cut a hole in the bonnet to allow the heater chimney to vent fumes to the atmosphere.

The heater was generally supplied as part of the winter-isation field kit.

Decontaminator

In 1941, the US Chemical Warfare Service developed a small refillable chemical decontaminator, known as 'Decontaminating apparatus, M2', which was designed to be carried in a bracket bolted to the sloping panel at the rear of the right-hand front mudguard. Suppliers included the Fyr-Fyter Company, General Detroit Corporation, and Badger Fire Extinguisher.

A similar decontaminator was frequently carried on the right-hand front mudguard of the M201.

De-froster

Manufactured by the Durkee-Attwood Company of Minneapolis, Minnesota, and the Fulton Company of Milwaukee, Wisconsin, the de-froster/de-icer kit consisted of a small (8 x 16in, 203 x 406mm) double-glazed panel designed to be attached to the Jeep windscreen in front of the driver using rubber suckers. The unit was connected to the Jeep electrical system, via a small switch fitted under the left-hand end of the dash, and heating wires between the panels were used to clear the screen of frost and humidity.

Desert cooling kit

Although the Jeep has a pressurised cooling system that effectively elevates the boiling point of the coolant, the system is not sealed and vehicles operating in hot climates tended to lose excessive amounts of cooling water. First developed as a field modification by British units such as the Long Range Desert Group (LRDG) and the Special Air Service Regiment (SAS) who were operating in North Africa, the 'desert cooling kit' included a surge tank that trapped water leaving the cooling system, allowing it to be drawn back in as the engine cools.

A proper factory kit was subsequently produced (Willys part number A-6490), which consists essentially of a cylindrical surge tank, bolted to a bracket attached to the front of the radiator grille, and connected to the radiator overflow by a combination of rubber hose and copper tubing.

Electrical slave receptacle

Willys part number WOA-11792 is a battery slave-cable connector that was part of the Willys winterisation field kit. It was designed to be fitted to the angular infill panel inside the right-hand front mudguard and allows one Jeep to provide a jump start for another. This is a very rare accessory.

Fire extinguisher

Second World War Jeeps frequently carried a small refillable carbon tetrachloride fire extinguisher in a bracket bolted to the inside of the body alongside the driver's left foot or on the sloping panel at the rear of the left-hand front mudguard. Suppliers included the Extinguisher & Chemical Company (Pyrene), the General Detroit Corporation (Quick Aid and SOS Fire Quand), American LaFrance Foamite Company (Fire Gun), and the Ford Motor Company. There are several different patterns of bracket.

(Note that carbon tetrachloride produces hazardous fumes when used and is no longer employed as a fire-extinguishing medium.)

First-aid kit

Most Jeeps carried a small steel first-aid box strapped into a bracket bolted to the rear of the dash behind the handbrake lever. Several types of first-aid kit exist, including one painted yellow, which was intended for the treatment of gas casualties.

Fuel primer kit

To prevent undue battery drain when attempting to start the Jeep in cold conditions, a fuel line priming kit was produced (Willys Part No WOA-7154). The kit re-routed the fuel supply from the fuel strainer unit to the carburettor via a hand pump installed on the dashboard. A few strokes of the pump, before attempting to start the engine, would ensure that the carburettor float chamber was full and avoid continuous cranking and the consequent battery drain.

Heater

Jeeps were famously inhospitable in cold weather, even if a full body enclosure was fitted, and a hot-water heater kit was available (Willys Part No WOA-11846), which might have gone some way to alleviating the problem. The heat-exchanger core was fitted under the dash just above the driver's feet and the heater was connected to the engine cooling system at the rear of the cylinder head, where the shut-off valve was located, and at the water pump.

Hull magnetic compass

The Hull Manufacturing Company of Warren, Ohio, produced bakelite-bodied magnetic compasses for use in aircraft and vehicles during the Second World War. The company was a major supplier to the US Army and the military compass was painted Olive Drab and was supplied with a simple mounting bracket, which could be attached to the windscreen frame of the Jeep. There are also a couple of different types of essentially-civilian Hull Streamline compasses that are correct for the Second World War time period.

Jerrycan

Although early Jeeps were not fitted with the holder, no standardised Jeep is really complete without a steel jerrycan at the rear. The rear jerrycan holder was sometimes doubled up, by mounting two holders back-to-back along the axis of the vehicle, and additional jerrycan holders were also sometimes fitted to one or both sides of the Jeep on the body step, and ahead of the radiator on the front bumper.

Examples of what became known as the jerrycan were first captured from the Germans by the British in North Africa, although there are those who claim that the design was actually Italian. With its secure cam-locked cap and 20-litre capacity, it was quickly realised that it was superior to the so-called 'flimsies' that were in use with the British Army at that time, and the design was copied and put into production in Britain and subsequently in the USA.

The American-made can was simplified to better suit American production methods, retaining the handles, size and shape, but with the centre weld replaced with rolled seams, top and bottom. The closure was also changed to a screwed bung, which was not only more prone to leakage,

ABOVE: Though, as its name suggests, the jerrycan was devised by the German Army, it was quickly adopted by the Allies who realised its superiority. No one had any qualms about using captured cans and this restored LRDG Jeep is equipped with a German water can as well as twin Vickers K machine-guns. *Phil Royal*

but also required a wrench and a funnel. From about 1943, the US Marine Corps used a hybrid style of can, which was manufactured like the standard American can, but was fitted with a British-style cam lock cap. Most cans carry a code that indicates the manufacturer, and are dated; American cans are also often marked 'G' for 'gasoline'. There were also cans for water, similar in design but often marked 'W' or 'water' and fitted with a different cap.

By late 1944, the Allies had manufactured literally millions of jerrycans and every vehicle that went ashore on D-Day, and after, carried spare fuel in jerrycans. However, during the advance to Paris in late 1944, the cans were being abandoned at the roadside at such a rate that there was actually a shortage. Nevertheless, jerrycans can still be found all over the world.

It is worth noting that for authenticity on a restored vehicle the can should almost certainly not be the exact same colour as the Jeep, but should certainly be appropriately dated.

Lubrication chart and holder

From the end of 1944, MB/GPW Jeeps were fitted with a lubrication chart holder bolted to the underside of the bonnet on the left-hand side. The corresponding lubrication chart, designed to fit into the holder, was LO 9-803.

Oil can and bracket

A small spring-loaded bracket was often fitted under the bonnet alongside the horn to carry a small pump-action oil can. Suppliers of the oil can included the Gem Manufacturing Company of Pittsburgh, NOERA, and Eagle.

There are similar French brackets and oil cans for the M201.

Rear stowage basket

Despite being considered to be a truck, the Jeep lacked sufficient stowage space for much of the kit required by front-line units, particularly airborne troops who were usually required to support themselves during the early stages of an operation, which meant that large amounts of kit had to be carried. It is for this reason that Jeeps employed on airborne missions were often fitted with large metal stowage baskets, or bustles, at the rear which necessitated removal of the standard jerrycan and spare-wheel mountings. Running the full width of the body at the rear, such baskets were fabricated from rectangular tube and steel strip, and were fitted with four or five footman loops across the top to allow the load to be secured or sheeted over.

Tandem towing hitch

On 20 December 1943, the US Army introduced the tandem hitch field kit (Willys Part No WOA-9183). This allowed two Jeeps to be coupled together to act as a tractor for the 105mm field gun, an operation normally assigned to the GMC 2½-ton 6 x 6 truck.

The main component of the kit was a substantial A-frame that was designed to be fitted in place of the standard front bumper. The A-frame equipped Jeep acted as the second vehicle in the line and was hitched to the towing pintle of the lead vehicle. During

ABOVE LEFT: The rear-mounted bustle provided a useful way of increasing the carrying capacity of Jeeps used in airborne, and other operations. The bumper markings identify this Jeep as belonging to the British 3rd Division, which re-entered France on D-Day and continued fighting until VE-Day. *Warehouse Collection*

ABOVE RIGHT: Photographed during trials for the tandem towing hitch, which allowed a pair of Jeeps to act as a tractor for the 105mm field gun, the tandem hitch also provides a useful way of towing a Jeep to a show behind a more modern vehicle. *Warehouse Collection*

RIGHT: The front mounted Braden capstan winch is one of the rarest and most sought-after Jeep accessories. With a maximum load of 5,000lb (2,272kg), it was intended for self-recovery. *Simon Thomson*

tandem operation, the maximum speed of the Jeep was restricted to 30mph (50km/h). When not in use the A-frame was strapped into a bracket attached to the top of the radiator grille.

Winch

Although it is not commonly seen, in March 1944 the US Army issued a capstan winch kit for of the MB/GPW. Constructed by the Braden Winch Company of Tulsa, Oklahoma, and identified as the company's Type J2 (Willys Part No WOA-9232), the winch had a maximum load of 5,000lb (2,272kg) and was intended for self-recovery. It was fitted into the space between the front extensions of the main chassis cross members, ahead of the radiator, and was driven via a propeller shaft that engaged with an extension to the crankshaft nose. The winch kit included new springs and a redesigned steering bell crank that lowered the tie rod inner ends to clear the winch drive.

Windscreen cover

Many Jeeps carried a canvas bag that was designed to be used as a windscreen cover. The lowered windscreen was inserted into the bag to prevent reflections from the glass, which might otherwise have made the Jeep visible from the air. The windscreen cover for the M201 differs from that for the Second World War Jeep since it must accommodate the sheet metal guard over the electric wiper motor.

Winterisation field kit and bonnet blanket

The winterisation field kit (Willys Part No WOA-11815) was developed for vehicles used in extremes of cold and consisted of thermal blankets designed to be attached to the bonnet and grille using press studs or turnbuckles, and an insulated battery box. The kit also normally included the cold-starting kit.

Wire cutter

After the D-Day invasion in 1944, the Germans developed an unpleasant habit of stringing thin wire across roads to decapitate, or injure, unwary Jeep drivers. A similar threat, albeit not deliberate, was posed by poorly-supported communications cables that could also dangle across roads. This was countered by fitting a wire-cutting bar on the front bumper. The bar was generally made from angle iron, extending above the height of the windshield, with a forward extension at the top designed to catch and cut any wires that would otherwise have posed a danger.

ABOVE: A well-armed and provisioned Jeep, complete with the airborne stowage bustle at the rear, tows an American 37mm anti-tank gun, broadly copied from the German PaK 36. Note the metal carbine holder on the inside of the folded windscreen. *Phil Royal*

LEFT: The tandem hitch field kit replaces the standard front bumper, and when the A-frame hitch is not in use it is tied back to a bracket on the radiator grille. *Phil Royal*

LEFT: After the invasion of Normandy, the Germans developed a nasty habit of stretching wires across roads to catch unwary Jeep and motorcycle riders. The angle iron on the front bumper was designed to counter the threat by pushing the wire up out of harm's way and then breaking it. *Phil Royal*

Chapter 4

The Soldier's View

'I have seen the Jeep everywhere, and though it is doubtless mere coincidence, for there must be many disabled or wrecked Jeeps, I myself in all my travels have never seen a Jeep that would not run.'

LIEUTENANT-GENERAL JOHN C.H. LEE, SHAEF SERVICES OF SUPPLY, 1943

It is as well to remember that, during the Second World War, soldiers lived, and unfortunately often died, in their Jeeps. Nevertheless, with so many examples of the vehicle in service, wartime Jeep anecdotes abound. Allied soldiers were frequently taught to drive by the Army and, for many, driving a Jeep was their earliest first-hand experience of a motor vehicle. While many saw the machine simply as a tool to get a job done – it was for good reason that other drivers became attached to the specific vehicle with which they had been issued.

And what tales we'd hear, if only those Jeeps could tell their own stories.

THE MILITARY JEEP EXPERIENCE

According to the US Army publication TM 9-803, the Jeep was a 'general purpose personnel or cargo carrier especially adaptable for reconnaissance or command...'. TM 9-2800 added a little more detail – describing the Jeep as being able 'to carry personnel, primarily for reconnaissance; to transport light cargo; (and) to tow (the) 37mm anti-tank gun' – but neither description even begins to convey the multitude of uses for which the vehicle was adapted throughout its years of service. Roles which, alongside the more usual military uses, included using the flat bonnet top as an altar or a map-reading table, fitting flanged wheels to provide a small railway locomotive, using the Jeep as an aircraft tug and as a snow plough, or dressing it in white to get the (military) bride to the church on time.

Bantam began deliveries of the BRC-40 reconnaissance car to the US Army in December 1940, where it was soon to be seen taking part in manoeuvres. Once American deliveries of the standardised Jeeps began the following year, very few of the Bantams, or for that matter the Ford GPs, remained in the USA and, one way or another most ended up either in Britain or the USSR.

The British Ministry of Supply (MoS) had taken delivery of the first of 56 Jeeps under Contract SM 2262 in July 1941. In truth, the British War Office would probably still have preferred motorcycles, but these Jeeps were the first to see any real action, being deployed in the Western Desert during 1941, and despite some initial reluctance, the vehicle was an almost immediate success. It seems that the possibilities for the Jeep were well understood right from the start. One of the first Bantam vehicles to be delivered was photographed by the MWEE armed with a Bren gun and equipped for desert patrol work. Soon the Jeep had been officially adopted as a

RIGHT: In true Hollywood style, the passenger dangles one leg lazily outside the Jeep. The canvas cover to the windscreen obviated reflections from the glass which might have been spotted by enemy aircraft. *Phil Royal*

LEFT: Seen here with a Harley-Davidson, the Jeep was a logical step forward from the military motorcycle, able to carry more personnel plus modest amounts of equipment or supplies. Although the German Army continued to favour motorcycles, the Allies tended to use them only for behind-the-lines duties. *Warehouse Collection*

TOP RIGHT: What more famous passenger in a Jeep could there be than Sir Winston Churchill, seen here lighting a trademark cigar and visiting the battlefront in France in June 1944. Montgomery sits beside the Prime Minister. *IWM, B5359*

BOTTOM RIGHT: Field Marshal Bernard Montgomery's Jeep passes lines of German prisoners of war at Creully on 8 June 1944. *IWM, B5179*

substitute for the motorcycle in areas where the latter's use was considered to be difficult. As supplies became more plentiful, the Jeep also started to replace the 4 x 2 light utility vehicles, which were generally known as 'tillys' and which were proving increasingly unsuitable for operational use.

Typical roles included reconnaissance and patrol vehicle, personnel carrier, mobile radio station, ambulance, signal layer, light recovery vehicle, and cargo carrier. Its small size and light weight meant that it was well suited to airborne operations and, suitably modified, was carried in gliders and transport aircraft, or later hung beneath helicopters; experiments were also carried out with air delivery by means of a parachute drop platform. It was regularly seen with a pedestal gun mount, armed with a Bren or a .50- or .30-calibre machine-gun, and vehicles were experimentally fitted with a variety of other weapons including anti-tank guns and rocket launchers. One of the vehicle's designated roles was to tow the carriage-mounted 37mm anti-tank gun, and photographs also exist showing Jeeps towing the 3in mortar complete with tripod and base plate mounted on a wheeled cradle, and the British also used Jeeps in tandem to tow the 25pdr field gun.

ABOVE CENTRE: The official caption to this still from a US Army training series stated that 'gasoline, oil and water capacity allows a normal day of operation without a refill'. *Warehouse Collection*

LEFT: It was fairly common practice during the Second World War for soldiers to give their personal Jeep a name, often the same name as their wife or girlfriend. If someone in the unit was handy with a paintbrush, the name would also be decorated with a painting of a scantily-clad girl. *Phil Royal*

T69

ABOVE: President Franklin D. Roosevelt riding in the passenger seat of a Jeep. Note the Stars and Stripes across the bonnet. Roosevelt, who was US President between 1933 and 1945, died on 12 April 1945, thus failing to see peace in Europe by just five weeks. *Warehouse Collection*

RIGHT: The unmistakeable profile of General Charles de Gaulle. The general was landed on the beach near Ouistreham on 14 June 1944 from a DUKW and was driven inland by a British Army Jeep. This was the first time that he had been in France since the German occupation. *IWM, B5476*

BELOW: Driven by Prince Bernhard and accompanied by Queen Juliana, this Jeep of the Royal Netherlands Army carries the four Dutch princesses. The date is 2 May 1957. *Warehouse Collection*

RIGHT: General Dwight D. Eisenhower, Supreme Commander of the Allied Forces in Europe, riding as passenger in a Jeep. The rear seat passenger, clearly enjoying a joke, looks like General Omar N. Bradley, commander of the US 1st Army after D-Day. *Warehouse Collection*

However, in the interests of fairness, perhaps it should also be pointed out that the Jeep suffered from two disadvantages. Firstly, even with the rear seat folded up out of the way, the lack of a rear tailgate made loading and unloading difficult and, without the matching ¼-ton trailer, Jeeps were little use as serious cargo vehicles. The other drawback was the general lack of proper weather protection. While the lightweight top was fine for keeping the occupants dry during a summer shower, without proper side curtains or doors, there was little protection against the Northern European winter.

THE JEEP IN ACTION

There can be few servicemen who rode in a Jeep who could forget the experience – even if it was not always for the right reasons. Firstly, there was inevitably the chance of being shot at, or encountering one of the wires that the Germans had a habit of stretching across roads at neck height in the hope of catching an unwary GI driving his Jeep with the screen folded down.

But, even without these dangers, no one could accuse a Jeep of being comfortable. Aside from the fact that the lack of any adjustment in the driving seat forced the driver to adopt a curious splayed-leg stance, there was also the bum-numbing, teeth-chattering, bone-shaking ride. US Army Lieutenant Colonel Manuel Conley rightly pointed out that there are just two ways to sit on those thinly-upholstered front seats, 'either bolt upright or slouched down to the middle of the backbone' – and Hollywood has subsequently taught us that no front-seat Jeep passenger rode with both legs inside the vehicle. It was no laughing matter. No matter how you chose to sit, the combination of rough ground and long hours in a Jeep caused many a case of pilonidal cyst disorder, which apparently became known as 'Jeep disease' by the US Medical Corps – and, since it required the serviceman to spend 60 to 90 days healing time before he could go back on duty, was a serious loss of manpower. However, you can get used to anything and Ernie Pyle, who was perhaps America's best-known war correspondent, said '... it doesn't even ride so badly after you get used to it!'.

If the discomfort of the ride wasn't bad enough, in winter the Jeep rightly earned its nickname as a 'pneumonia wagon'. This was perhaps unavoidable since many soldiers chose to always keep the top down when riding in a combat zone, which certainly ensured that the driver remained alert even if he was unable to keep warm.

Nevertheless, the Jeep was a great leveller and prominent Allied leaders seemed keen to be photographed riding on that thinly-upholstered front seat. President Franklin D. Roosevelt, Winston Churchill, Charles de Gaulle, King Farouk of Egypt, and even Queen Elizabeth, later the Queen Mother, were all seen and photographed by the press as Jeep passengers. Although General Bernard Montgomery preferred his big Humber staff car, leading US Army generals like Dwight D. Eisenhower and Douglas MacArthur chose to ride in the Jeep rather than the more luxurious vehicles that were generally at their disposal. George S. Patton's personal Jeep was fitted with a large red leather seat and had two long brass horns mounted on the hood to announce his presence.

ABOVE: 'Get me to the church on time!' The Jeep was draped in white cloth especially for this all-military marriage, which took place in the Lebanon in August 1944. The wedding was between Miss Anne Butterfield QAIMNS (Queen Alexandra's Imperial Military Nursing Service) and Major C.T. Overman RASC. The Jeep was pulled by 20 men. *IWM, E29410*

Colonel John Weeks described the Jeep as 'the saviour of battlefield mobility for the Allied airborne forces' since it allowed the troops to also carry radios and heavier support weapons. General Maxwell D. Taylor, Commander of the US 101st Airborne Division, who parachuted into Normandy with his men on D-Day, jumped onto the bonnet of his Jeep to welcome reinforcements to his unit in Germany in 1945. Lieutenant-General John C.H. Lee, in charge of SHAEF

RIGHT: A nicely restrained British-marked Jeep of the 50th (Northumbrian) Division. The red 'TT' on the windscreen panel stands for 'Tyne' and 'Tees'. *Warehouse Collection*

BELOW: If all else fails, it is possible to wriggle under the Jeep to provide cover and a useful firing position. The photograph was taken on 25 June 1944 in France and shows Rifleman Brett from Newport, Isle of Wight, trying to eliminate a sniper. *IWM, B5998*

Services of Supply, said 'I have seen the Jeep everywhere, and though it is doubtless mere coincidence, for there must be many disabled or wrecked Jeeps, I myself in all my travels have never seen a Jeep that would not run'. He was not alone in this view of the almost magical power of the Jeep and one officer, reputedly British but, like Chinese whispers, these stories have a habit of growing and changing in the retelling, apparently said of his Jeep that 'it can do everything but bake a cake'. And, back to Ernie Pyle, who described his Jeep as 'a divine instrument of military locomotion'. He said that 'I don't think we could continue the war without the Jeep... it does everything... it goes everywhere... it's as faithful as a dog, as strong as a mule, and as agile as a goat'.

In *Hail to the Jeep*, a factual and pictorial history of the Jeep originally published in 1946, Albert Wade Wells wrote that 'of all the millions of pieces of military equipment that America, the "arsenal of democracy", poured forth from her prodigious industries for use in the Second World War, no other implement of war became so famous. In winning the favor of United Nations [meaning Allied] troops everywhere, the Jeep became America's foremost goodwill ambassador in the war.'

The press was equally enthusiastic about the vehicle. In 1941, the US magazine *Parade* called the Jeep '...the Army's most intriguing new gadget' and was so excited that it devoted three full pages to the vehicle. *Life* magazine was no less effusive and the July 1942 issue carried a six-page piece extolling the amazing performance of the machine. 'Boy, oh Boy' said the reporter, 'any car that can do these things must be a lulu' – which, in this case, was a good thing. And as regards its appearance – well, they say that beauty is in the eye of the beholder. How else can we explain that an unknown writer on the English *Ford Times* called the Jeep 'the ugliest motor vehicle in the world', while a staff writer for the British Army magazine *Soldier*, in describing Britain's post-war attempts at developing a replacement for the Jeep explained that 'unlike the (original)... it was not a thing of beauty'. John Keegan, who subsequently became a respected military historian, remembered 'the tiny entrancing Jeeps' that he saw during his West Country childhood, 'caparisoned with whiplash aerials and sketchy canvas hoods'.

The British humourist Jon was author of *The Two Types*, a series of cartoons that featured a pair of elaborately moustachioed 8th Army officers. With their eccentric dress code and modified Jeep, these two unlikely characters came to typify the desert army. American cartoonist Bill Mauldin named his vehicle 'Jeanie' after his wife, and also often included the Jeep in his cartoons. After travelling 1,000 miles (1,600km) across Italy and France, Mauldin's mount was described by his mechanics as 'the most neurotic Jeep in Europe'. Mauldin was not alone in naming his Jeep; many soldiers adorned their personal Jeep with a name that would

ABOVE: US Army military vehicles attempt to make progress through a shattered Italian town in this photograph dated 1944. *Warehouse Collection*

BELOW: This Jeep is bogged down and abandoned on 'The sands of Iwo Jima'. *Warehouse Collection*

ABOVE LEFT: On foot and riding in Jeeps and armoured vehicles, at times it must have seemed to the enemy that the US Army was unstoppable. *Warehouse Collection*

ABOVE RIGHT: Loading a Jeep into an Airspeed AS.51 Horsa glider. The windscreen has been removed to reduce the overall height of the vehicle. *Warehouse Collection*

ABOVE: Practising loading a Jeep into a mock-up of an aircraft. The photograph was taken at Fort Benning in the USA, on the border of Georgia and Alabama. *Warehouse Collection*

RIGHT: Despite its 'go-anywhere' reputation, a Jeep can actually be defeated by mud. *Simon Thomson*

RIGHT: Bearing in mind the crates that are being handled, wouldn't it be serendipitous if this railway Jeep and trailer, photographed in New Zealand, were a Ford GPW? The railway wheels on the trailer are very unusual. *Warehouse Collection*

BELOW: The Jeep survived in service with the British Army until it was superseded by the Austin FV1801 Champ and the Land Rover Series I. This Jeep and trailer has just been successfully air-dropped in the Universal Freight Container from a Handley Page Halifax A Mk VII. *Army PR*

remind them of wives or girlfriends who were often thousands of miles away. Even the Reverend J.K. Best, Chaplain to SHAEF ETO, adorned his Jeep with the name 'Our Lady of Victory'.

There is little doubt that the Jeep was held in the highest regard by all who drove or rode in it.

The British SAS modified Jeeps for interdiction raids behind enemy lines, loading them to within an inch of their lives with water, fuel, weapons and ammunition.

The Belgian Major (later Lieutenant-Colonel) Vladimir Peniakoff, nicknamed 'Popski' by the LRDG's Intelligence Officer, Captain Bill Kennedy Shaw, was equally enthusiastic about the Jeep's abilities. In North Africa, Popski's Private Army (officially, No 1 Demolition Squadron, PPA) operated a fleet of modified Jeeps, each fitted with twin Vickers K 0.303in machine-guns and racks to carry 12 x 4gal petrol cans, giving them a range of between 600 and 700 miles (1,000–1,135km). Operating as part of the 8th Army, Popski attacked Rommel's

LEFT: This is what happens to an air-dropped Jeep if the parachutes fail to open properly. *Warehouse Collection*

ABOVE: If you need to know, there are 11 of them – but I've no idea why! *Warehouse Collection*

BELOW: Members of the US Army's 101st Airborne Division, 327th Glider Infantry Regiment, pause for a spot of sightseeing in the Bavarian Alps, near Berchtesgaden. *David Doyle*

fuel supplies at the time of the Battles of El Alamein. When the fighting in Africa was over, Popski took his Jeeps to Italy by sea and managed to get a patrol of five vehicles behind enemy lines with the task of checking the strength of opposing German units. Later, a second PPA patrol was formed under the command of Captain Yunnie. In the spring of 1945, nine PPA men in three Jeeps fooled the entire 700-man German garrison at the seaside town of Chioggia near Venice into surrendering, complete with two batteries of 88mm guns and 120 heavy machine-guns. Popski subsequently sailed into Venice where he moored on the Canal San Marco and led his Jeeps into Piazza San Marco, which he circled seven times, describing this in his autobiography as 'my hour of triumph'.

One US Cavalry veteran was heard to state that he believed that his Jeep could get into more places than a mule: 'Lots of times a mule will baulk if he doesn't think his leader is using good judgment,' he said, 'but a Jeep will always *try*.' When the US Marines landed at Guadalcanal in August 1942, one soldier described the performance and utility of the Jeep as 'a godsend'. Two American war correspondents, Daniel DeLuce and Darrell Berrigan, escaped from Burma to India when the Japanese invaded and travelled across 1,300 miles (2,100km) of land by Jeep. When they arrived in Imphal, there were those who disbelieved their story, pointing out that there were no roads in the area they had crossed. 'Shhhh! Not so loud,' one of them said, 'our Jeep hasn't found out about roads yet, and we don't want to spoil it.'

ABOVE LEFT: It seems that every Second World War soldier who was issued with a Jeep wanted to be photographed with it. *Warehouse Collection*

ABOVE RIGHT: Another 'soldier's snap'. The reverse of this photograph bears the curious inscription 'yours truly, but what am I made of?'. *Warehouse Collection*

RIGHT: A US Army Corporal with caricatures of Mussolini, Hitler and Hirohito and painted on the side of his Jeep. The Mussolini image bears the legend, 'Benito, finito'. *Warehouse Collection*

It wasn't just the Americans and the British who so admired the Jeep. Both the Chinese and the Russians received supplies of the vehicle under the American Lend-Lease arrangements and both quickly fell under its spell. The Soviets had originally asked the US Government for motorcycle combinations and, back in 1941, the iconic Harley-Davidson WLA was prototyped for possible desert use with a driven sidecar wheel in the style of the big German motorcycle outfits of the time; this would probably have suited the Red Army just fine. However, the Soviet Ambassador, Maxim Litvinov, was told that the US Army preferred the Jeep to the motorcycle and, since it would have taken far too long to put sufficient sidecars into production, the Russians agreed that they would also try the Jeep. Perhaps, it should also be pointed out that the Red Army never quite gave up on the notion of using American motorcycles and a second Harley-Davidson 3 x 2 prototype appeared in 1944, which was intended especially for conditions on the Russian Front. By this time, however, the Soviets had received more than 20,000 Jeeps and apparently had discovered that, indeed, it did fill the bill exactly. During a visit to a Soviet front-line artillery regiment, an Associated Press reporter is said to have asked the Russian driver of the Jeep in which he was being carried across the muddy and shell-pocked ground what he thought of the vehicle. '*Zamechatelno,*' replied the grinning driver – which, apparently, means that he liked it just fine.

Even at rest, the Jeep remained useful. The flat top of the bonnet could serve as a sniper's firing position, a meal table, a map table, a surface on which to play cards, or even an altar, and more than one commander stood on the bonnet to address his men. *Soldier* magazine published a photograph showing a British soldier balancing on a pile of jerrycans on the bonnet of a Jeep, attaching a sign to a post. Definitely not one to be tried at home.

ABOVE LEFT: This photograph is captioned 'Slim Glasgow, 1946', but the snow and the makeshift hardtop tell their own story. The location is not known, but 'NAF' means Naval Air Facility and, clearly, Slim was a Master at Arms since the Jeep says so. *Warehouse Collection*

ABOVE RIGHT: Tall men usually found that their heads came into contact with the canvas top which, at speed, could be very irritating. In the absence of any seat adjustment, one solution was to raise the height of the top of the windscreen by using a strip of wood – this also raised the canvas top. *Warehouse Collection*

RIGHT: Shots of the Willys MA in service are rare, and the low-cut sides clearly encourage the characteristic stance of the front seat passenger with one foot outside the vehicle. Notice how the photograph shows the steering column-mounted gear-change lever. *Warehouse Collection*

It was said that the heated radiator water could be used for shaving and canned combat rations could be heated on the manifolds during a long run. Campbell Soups even featured a Jeep in a 1943 advertisement showing soldiers using the heat of the Jeep's engine to prepare a can of soup. According to Willys-Overland it could also make ice cream. Some enterprising GIs apparently used a stationary Jeep to power a refrigeration device. And in a similar vein, there are photographs showing stationary Jeeps driving machinery by means of a flat belt running on the brake drum.

Despite the sparseness of the upholstery, it was even possible to fall asleep in a Jeep – but, there again, exhausted soldiers quickly learned the knack of falling asleep anywhere.

But, running a Jeep in wartime wasn't all plain sailing, even when Uncle Sam was picking up the bill. In the face of shortages of rubber, fuel, lubricating oil and even essential parts, keeping a military Jeep on the road sometimes called for a little ingenuity. Between March 1940 and September 1945, the US Army publication *Army Motors* published tips and advice to help Army drivers and mechanics to continue to get the best out of the vehicle, even if this included practices that these days would be considered unsafe or even illegal. Never afraid to dumb-down, the US Army often used cartoonist Will Eisner's relentlessly incompetent Private Joe Dope character in *Army Motors* to help get the point across and, from April 1942, the aptly-named Sergeant Halfmast McCanick encouraged readers to write in with their day-to-day problems and the solutions that they had found.

Consider the story in *Army Motors* of Corporal Farrell Carpenter of 551st SAW Company who, faced with a shortage of tail lamp units, described how a burnt-out unit could be cut open and 'repaired' using a separate bulb. Or Corporal Frank S. Payerle who discovered that a standard 3in (76mm) split pin could be opened out and bent into a makeshift tool to remove the lock washer from inside the Jeep hub. Lieutenant W.F. Zadrozny, stationed in the Netherlands, suggested that the driver and crew of a Jeep could keep most of the mud away by using discarded oil drums to make 'fender extensions running from the leading edge of the fenders down to the bumper bar' – and many made such modifications, some even going so far as to construct a complete enclosure for the Jeep using parts of aircraft cockpit covers or whatever materials came to hand. Or, how about First Lieutenant Robert S. Vogt, who was faced with two Jeeps that had 'lost their brakes' after a spell across country. On inspection he discovered that the starter-crank nut on the lower fan pulley had been hitting the brake pipe, which

ABOVE: Jeeps in the French town of Marigny, the objective of the US 1st Infantry Division during Operation Cobra in 1944. *Warehouse Collection*

LEFT: US Army Jeeps and trailers loaded onto railcars during the Korean War. *Warehouse Collection*

LEFT: Making slow progress across a flooded river in Italy during 1944. *Warehouse Collection*

BELOW: Airborne Jeep demonstrating how three stretchers can be carried, albeit at some discomfort to the occupants. *Simon Thomson*

LEFT: If you are sufficiently tired, it is possible to sleep in a Jeep. If you don't need to sleep, at least there are sufficient flat surfaces, aside from the seats, to be able to sit down. *Warehouse Collection*

BELOW: Photographers of the Army Film and Photographic Unit (AFPU) dismount from their Jeep near Cairo. The man in bandages had been badly burned. Note the RAF roundel on the bonnet top. *IWM, E19971*

is clamped across the front diff casing – repositioning the pipe further forward solved the problem.

Troubled with electrical gremlins – well, why not slip a length of garden hose over the terminal end of the battery cable to prevent it being chafed through on the hold-down bracket?

Lieutenant James Tom, stationed in the South Pacific, came up with an interesting modification that did away with the conventional exhaust silencer, which was easily damaged or even ripped right off by rocks or tree stumps during serious off-roading. Tom devised a way of constructing an improvised square silencer that wrapped around the down pipe almost directly under the manifold. This ensured that it was tucked right up against the engine, out of harm's way, even if it did increase the under-bonnet temperature a fair bit. This was later ratified as an official field modification (TB 9-803-FE3) before the development of the deep-mud exhaust system.

Advice was even available on how to remove grease spots from matt paint – although you'd imagine that there were more important issues than spotty Jeeps. Well, it seems the short answer is that it can't be really done without creating light spots on the paintwork. Corporal Chester G. Pehl suggested that the best thing to do was to wash the entire panel in solvent; this removed the spots, even if it did make the paint a little lighter in colour.

And there were plenty of questions regarding the propensity of the Jeep to swerve to the left under heavy braking. While some of this is built into the steering geometry, Sergeant Halfmast McCanick's advice was to ensure that the front-end geometry was as near perfect as possible.

RIGHT: The open mudguards of the Jeep ensured that, should the vehicle be driven through floods or deep mud, then a fair proportion of mud or water would be thrown at the driver. Servicemen who were regularly subjected to unwanted showers often found that it was possible to use sheet metal to construct a defensive barrier. *Warehouse Collection*

Everyone who used a Jeep must have had their own story and Jeeps were used by all of the Allied armies, including the American, British, Chinese, Russian, Australian, Indian, French and New Zealand armies. Manuel Conley summed it up well when he described the Jeep as 'versatile, reliable, and virtually indestructible', going on to say that 'this magic motor vehicle bounced to glory as one of the Second World War's most enduring legends'. And if the number of Allied soldiers who had themselves photographed with their Jeep is any sort of testament, then clearly the Jeep was considered to be something special.

ABOVE: A well-armed patrol vehicle. Note the non-standard invasion star on the body side. *Warehouse Collection*

RIGHT: The hand-written caption on the reverse of this photograph reads 'to Shirley-Ann Wilson… love Daddy… Delano, California, 16 May 1943'. *Warehouse Collection*

BELOW: Popski's Private Army equipped at least one Jeep with the flame-throwing equipment from a Canadian Wasp universal carrier. It is said that the first time the equipment was used in anger the operator singed his eyebrows. *Phil Royal*

Chapter 5

The Owner's View

'I drive a Jeep. An old Jeep – so nobody will say I'm driving a BMW anymore.'

BOB MARLEY, 1980

A Jeep is classless and unpretentious, and thousands of owners worldwide see it as an ideal fun vehicle that opens up a world of shows and re-enactment events. It is small enough to fit into the average lock-up and presents no particular difficulties on the road or in repair or maintenance. And, if you can disregard those thin seat cushions and the somewhat firm ride, a Jeep will generally be a pleasure to drive.

It is also a textbook example of how 'form follows function' and is considered by many to be a genuine design icon. A Jeep appeared at the prestigious New York Museum of Modern Art in the 'Eight Automobiles' exhibition in 1951 alongside the MG TC, the Lincoln Continental and the Cord 810, and the museum described the vehicle as 'a masterpiece of functionalist design'.

What's more, a Jeep is also an excellent investment.

BUYING A JEEP

Although the expression 'time spent in reconnaissance is seldom wasted' is generally attributed to the Duke of Wellington, it seems more likely that it was first said by the Fourth Century Chinese warrior Sun Tzu – but, of course, he said it in Chinese, which makes him rather less quotable. But, regardless of who first made this observation, it holds equally good when undertaking the purchase and restoration of a Jeep, as it would for those bent on world domination.

As regards where you buy, it all comes down to personal preference. Jeeps can still be found in the backs of barns, particularly in rural France, but the vehicles are definitely no longer available direct from any Western armies – even the French have reputedly sold all that they had. However, there are plenty of dealers (see Useful contacts, page 183) and there are plenty of private sales advertised in the military vehicle and club magazines. Be slightly wary of buying from mainstream classic car dealers or classic car auctions, where values tend to be over-inflated and the vehicles often over-restored.

ABOVE: Muddy but extremely well-equipped Jeep with bags and tools covering every flat surface. Note the .50in Browning M2HB heavy barrel machine gun. *Phil Royal*

ABOVE LEFT: Dozens of Canadian Army Jeeps marked up and ready for auction. *Warehouse Collection*

ABOVE RIGHT: More surplus Jeeps – this time, cast aside by the US Army. *Warehouse Collection*

TOP LEFT: Some owners take pride and pleasure in refinishing the Jeep to match vehicles used by a particular unit at a specific time, as well as dressing the part themselves. These Jeeps are re-enacting the SAS, which was formed in 1942, initially to operate in the Middle East. *Phil Royal*

BOTTOM LEFT: If only! This 1941 photograph shows an impressive line-up of Willys MA Jeeps on Crissy Field at the Presidio in San Francisco. *Warehouse Collection*

ABOVE: There are plenty of dealers in military surplus Jeeps and vehicles are advertised regularly in the enthusiast and club magazines. The occasional vehicle also turns up for sale at the major military vehicle shows, but this rare slat-grille Willys will not be cheap, particularly since it is fitted with the proper Braden winch. Although this vehicle is finished in RAF livery, the red white and blue roundel was also used as an aerial identification symbol during the first years of the war. *Simon Thomson*

WHAT TO LOOK FOR WHEN BUYING

Engine

All three Jeep models use essentially the same engine – the Willys Go-Devil. Despite being a rather dated side-valve design, it is robust and surprisingly powerful. It should idle cleanly and pull well in all three gears up to about 60 or 65mph (100–110km/h). A smoky exhaust on acceleration indicates worn bores or rings, and smoke on the over-run means that the valve guides are worn. Don't worry if an M201 exhibits a slight irregularity during idling, which manifests itself as an occasional chuffing sound, 'they all do it'.

As with any engine, low oil pressure means that the bearings are worn or that the oil pump needs reconditioning. Both the main and big-end bearings use steel-backed shells and these are available in a range of oversizes for use with reground crankshafts. Overheating, generally resulting from a silted-up block or radiator, can lead to warping of the cylinder head, or even the block face, which will manifest itself in blown head gaskets. The modern, non-asbestos, gaskets are particularly prone to failure between the pairs of cylinders if there is any warping of the head. Externally, the engine should be oil-tight and clean, but you should look carefully at the water jacket casting below the distributor for cracks where Ford-built engines are said to be susceptible to frost damage.

Workshop rebuilt Go-Devil Type 442 engines are still available at around £5,000–£6,500, courtesy of the French Army.

Transmission

The transmission consists of a three-speed Warner gearbox coupled directly to a two-speed Spicer transfer box, the latter interlocked with the front-axle drive. Although the synchromesh will become less effective as the miles are clocked up, and a worn gearbox may start to jump out of second gear on the over-run, neither unit is particularly troublesome. However, be sure to check that front-wheel drive can be selected, and that the selection levers have not seized due to a lack of use. Repair parts and reconditioned units are readily available if necessary.

The M201 runs on larger-section tyres. There should be a small right-angled gearbox attached to the speedometer drive output gear on the transmission to which the drive cable is attached in order to correct the speedometer and odometer readings. Check that this is present and that the drive is not broken.

Axles

The Spicer front and rear axles do not suffer any particular faults. At the front, check for wear in the constant-velocity joints and steering swivels, and check for unacceptable wear in the final drive (crown-wheel and pinion), and wheel bearings on both axles. Check the universal joints in the propeller shafts for undue wear.

Brakes

The brakes should pull the Jeep up efficiently, and in a straight line. Particularly hard braking may result in the vehicle pulling to one side as the axle rolls forward under the braking forces, taking the drag link with it. This is normal, albeit a little alarming.

The master cylinder is under a small inspection cover beneath the driver's feet, which means that it tends to get neglected. You should anticipate changing the brake fluid on a newly-acquired vehicle and, if you can afford it, silicone brake fluid (DOT-5) is a better proposition than the normal alcohol- or glycol-based fluid since it is non-hygroscopic and reduces the chances of wheel cylinders seizing during long-term storage. However, the two types of fluid should not be mixed and you should flush-through the entire braking system if you are contemplating making the change.

The handbrake (parking brake), fitted to the rear of the transfer case, is not particularly effective simply because it is so hard to pull the brakes up tight. Most wartime Jeeps use an external contracting brake, while very late-Second World War Jeeps, and the M201, use an internal expanding system that is rather prone to contamination of the linings by oil leaking from the rear seal of the transfer case.

Steering and suspension

The steering box is a cam and twin-lever unit and is coupled to the wheels via a drag link, an axle-mounted bell crank, and a pair of tie rods. Between the drop arm of the steering box and the front wheels there are six ball joints and a pair of needle bearings – with more than a few miles on the clock, the system will exhibit a degree of in-built backlash, which would seem unacceptable to those more used to a modern rack-and-pinion unit. Excessive wear in all of these joints, and in the box itself, will result in decidedly vague steering characteristics. Up to a point, the steering box and the drag-link joints can be adjusted to compensate for wear, but new steering boxes, bell cranks and ball joints are readily available.

The suspension is thoroughly conventional, using multi-leaf semi-elliptical springs, which are attached directly to the chassis at one end, via fixed bushed shackles, with U-shaped swinging shackles at the other end. There is a helper spring on the left-hand side to compensate for the offset weight of the engine. The spring leaves were never enclosed by gaiters. Problems are confined to wear in the spring shackle pins and bushes, loss of temper in the leaves, which results in flattening of the springs, and failure of the shock absorbers. None of these are serious problems.

Hydraulic telescopic shock absorbers are fitted front and rear, and these should be replaced as a matter of course during a rebuild.

Wheels and tyres

Almost all wartime Jeeps were shod with two-piece steel combat wheels. Steel hinged bead locks were fitted inside the rims to prevent a deflated tyre from leaving the rim if the driver was unable to stop. In theory, these bolted rims made it easy to change a tyre in the field without special equipment and, although these combat wheels are considered desirable by Jeep enthusiasts, if they are rusty they can be very difficult to work on. In extreme cases, it is impossible to remove the tyre from the rim without damage unless the two halves of the wheel can be separated. If you must have them, new combat wheels are available at about £175 each – the bead locks are best thrown away.

The M201 uses a conventional well-base one-piece wheel, which is less likely to lead to difficult conversations about bead locks at the local tyre depot.

The standard tyres for wartime Jeeps are 6.00-16 cross-ply bar-grips – original pattern bar-grips are still available at around £90 each. The M201 should wear Kleber-Colombes 6.50-16 radials, which are now extremely hard to find.

Body

Rust is the biggest problem with the body, but the panels are mostly flat and it is simple enough to produce repair sections or to use the reproduction repair sections that can be purchased from Jeep dealers. A body that is totally beyond salvation is rare, but complete new tubs and component parts are available so this should be no bar to restoration.

Look for rust, filler or evidence of bodged repairs in these places:

- front floor, where it meets the side panels
- rear floor, where it meets the heel panel in front of the rear seat
- lower edges of the side panels
- rear outer corners of the front mudguard flanges, where the top panel meets the back panel
- inside the toolboxes in the inner rear wings
- in the 'top-hat' sections, which brace the floor; these sections are under the floor and run diagonally towards the mudguard step panels
- fuel tank well; the space between the fuel tank and the well is narrow and can become packed with mud which, if it remains damp, will cause both the tank and the well to rust through.

Don't be put off an otherwise very presentable Jeep by the condition of the upholstery and hood; new canvas is not especially expensive (budget £250 for the hood, and £270 for a seat cover set, including hip pads) and makes a world of difference to a tired-looking vehicle.

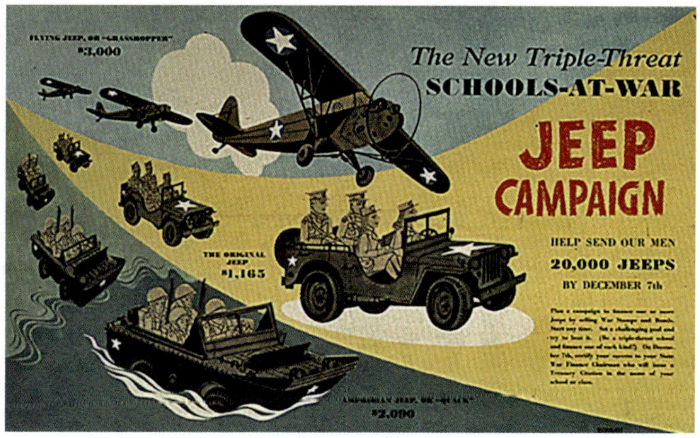

ABOVE: This poster was produced by the US Government to encourage war savings in schools. Note how the amphibious GPA is referred to as 'Quack'. *Warehouse Collection*

LEFT: For many, part of the fun of military vehicle shows is the opportunity to devise and construct period scenarios that allow nostalgic members of the public to see how things were back then. *Warehouse Collection*

Chassis

Unless a Jeep has led a particularly hard life, problems in the chassis are likely to be confined to the exposed chassis members ahead of the radiator, the front bumper gussets, and the radiator cross member. Repair pieces are available, as are complete chassis.

Note that the chassis allows considerable torsional flexibility and this can lead to cracking of the welds in the body at the bottom edge of the dashboard where it joins the body side panels.

DRIVING AND HANDLING

A good Jeep drives like a pre-war car – which is effectively what it is – and, in this respect, it is as practical as any 50-year-old classic car, which means that in modern terms it isn't very practical at all. However, no less an authority than Enzo Ferrari is said to have described the Jeep as 'America's only real sports car' and the long-time British editor of *Motor Sport*, Bill Boddy, was of a similar view. But, in truth, while it might be fun, it's no sports car and the handling is decidedly unlike a sports car.

Indeed, the question of handling is almost academic – you don't buy a Jeep for its road-holding. Off the road a Jeep will go practically anywhere and is both surefooted and communicative, but its road manners are somewhere short of perfection. Acceleration is acceptable up to about 45mph (75km/h) and the Jeep can keep up with A road traffic without much difficulty. However, the ride is harsh and the steering vague, with lots of turns of the huge wheel to get from lock to lock. The centre of gravity is high, which discourages over-exuberant cornering, and with a surprisingly small rubber surface on the road, the standard NDT bar-grip tyres don't hang on too well, particularly in the wet when they can provoke poor braking and understeer.

As regards the driving position, the first thing to say is that no one should be put off by the left-hand driving position on such a small vehicle. You won't be overtaking much but, if you are driving on the left-hand side of the road, it is advisable to fit a second external mirror on the passenger side. With a pair of mirrors, all-round visibility is excellent due to the open body and there are no blind spots. However, the Jeep is best suited to those of average height or below and, even then, you will find that your knees are splayed out either side of the steering column and you may have to hunch down slightly to get a clear view out of the top of the windscreen, particularly with the slightly thicker seat cushions of the M201. Unfortunately, if you are tall, or more than a bit overweight, you will probably find that the lack of any adjustment in the driver's seat means that the steering wheel will be uncomfortably close to your chest. Here, once again, the M201 might prove to be more of a problem with its slightly larger wheel.

Sitting in the driver's seat, the pedals are nicely placed and the gearbox allows quick changes, even if downshifts call for double-declutching. The brakes are good and, except in a real emergency-stop situation, will pull the vehicle up in a straight line. There is a quirk in the design of the steering gear that causes the vehicle to turn in to the left under very heavy braking, but consider it to be simply a fact of life and learn to live with it.

On the comfort side – forget it. There is no comfort as we would know it. The seats are firm and virtually unsprung, and the combination of these thin seat cushions, the cart-spring suspension and stiff-walled tyres ensures that the occupants feel every bump in the road. The French Jeeps fare slightly better – the seat cushions are a little thicker and the radial tyres more compliant.

The biggest downside is that weather equipment is minimal, which makes it a fair-weather car. If you are unfortunate enough to get caught in really heavy rain, you will find that

ABOVE: This high-level three-quarter rear view shows the compact nature of the Jeep, in this case an American-marked M201. Note the obligatory canvas bucket under the jerrycan strap. *Simon Thomson*

LEFT: Inside, the upholstery of this M201 is serviceable but mismatched, with a mix of grey and green plastic-covered cushions at the front, and canvas at the rear. As it happens, a complete upholstery set is both cheap and easily fitted and this is one of the things that can bring an immediate transformation to a tired-looking Jeep. *Christophe Muller*

both sides of the windscreen will get wet – the inside catching spray kicked up from the front wheels and from passing traffic – and most Second World War Jeeps have nothing more than hand-operated wipers. Side-screens and doors can be fitted, but the result is rather like driving a mobile tent. But, providing the weather is warm and the traffic fairly light, there is no doubt that most would agree that a Jeep is fun to drive. The engine is willing, the brakes are good, and you will have no trouble keeping up with the traffic up to about 60mph (100km/h). However, think carefully about your selected route when out for a spin. It isn't fun to have huge trucks continually blasting past you but, if you keep away from motorways and dual carriageways, driving a Jeep is going to be a happy experience.

RIGHT: An interesting half-enclosure made from timber, which could be easily reproduced. Note that the Jeep, one of 1,798 Ford GPWs supplied to the British Army under contract SM 2275, appears to have had the bonnet and windscreen panel painted matt black. *IWM, KID3053*

LEFT: A total of 12 men crewed the atomic bomb-armed B-29 Superfortress 'Enola Gay' on that first iconic run to Japan, and this photograph would seem to suggest an idea for a group of 12 re-enactors. However, it would possibly not be in tune with modern views on the subject. *Warehouse Collection*

In colder weather you will need to think very carefully about what you wear, Jeeps weren't dubbed 'pneumonia wagons' for no reason. If you plan to travel any distance you will need thermal underwear, a hat with earflaps and good gloves but, having said this, there are plenty of enthusiasts who think nothing of taking the Jeep out for a run on the coldest days of the year. Just don't underestimate how cold your extremities will become when exposed to freezing wind at speed.

And while insurance may be cheap, the little beast's fuel consumption means that you will be putting as much as £115 worth of petrol into the tank every 175 miles (280km) or so – and don't forget that you will need to avoid E5 fuels, which means using the more expensive E10 grade. Nevertheless, driving a Jeep is guaranteed to put a smile on your face – and to those of passing pedestrians.

Safety

Let's face it – on the safety front, the Jeep would achieve no Euro NCAP stars and would guarantee nightmares to Ralph Nader.

As regards passive safety systems, there are plenty of sharp-edged projections on the dashboard and windscreen panel, there are no seat belts or air bags and there is no crash padding at all. The steering wheel is too close to the driver's chest, although at least the steering box is tucked well behind the front axle. The 'safety straps' across the doorway openings seem to be there simply to provide something for the passenger to hang onto and would certainly offer no protection of any kind in an accident.

Nevertheless, proper seat belts can be fitted and indeed, some French Jeeps were latterly fitted with a full roll-over cage, which provides very secure belt mountings as well as stiffening up the chassis.

ABOVE: More re-enactment fun. *Warehouse Collection*

LEFT: During the 1951 General Election, which the Conservatives won, the Browne family used this civilian-registered Jeep for a spot of electioneering in the constituency of Leicester North East. Sadly, it was not sufficient to sway the voters. *Warehouse Collection*

TOP RIGHT: Five people, representing three generations, enjoy a Jeep ride at the annual War & Peace Revival event. The stick-on bullet holes are perhaps not in the best possible taste. *Warehouse Collection*

CENTRE RIGHT: This California-registered Jeep has been crudely extended at the rear to increase its carrying capacity. Look at the picture carefully and you will see that free-wheel hubs have been added at the front, presumably to reduce fuel consumption. *Warehouse Collection*

BOTTOM RIGHT: Jeep owners from across the world attend the annual D-Day commemoration events in Normandy. Judging by the flag draped across the bonnet, this Jeep hails from Norway. *Simon Thomson*

While the French radial tyres are fine, the wet-weather performance of the NDT tyres is decidedly marginal. This can be improved without too much of a compromise in appearance by a process known as 'siping', whereby slits, or 'sipes', are cut into the tread bar perpendicular to the direction of rotation. The process, which is named after its inventor John F. Sipe who patented the process in 1923, is popular with some off-roaders and, at least in the USA, the process is offered by some tyre retailers who use a siping machine. Hand-siping tools can also be obtained, but it is a laborious process. Don't forget to tell your insurance company that your tyres have been modified.

VALUES AND INSURANCE

While 'past performance is no guarantee of future results', over the years the wartime Jeep has proved itself to be a surprisingly good financial investment. Prices have certainly risen over the last couple of decades.

At the time of writing (late 2021) a realistic budget for a good, usable Jeep is around £15,000, but plan to spend another £2,000–£3,000 over a period to bring it up to scratch. It is still sometimes possible to buy a 'basket case' for below £10,000, but the restoration costs will almost certainly amount to two or three times this figure. Alternatively, if you really must have a '100-point' vehicle, be prepared to pay £28,000-plus. A Hotchkiss M201 will generally sell at around £1,000–£1,500 below the figure for a comparable Second World War Jeep. Prices in the USA and on mainland Europe are similar.

Note that prices tend to rise in the two or three months leading up to the summer show season and fall back slightly in the autumn. And, of course, you will generally pay more from a dealer but, naturally, you get a greater degree of legal protection should something prove to be not as described.

A number of insurance companies offer special, low-cost schemes for military Jeeps. It should be possible to obtain comprehensive cover for around £120 per year, subject to factors such as the age of the driver, the value of the Jeep, its location, and the provision of secure, storage. Quotations can vary wildly so it makes sense to shop around for the best price. Be careful that the vehicle is covered for its full replacement value, including all accessories and spare parts, and that, should there be a total loss, it is possible to buy back or retain title to the wreckage.

Chapter 6

The Mechanic's View

'In your possession is a motor vehicle that has been thoroughly tested and inspected... like any other piece of machinery, to maintain it in first class condition, you should lubricate it at the time prescribed with the proper grade of oil and grease... .'

WILLYS-OVERLAND CORPORATION, 1946

A military Jeep is a simple and very basic motor vehicle with any complexity restricted to the four-wheel drive system. It is sufficiently old-fashioned to allow it to be maintained by the average home mechanic, but it is also well-built and reliable and perfectly capable of everyday use – if you don't mind a degree of discomfort.

Perhaps the only real downside is that the vehicle requires much higher levels of regular maintenance than the average modern car, but most components are easily accessible and there is little need for specialised tools or equipment.

LEFT: HRH the Princess Royal, the daughter of King George VI, inspecting Motor Transport Company Jeeps of the Eastern Command, Auxiliary Territorial Service (ATS). *IWM, H34159*

SAFETY FIRST

It hardly needs to be said that a motor vehicle can bite if treated without respect. Even during maintenance and repair operations there are all kinds of potential perils, some of which can result in serious personal injury.

Personal protection

- Before starting work, make sure that you are wearing proper mechanic's overalls and stout boots or shoes, preferably with steel toecaps. Tuck any loose hair, neckties or other clothing out of harm's way. Remove rings or other jewellery to avoid the possibility of causing accidental electrical short circuits
- Never work under a vehicle that is not properly supported on axle stands
- Keep your hands and fingers away from the fan if you need to work under the bonnet with the engine running
- Remember that the exhaust system and radiator become very hot when the engine is running and can cause skin burns
- Do not attempt to lift heavy components without adequate assistance. The Health & Safety Executive suggests that men should not try to lift more than 55lb (25kg) single-handedly. The figure should be reduced if the load is awkward or sharp-edged, if it needs to be held at arms' length, or if you are forced into an uncomfortable working position.
- Always wear suitable eye protection when using a grinding wheel or powered abrasive discs, etc

LEFT: Don't try this at home – there are better ways to support a Jeep just as surely as there are better ways to get exercise! *Warehouse Collection*

BELOW: Fitters at the British 5th Army Jeep Service Station in January 1945 adopt a curious approach to servicing the rear axle of a Jeep. Despite appearances, the work in progress cannot have been too serious since the unit apparently passed all 'serious repair work' to the main Divisional Workshops. *IWM, NA21593*

- Do not strip paints and surface coatings without proper respiratory protection. Old paints can contain lead compounds, which are potentially injurious
- Do not spray paints or other fluids without proper respiratory protection.

Potential hazards

- Never run the engine in a closed space. Carbon monoxide exhaust gases are poisonous and can cause permanent brain damage and death
- Battery acid is corrosive to metal and will burn skin and clothing. Make sure it stays inside the battery!
- The gases produced by an open-vented battery during charging and discharging are highly inflammable and can easily ignite
- Be careful of short-circuiting the batteries. There is sufficient voltage and current available, particularly with the 24V Hotchkiss M201, to cause the battery casing to split, to start a fire in the wiring, or to cause serious skin burns
- Petrol vapour is highly flammable, with a flashpoint of −23°C (−10°F) which means that it is liable to ignite in any normal ambient conditions. Do not expose such vapours to a naked flame and never introduce any flame, or any apparatus that can produce a spark, into an empty fuel tank
- Do not allow oils or greases to come into contact with the skin; old engine oil, particularly, contains carcinogenic compounds. Wear disposable gloves or use a skin barrier cream.
- Be careful not to accidentally put the vehicle into gear with the engine running or to start it with first gear engaged

- Dispose of used fluids in a responsible manner. Most local authority waste disposal sites have facilities for old oils.

TOOLS AND WORKING FACILITIES

Get hold of a proper military parts list, and a user manual or a maintenance manual. These books will repay you time and again in reducing frustration and wasted effort. Reproductions are readily available and are preferable for use in the workshop anyway, since they are liable to become well thumbed and greasy. Keep the originals indoors out of harm's way.

As regards tools, for day-to-day maintenance, a good selection of imperial 'AF' ('across flats') spanners and

ABOVE: Sand and dust are not the best friends of motor vehicles, clogging air filters and getting into every possible crevice. Nevertheless, here, Lieutenant-General Sir Ronald MacKenzie Scobie watches a parade of Arab Legion vehicles from his Jeep in Palestine, May 1944. *IWM, E28321*

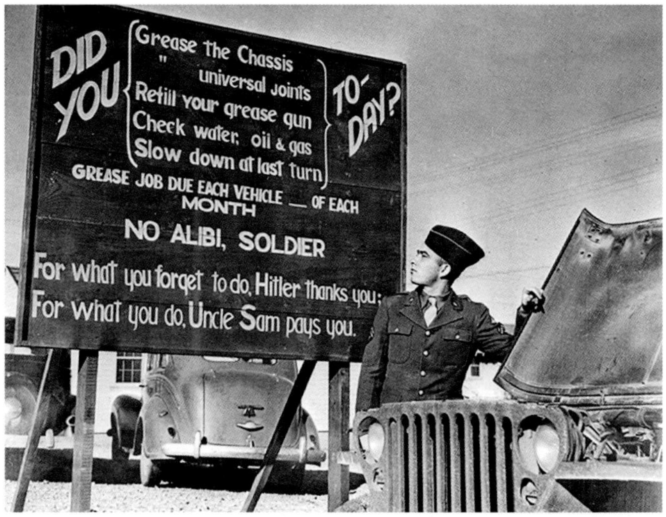

ABOVE: The importance of regular maintenance cannot be over-emphasised. *Warehouse Collection*

sockets will be required, as well as a lever-operated grease gun, and other standard hand tools such as pliers, feeler gauges, screwdrivers, hammer, etc. More specialised work will involve the use of a torque wrench, and there are two special tools available that are essential. One is the large box spanner, which is required to loosen the hub bearing lock nuts (Willys Part No WOA-348); the other is the puller for the front hub driving flange (Willys Part No WOA-1339). Both can easily be found.

Threaded fastenings on the vehicle use either American NF (SAE National 'fine') or NC (SAE National 'coarse') thread forms, more usually rendered as UNF and UNC these days. This is equally true of the French-built Hotchkiss where the only metric thread forms seem to be in the leads to the spark plugs.

It is always good practice to use new fasteners when re-assembling parts after maintenance or replacement, and the military parts list is invaluable in this respect since it itemises every fastening used on the vehicle, giving details of head, material and finish, diameter, thread form and length. For example, the parts list description 'bolt, S, hex-hd $\frac{7}{16}$-20NF x $1\frac{1}{2}$' translates as a $\frac{7}{16}$ in diameter steel bolt, $1\frac{1}{2}$ in long, with a National fine thread having 20 turns to the inch, and a hexagonal head.

MAINTENANCE AND REPAIRS

Unlike a modern car where bearings and bushes are sealed for life and service intervals have stretched almost beyond credibility, a Jeep requires regular attention from the grease gun to keep the suspension and steering bushes in peak operating condition. Similarly, the engine, transmission and other components need to be regularly checked and the oils changed or topped-up. Stick to the manufacturer's recommendations and keep a proper maintenance schedule and your Jeep will give you years of fun.

Lubrication

Points that require attention include:

- Cooling water and engine oil levels should be checked every day that the Jeep is used, and the battery level should be checked weekly
- *Chassis and suspension bushes, steering tie rods, propeller shafts and transmission control levers*: 29 grease nipples (zerks) require attention with high melting point grease (NLGI grease number 1) every 1,000 miles (1,600km)
- *Steering box and steering knuckles*: check the oil level every 1,000 miles (1,600km), and top up with high melting point grease (NLGI grease number 1)
- *Clevis pins, yokes and cables*: lubricate with light oil (SAE 10W) every 1,000 miles (1,600km)
- *Engine oil and filter*: change the oil and filter every 2,000 miles (3,200km); original oil grade, SAE 30; filter, Fram C3 or Purolator Junior
- *Air cleaner*: drain, clean and refill every 2,000 miles (3,200km); original oil grade, SAE 10W
- *Distributor oil cup, shaft wick and pivot for the breaker points*: lubricate with light oil (SAE 10W) every 2,000 miles (3,200km)
- *Transmission (gearbox and transfer case)*: check the oil level every 6,000 miles (10,000km); original oil grade, SAE 90
- *Front and rear axles*: check the oil level every 6,000 miles (10,000km); original oil grade, SAE 90EP
- *Wheel bearings*: clean and repack every 6,000 miles (10,000km) with high melting point grease (NLGI grease number 1)
- *Steering knuckles*: remove, clean and refill every 12,000 miles (20,000km) with high melting point grease (NLGI grease number 1).

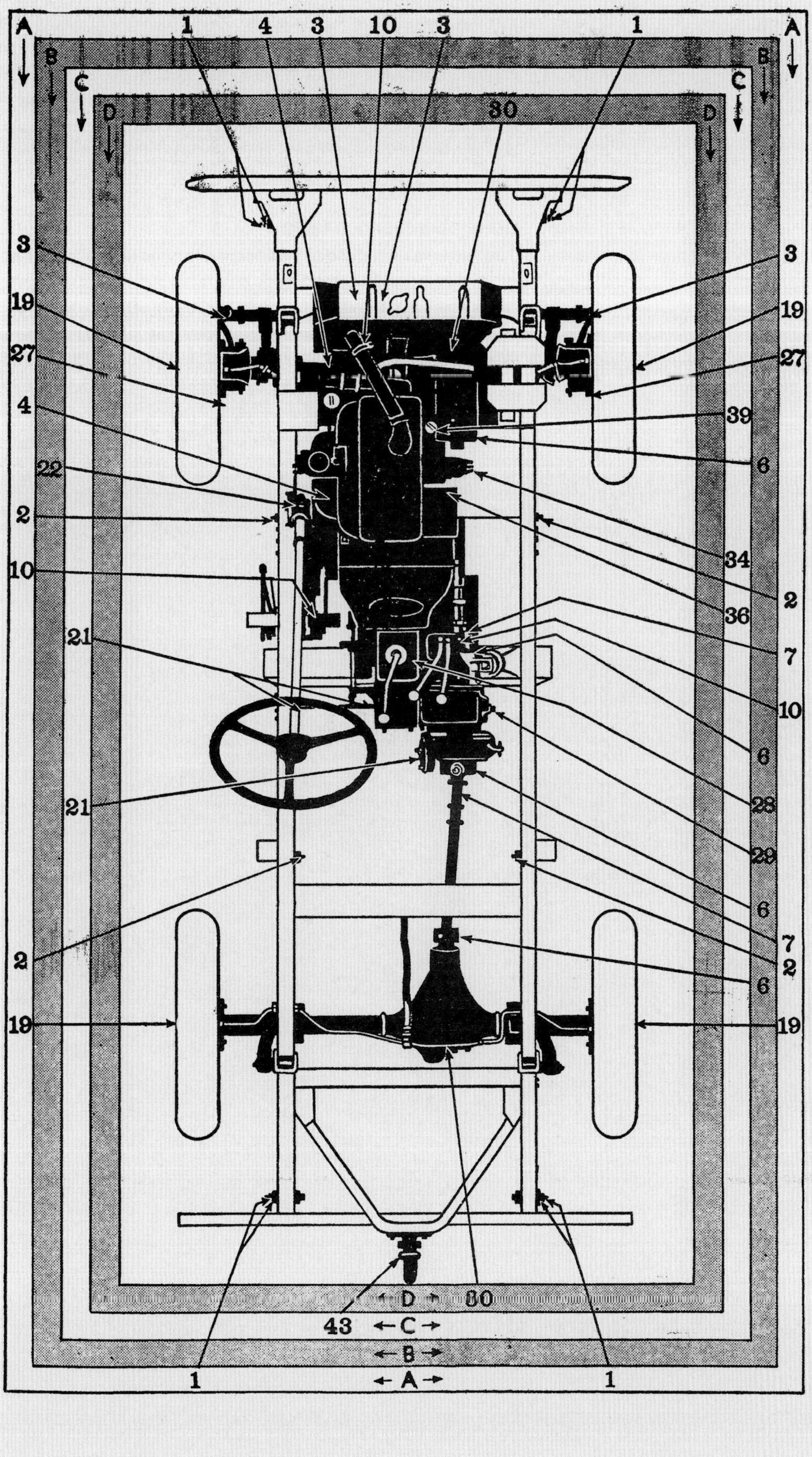

LEFT: Official lubrication chart. Note that some of the references are missing on the original. *Warehouse Collection*

1 Spring shackle
2 Spring bolt
3 Tie rod
4 Drag link
6 Universal joint needle bearings
7 Propeller shaft splines
10 Lever shaft, transfer case, clutch shaft and brake pedal and steering bell crank
19 Wheel bearings
21 Linkage
22 Steering gear housing
27 Front axle universal
28 Transmission
29 Transfer case
30 Axle housing
34 Distributor
36 Starter
39 Engine crankcase
40 Pintle hook

Lubricants

Frame A: chassis lubricant

Frame B: mineral oil gear lubricant

Frame C: engine oil

Frame D: hypoid gear lubricant

Instructions

Clean and lubricate all points in the order indicated, except those which require disassembly. Clean all vents. Check and adjust level in housings. Disassemble as separately instructed. Drain as separately instructed.

Capacities

Engine sump: including filter change, 0.875gal (3.97 litre); refill, 0.75gal (3.2 litre)
Air cleaner: 0.6 pint (0.33 litre)
Gearbox: 0.22gal (1 litre)
Transfer box: 0.3gal (1.4 litre)
Front and rear axles: 0.25gal (1.1 litre)
Front axle steering knuckle: 0.5 pint (0.25 litre)
Steering box: 0.5 pint (0.25 litre)
Radiator and cooling system: 2.3gal (10.5 litre)
Fuel tank: 12.5gal (57 litre).

Always make sure that you are using the correct lubricant for the job – as *Army Motors* said back in 1941, 'the right lubricant in the right place at the right time does the right job'. And, as regards engine lubrication, do not assume that modern synthetic oils will necessarily be an improvement. A Jeep engine does not generate the same temperatures and stresses as a modern engine, and was designed to run on a straight SAE30 grade oil; the most appropriate modern oil is probably a high-quality 20W-50 multigrade.

Other maintenance tasks

The Jeep was intended to be able to continue to operate reliably in a harsh and demanding environment – one where a breakdown could result in injury, death or capture of the crew – and the military maintenance schedule is similarly rigorous. Aside from the regular attention outlined above, there is a laid-down regime of checks, which need to be made at 1,000, 6,000

BELOW: What could be a better bet for recovering a broken-down Jeep than a Jeep-based recovery vehicle? *REME*

and 12,000-mile (1,600, 10,000 and 20,000km) intervals. For example, every 1,000 miles (1,600km), the schedule requires that the wheel alignment should be checked, that wiring connections be checked for tightness, and that the bolts securing the axle shaft flanges, the manifolds and the sump have not started to loosen. Similar attention should be paid to the carburettor flanges and to the cylinder head bolts at 6,000-mile (10,000km) intervals.

Maintaining a Jeep properly is not a task for the faint hearted.

DAY-TO-DAY PROBLEMS AND RELIABILITY ISSUES

A well-restored Jeep will still be sufficiently reliable for daily use, should you be so brave, and issues of comfort aside, requires very little in the way of compromise. It certainly does not need nursing along, and there are few potential problems, beyond those likely to be encountered with any older vehicle that has led a hard life and is only used infrequently.

Watch for the following:

- Blown head gaskets can be an issue. The modern composite head gaskets are not as reliable as the old copper-asbestos sandwich type and these gaskets are less forgiving of slight distortion in the cylinder head, which can lead to failure of the metal bow-tie link between cylinders
- The use of anti-freeze is essential. If the water in the block is allowed to freeze there will be damage to core plugs and the possibility of cracks appearing in the block itself, particularly beneath the distributor mounting
- Although the radiator is generously sized, over a period of time it can become silted up, which will cause overheating problems
- If you are tempted to replace the metal pipes that are connected to the radiator hoses, be sure to use a stiff or reinforced hose; soft hoses can be sucked flat with the engine running at speed, which will restrict the flow of water and cause overheating
- Air being drawn into the joint at the fuel filter bowl can lead to frustrating fuel-starvation problems. Similar problems can arise if this filter is allowed to become blocked
- An accumulation of mud in the sump under the fuel tank can cause the tank to rust through
- Abusing the clutch in off-road situations can lead to breakage of the torque springs and possible damage to the driven plate and flywheel faces
- If the clutch cable needs replacement, be very careful when feeding the ball end of the new cable into the clutch housing. It is very easy to knock the clutch fork off its pivot, meaning that the engine must come out to replace it
- The 6V electrical system of the Second World War Jeep must be kept in good condition if the lights are to be effective
- The contacts on the foot operated starter switch of the Second World War Jeep can become burned out through arcing and this will lead to erratic operation of the switch

Supplement to "The Motor Trader," September 15th, 1943 i

"TRADER" SERVICE DATA No. 119

Articles in this series are written by the Technical Staff of "The Motor Trader" and checked by the service managers of the vehicle manufacturers or importers.
Next article—
CLETRAC HG TRACTOR

Servicing the Jeep

Model GPW— Ford and Willys

SINCE the design of the Jeep—as the U.S. Army ¼-ton truck has become universally known—was finalised in 1941, the vehicle has been produced by Willys and Ford to the same blueprints. Very minor differences, chiefly in the details of frame construction, are discernible, but all units are interchangeable between the two makes.

Previous types produced by Willys (Model MA) and Ford (Model GP) differed in many respects and were not interchangeable.

As the vehicle is of severely utilitarian design, there are no special difficulties in servicing it. A certain amount of added complication is inevitable with the four-wheel drive, including as it does a transfer gearbox with auxiliary two-speed gear and provision for disconnecting the front drive. Apart from the drive through the steering knuckles, the front axle is a replica of the rear. It should be noted that some vehicles are equipped with radio suppressors, involving extra connections.

No special tools are needed other than a set of SAE spanners.

Instruments and Controls :—

1. Lighting switch
2. Choke
3. Horn button
4. Screen wiper hand controls
5. Ignition switch
6. Hand throttle control
7. Panel light switch
8. Petrol gauge
9. Dash lamps
10. Oil pressure gauge
11. Speedometer
12. Ammeter
13. Handbrake lever
14. Water temperature gauge
15. Starter switch
16. Transfer box lever (low and high)
17. Front axle drive lever
18. Gear lever
19. Accelerator
20. Brake pedal
21. Clutch pedal
22. Headlamp dipper switch

ENGINE

MOUNTING AND REMOVAL

Extended front engine plate rests on moulded rubber blocks on either side, bolted to brackets on chassis frame.

ENGINE DATA.	
No. of cylinders ...	4
Bore and stroke : mm.	79.38 × 111.13
ins.	3⅛ × 4⅜
Capacity : c.c.	2199
cu. ins.	134.2
R.A.C. rated h.p.	15.6
B.H.P. at 3600 r.p.m.	60
Max. torque at 2000 r.p.m. lbs. ft. ...	105
Compression ratio	6.48
Firing order	1 3 4 2
Tappet clearance (cold), both	.014"
Contact breaker gap	.020"
Plug : Make	Champion
Type	QM-2
Size	14 mm.
Gap	.030"

Third mounting below rear of gearbox on rubber block bolted to cross-member. Fourth rubber block, bolted to bracket on transfer box and resting on offside of cross-member, acts as stabiliser.

Engine can be removed leaving gearbox and transfer box in place. Raise bonnet top and disconnect battery earth wire, wires from dynamo and main feed wire from starter to regulator. Disconnect headlamp wire on near side at front (one screw terminal and one push-in connector) and undo two clips to wing. This is preferable to disconnecting wire from junction box on dash. Remove front grille and wing assembly (bolts each side to body and two bolts at front to frame). Detach radiator top hose from radiator and engine, and bottom hose from engine only. Remove radiator (tie rod at top, two studs at bottom. Note earth connection which goes between two nuts on bottom stud). Disconnect air cleaner hose from cleaner, and all pipes, controls and wires, including heat gauge and oil gauge pipes, wire from coil to switch and earthing strap between cylinder head and dash. Detach handbrake cable conduit from clip on flywheel housing. Detach front engine mountings from frame brackets (do not remove from engine plate). Attach short chain between front and rear centre cylinder head studs and sling at point of balance. Take out bolts round bell-housing flange, draw engine forward clear of clutch spigot and lift out.

Before reassembling engine remove starter motor, which comes out with engine but must be refitted separately.

CRANKSHAFT

Three main bearings, steel-backed, white metal-lined shells located by dowels. Running clearance .0015in.-.002in., end float .004in.-.007in., controlled by front bearing, flanged both sides, thrust washer being fitted behind timing sprocket with shims for adjustment. Bearings must not be scraped or caps filed to take up wear. For reground shaft bearings are available in .010in., .020in. and .030in. undersizes.

Main bearing shells can be changed without removing crankshaft, but practice is not recommended. Remove one cap at a time and slacken others sufficiently for crankshaft to drop so that upper shell will clear dowel. Bolts round bell-housing flange should be slackened slightly.

Flywheel attached to flange at rear end of shaft by two dowel bolts and four setscrews. Starter ring gear shrunk on.

Front end assembly consists of shims against shoulder of front bearing journal, thrust washer, distance

CRANKSHAFT DATA				
	Main Bearings			Crank-pins
	No. 1	No. 2	No. 3	
Diameter	2.334"	2.334"	2.334"	1.9375"
Length...	1.920"	1.8125"	1.75"	1.9375"

ABOVE: Service bulletin produced as a supplement to Motor Trader magazine. Rather than being a post-war publication, which is what you might expect, the date of publication is 15 September 1943, which would suggest that civilians were often called upon to service Jeeps. *Warehouse Collection*

- The current-voltage regulator units on M201 Jeeps have become hard to find and it is possible to buy an electronic unit that fits inside the casing, thus retaining the original appearance
- Infrequent use of the vehicle will encourage seizure of the brake cylinders
- The brake lights are operated by a pressure switch screwed into the cast body of the master cylinder. This can become seized with infrequent use
- Infrequent use of the four-wheel drive system may lead to seizure of the operating mechanism
- A worn gearbox, or loose attachment of the bell housing to the engine, will cause the vehicle to jump out of third gear on the over-run
- The later design of internal contracting handbrake is prone to oil contamination from failure of the rear seal on the transfer case. This is particularly a problem with original type leather seals that have been allowed to dry out.

Finally, here's a couple of 'get you back to base' repair tips from the US Army's *Army Motors* magazine that certainly shouldn't be tried at home. Apparently, a short circuit in the ignition system due to the engine being drowned could be remedied by squirting carbon tetrachloride from the vehicle's fire extinguisher onto the wet cables. As an emergency expedient for wet spark plugs, 'a short stick attached to the terminal will form a spark gap, which builds up line potential and causes a plug to fire even when wet'. And if the spring contact on your rotor arm should become lost or damaged it can temporarily be replaced with a piece of wire attached to the rotor with adhesive tape.

ABOVE: A well-serviced Jeep should be reliable – and being methodical is the key to proper servicing. *Warehouse Collection*

RIGHT: Under-wing view shows the lever-arm shock absorbers (dampers) that were fitted to the Ford GP. *Warehouse Collection*

ABOVE: A British soldier of the Royal Electrical and Mechanical Engineers REME services the front brakes. *IWM, NA16522*

LEFT: The scuttle top, or bonnet, provides a handy flat surface. Here, it is being used to serve lunch, but it was equally at home as a work bench. Note the relocated spare wheel mount. *Warehouse Collection*

Chapter 7

German 'Jeeps'

'Of unconventional design throughout, this Light Aid Detachment vehicle is based on the Volkswagen "Peoples Car", and employs a rear-mounted horizontally-opposed four-cylinder air-cooled engine.'

AUTOMOBILE ENGINEER MAGAZINE, JULY 1944

During the Second World War the German *Wehrmacht* had no vehicle that could be directly compared to the Jeep. In fact, aside from the vehicle's thirst for fuel, which was often complained about, captured Jeeps made a very welcome addition to the German fleet, being pressed into service under the *Beutefahrzeuge* (literally 'Loot Vehicle') scheme for captured enemy vehicles.

The closest thing available was the Volkswagen *Typ 82 Kübelwagen* – more correctly described as the *Leichten Kraftpersonenwagen, Kfz 1* – and its amphibious cousin, the *Schwimmwagen*.

GERMAN MILITARY MECHANISATION

Mechanisation of the German Army had started in the mid-1930s, but the provision of logistical vehicles remained poor throughout the war years and the *Wehrmacht* had no small four-wheel drive utility vehicle that could be considered as directly equivalent to the American Jeep. However, the Jeep and the *Kübelwagen* were often compared to one another since the two vehicles were used in similar roles.

LEFT: The air-cooled *Kübelwagen* was the closest thing that the *Wehrmacht* had to the American Jeep and, although it lacked four-wheel drive, its light weight was very much in its favour when off-road. *Simon Thomson*

ABOVE: The 'beetle'-based VW *Typ 82 Kübelwagen* was the closest thing that the *Wehrmacht* had to the American Jeep. Although it lacked all-wheel drive, its light weight and low gearing gave it a reasonable level of off-road performance, despite the lack of front-wheel drive, while the air-cooled engine meant that it was equally happy in extremes of heat or cold. *Warehouse Collection*

RIGHT: The rear-engined *Kübelwagen* was constructed almost entirely from flat panels, with pressed-in reinforcing ribs to provide strength. *Simon Thomson*

KÜBELWAGEN

The *Kübelwagen* was effectively a militarised version of Ferdinand Porsche's iconic 'beetle', whereas the Jeep was a purpose-made military vehicle. The name is contracted from *Kübelsitzwagen* and simply means 'bucket car' in recognition of its original bucket seats.

Work on the development of a military version of the beetle had begun in 1938 and the first prototype was ready by the end of the year, with early pre-production models appearing in December 1939 in time for the invasion of Poland. Standard production examples – described by Porsche as the *Typ 82* – were manufactured from February 1940, with the first 25 vehicles being built in Stuttgart. From May 1940 onwards, production took place at the Fallersleben factory on the outskirts of Wolfsburg. The vehicle saw its first real action in Russia and North Africa in 1941, where the air-cooled engine ensured that it was equally at home in either climatic extreme.

The *Kübelwagen* shared its backbone-and-platform chassis with the standard beetle and, with some modification, derived all of its mechanical components from the same source. The engine was a horizontally-opposed four-cylinder air-cooled unit, initially, of 985cc (60in^3) mounted in a fork between the

ABOVE: When reviewing the *Kübelwagen* in July 1944, *Automobile Engineer* magazine rather churlishly stated that 'notwithstanding the freedom of the design and the unconventional vehicle produced, very little advantage appears to have been obtained in production economy. While neither in performance nor weight are any special benefits achieved.' Hardly fair but, there again, we were at war. *Simon Thomson*

chassis members, low down at the rear. The engine was bored out to 1,131cc (69in³) in March 1943, increasing the output from 23.5bhp (17kW) to 25bhp (19kW). The drive from the engine was transmitted forwards through a single dry-plate clutch to a four-speed non-synchromesh gearbox with an overdrive top gear, and then turned through 180° to drive the rear wheels through a ZF self-locking limited-slip differential. Reduction gears were used at the rear hubs, but, nevertheless, the *Kübel* was capable of a top speed of 50mph (81km/h) on the road. Suspension was independent at all four wheels by means of laminated torsion bars.

The angular, flat-panelled open body was constructed by the American company Ambi-Budd Pressworks in their Johannesthall factory in Berlin. Offering perhaps a tad more creature comfort than a Jeep, it was, nevertheless, little more than a rectangular tub of pressed steel, with curved projecting mudguards covering the wheels at the four corners. A simple, top-hinged flat cover was provided for the engine compartment at the rear, and the spare wheel was placed on top of the sloping

BELOW: The *Kübelwagen* was in production from 1940 until 1945, with a total of 53,000 examples produced; 2,490 of these were supplied to the British Army in 1945. *Simon Thomson*

front compartment, either in a recess or on a boss. There were four un-trimmed steel doors, hinged on the centre pillar, and the body was reinforced by means of a transverse strut between the pillars, which also served as a grab rail. Small headlamps were mounted on the front mudguards, with a *Notek* blackout light on the left-hand side of the front panel.

Inside, there were four thinly upholstered seats covered with coated cloth, while wooden duckboards covered the floor. Instrumentation was minimal. A canvas hood, supported on a folding frame, provided weather protection, and side-screens could be attached to the door tops to make a complete enclosure.

During six years of production, 48,454 examples were constructed. Alongside the basic four-seater personnel car, standard variants included a three-seat command car (*Kfz 3*), radio communications vehicle (*Kfz 2*), and an automotive repair car (*Kfz 2/40*); there were experimental variants produced as a dummy tank. In the manner of the Jeep, there was also a field ambulance conversion. Four-wheel drive prototypes were also developed (*Typ 86* and *Typ 87*), and there were experiments with a half-tracked version (*Typ 155*), but there was no production of either.

While the *Kübelwagen* was certainly no match for the Jeep off the road, the limited-slip differential helped with traction in the rough, and the light weight meant that it performed well on most surfaces, although, despite the use of special balloon tyres, it was never particularly good on loose sand. And, although it was not as lively as the Jeep on the road, the independent suspension ensured a higher standard of road-holding, combined with better fuel economy.

However, while the official *Wehrmacht* line was that that the Jeep was inferior to the German *Kübelwagen*, clearly not all of the soldiers agreed and to prevent a disabled Jeep from falling into enemy hands, the US Army issued specific instructions on how the vehicle should be destroyed before it was abandoned. Nevertheless, the Germans managed to get hold of more than one example, and there were incidents where German soldiers believed that they could pass themselves off as GIs more easily by riding in a Jeep. In 1944, using 57 captured Jeeps, as well as trucks and armoured cars, German soldiers disguised as GIs got behind American lines during the battle for the Ardennes. Not realising that most Jeeps used by American forces at this time carried only one or two men, most of the German crews were quickly rumbled at US checkpoints because they put four men in each Jeep. In what was essentially the reverse of this ploy, the British SAS Regiment also disguised a Jeep as a *Kübelwagen*, the better to get behind German lines.

In passing, the Italian Army had much the same view of the value of Jeeps and, during the fighting in North Africa, any Italian soldier who could capture a Jeep intact was offered a bounty of 2,000 Lire and the possibility of leave.

SCHWIMMWAGEN

If the *Kübelwagen* is to be compared to the Jeep, then the *Schwimmwagen* must be likened to the amphibious Ford GPA.

Also designed by Ferry Porsche, and notwithstanding features that included a welded steel watertight body tub manufactured by Ambi-Budd, all-wheel drive, a five-speed gearbox, and self-locking differentials, the amphibious *Schwimmwagen* shared

BELOW: *Schwimmwagen* prototype climbing out of the water. *Warehouse Collection*

ABOVE: Overhead view of the four-wheel-drive amphibious *Schwimmwagen*, of which a total of 14,265 examples were constructed between 1942 and 1944. *Simon Thomson*

several features with the original *Kübel*. The engine was the same horizontally-opposed four-cylinder unit producing 25bhp (19kW) from a capacity of 1,131cc (69in³), and there was independent torsion-bar suspension at all four wheels.

With an all-up weight that was less than a third of that of the GPA, the *Schwimmwagen* – or *Schwimmer* for short – could produce a maximum road speed of 50mph (81km/h) from a smaller power unit. In the water, a hinged three-bladed propeller at the rear could be swung down and locked to engage with a dog drive on the crankshaft, giving a maximum speed of 6mph (10km/h).

Although development had started in July 1940, with what was originally described as the *Typ 128*, the final production version of the *Schwimmwagen*, the slightly-smaller *Typ 166*, was not put into production until early 1942. The total number of vehicles constructed was 14,265 before production was terminated in 1944.

RIGHT: In the water, the *Schwimmwagen*, which was powered by what was essentially the engine of the *Kübelwagen*, used a hinged three-bladed propeller at the rear that could be swung down and locked to engage with a dog drive on the crankshaft. Maximum speed was 6mph (10km/h). *Warehouse Collection*

AFTER THE WAR

Production of the *Kübelwagen* continued until 1945, although the *Schimmwagen* production line was closed down during the previous year owing to materials and labour shortages.

The Volkswagen Company scarcely survived the end of the war. If it hadn't been for one Major Ivan Hirst, an officer in the British Army's REME, the bombed-out Wolfsburg factory would probably have been pulled down. Hirst apparently found a pre-war prototype beetle in a remote workshop and realised that, despite the British Humber company stating that the vehicle was of 'no value', it could be put back into production to provide transport for the British Army who were short of light transport vehicles. In September 1945 the Army placed an order for 20,000 cars – and the rest, as they say, is history.

The beetle went from strength to strength, surviving in production in Mexico until 2003, by which time a total of almost 21 million vehicles had been built. You might even consider that the *Kübel* was put back into production in 1978 when the West German *Bundeswehr* took delivery of the first of almost 10,000 examples of the *Typ 183 Iltis.*

Following the acquisition of Audi in 1965, Volkswagen, of course, went on to dominate European car production.

BELOW: Captured *Schwimmwagen* in the hands of the US Army. *Warehouse Collection*

Chapter 8

Post-war Military 'Jeeps'

'There'll always be a Jeep – even if it is called by some other name.'

SOLDIER MAGAZINE, AUGUST 1950

The American author Robert A. Heinlein, writing in his novel The door into summer, said that 'when railroading time comes you can railroad – but not before'. What he meant by this is that inventions generally rely on the availability of appropriate technology – you can imagine a helicopter, as did Leonardo da Vinci, but without metallurgy and suitable power units, for example, you won't be able to build one. And once the technology is available, everybody wants to build one.

This notion can be applied to the concept of the Jeep – once Bantam, Willys and Ford had shown the way, manufacturers in half a dozen countries believed that they could do better. In post-war Britain, Jeep-shaped machines came out of the factories of Austin and Land Rover, in France it was Delahaye, in Germany there was the Auto Union Munga, and in Italy, Fiat, and even Alfa Romeo, joined the party. And on the other side of the Iron Curtain, large numbers of similar all-wheel drive light utility vehicles were produced in the factories of GAZ and UAZ – and then went on to be licence-built in China.

POST-WAR US ARMY JEEPS

The Jeep set a new fashion – if that's the word – in military vehicles, and in 1950, *Soldier* magazine put it on record when it wrote that 'a modern army is incomplete without a midget car tough enough to tackle tank country and powerful enough to do the work of a small lorry'.

LEFT: The rubber-suspended Austin Gipsy was typical of post-war efforts to improve on the Jeep, and although trialled by the British Army, the only serial purchases went to the Home Office Auxiliary Fire Service as part of the nation's civil defence service. *Simon Thomson*

However, production of the MB/GPW was terminated before the end of the war. Ford resumed building passenger cars, but Willys believed that there was a future for the Jeep concept outside of the military and, in 1948, launched the first civilian Jeep – the CJ-2A. Aside from the inclusion of a tailgate, which necessitated moving the spare wheel, it was little different to the military Jeeps that had gone before. But, don't get the idea that Willys had abandoned the military market, because examples of the CJ-2A went on to be purchased for military use by the South African, Swedish, Swiss and US armies.

In 1949, the CJ-2A was followed by the lightly-modified CJ-3A, examples of which were purchased by the armies of Belgium, India, the Netherlands, Sweden, and the USA, and then by the militarised M38, which also found itself in US Army service, as well as being licence-built by Ford in Canada.

Big changes came in 1952 when the redesigned M38A1, or MD, was introduced. This was the first Jeep to depart significantly from the pattern of the Second World War original, with the trusty Go-Devil engine ousted in favour of the new Hurricane, which had its inlet valves in the head and the exhaust valves in the block. Alongside the basic utility vehicle, there was a factory-produced long-wheelbase ambulance version, designated M170 or MDA, and a recoilless rifle carrier, designated M38A1C. The design of the basic M38A1 was also licensed to NEKAF (Nederland-Kaiser-Frazer) in the Netherlands, and there was a Canadian-built version designated M38A1CDN.

ABOVE: Although the US Army purchased small quantities of CJ2A and CJ3A Jeeps, the M38 was the first of the post-war military Jeeps. The electrical system was wired for 24V but, aside from this, most of the automotive details were similar to the Second World War Jeep. *Warehouse Collection*

BELOW: In 1952, the M38 was superseded by the updated M38A1. The major change was the substitution of the Willys Hurricane engine in place of the original Go-Devil, the height of which necessitated changes to the front-end sheet metal. *Warehouse Collection*

LEFT: A licence-built version of the M38A1 was produced in the Netherlands under the name NEKAF (Netherlands Kaiser-Frazer). These Dutch-built Jeeps can be identified by the smaller headlights. *Warehouse Collection*

BELOW: In India, Mahindra & Mahindra, based in Mumbai, produced a licence-built version of the CJ3B Universal Jeep, many of which were sold to the Indian Army. *Warehouse Collection*

LEFT: A version of the CJ3B was also constructed in Spain by VIASA; owing to the retention of the wartime Go-Devil engine rather than the Hurricane, these Jeeps were properly referred to as the MB-CJ3B. *Warehouse Collection*

BELOW: Developed by the Ford Motor Company and introduced into production in 1960, the frameless M151 was a wholly new take on the Jeep concept. Handling problems led to the introduction of the M151A1, seen here, in 1964. *Warehouse Collection*

ABOVE: Powered by a V4 air-cooled engine, and weighing just 1,700lb (772kg), the lightweight M422 'Mighty Mite' was developed by American Motors for the US Marine Corps. A total of 1,250 examples were constructed. *Simon Thomson*

LEFT: The M151A2 was introduced in 1970 with further improvements made to the suspension to reduce the vehicle's tendency to roll over if cornered too fast on hard surfaces. *US Department of Defense*

A year later, a militarised version of the CJ3B was introduced, powered by the Hurricane engine. This version saw service with the armies of the Congo, Philippines and South Vietnam, and the design was also licensed to Mitsubishi in Japan and to Mahindra and Mahindra in India. The CJ3B was purchased by the armies of Australia, Denmark, India, the Netherlands, Switzerland, and the USA. There was also a proper military version, designated M606, intended for the US Military Aid Program (MAP), with larger-section tyres, blackout lights, and a military-style rear tow hitch.

The launch of the unitary-bodied M151 in 1960, and its subsequent A1 and A2 variants, spelled the end of the original Second World War style Jeep. Although it was developed by Ford, the M151 was also constructed by AM General, Kaiser Jeep, and Willys.

EUROPEAN MILITARY JEEPS

Supplies of new Jeeps to Britain and Europe generally dried up with the end of Lend-Lease, but during the decade or so following the end of the war, most European countries were sufficiently fired up about the Jeep to contemplate designing

ABOVE: Despite the modifications made to the suspension, the M151A2 was never entirely satisfactory. Nevertheless, the vehicle remained in service until the introduction of the AM General 'Humvee' (HMMWV) in 1983. *US Department of Defense*

ABOVE: The *Matta* was manufactured in military and civilian versions. Production was terminated in 1954 by which time the total number of vehicles produced was 2,007 for the Italian Army and 154 civilian. *Warehouse Collection*

and building one of their own – didn't Oscar Wilde say that 'imitation is the sincerest form of flattery that mediocrity can pay to greatness'?

Alfa Romeo 1900 *Matta*

What eventually ended up as the Alfa Romeo 1900 *Matta* was prototyped in 1950 under the designation 1900R. It was powered by a dry-sump twin overhead-camshaft four-cylinder engine based on that used in the contemporary Alfa Romeo 1900, producing 65bhp (48kW) from 1,884cc (115in³). Like so many of the supposedly 'improved' Jeeps there was independent suspension by torsion bars.

BELOW: Based on the earlier Alfa Romeo 1900R *Folle*, the Italian *Matta* dates from 1952. *Warehouse Collection*

The improved and restyled *Matta* appeared during the following year. The power unit was unchanged, as was the 4F1Rx2 transmission, but the suspension was simplified, with independent springing at the front and a rigid leaf-sprung axle at the rear. Improvements were made to the front mudguards, the radiator grille, and the engine compartment cover, and the doors, originally of canvas, were now pressed steel.

Eventually, a total of almost 2,200 were constructed for the Italian Army (known as Model AR51 like the Fiat *Campagnola*) and Airforce (AR52) before the production line was shut down in 1955. A small number were also produced for civilians.

Auto-Union DKW *Munga*

The Auto-Union DKW F91/4 *Munga*, a four-seat field car produced between October 1956 and the end of 1968, is a possible contender for the title of the oddest of the Jeep look-alikes. Easily identified by virtue of its wedge-shaped nose, which did, at least, provide more effective mud control than the original, the vehicle shared the typical Jeep features of a folding windscreen, open sides, and a folding top.

Power was provided by a three-cylinder two-stroke engine of just 887cc (54in³), producing 38bhp (28kW); this was subsequently uprated to 974cc (59in³), with a power output of 44bhp (33kW). The engine was coupled to a four-speed gearbox with an overdrive top gear, and two-speed transfer case. Early examples had selectable front-wheel drive, but, for most, all-wheel drive was permanent. There was rack and pinion steering, and independent suspension for all four wheels by means of transverse leaf springs with lower wishbone arms. Maximum speed on the road was 60mph (95km/h).

ABOVE: Based on the German DKW Junior, the three-cylinder two-stroke *Munga* (*Mehrzweck Universal Geländewagen mit Allradantrieb*) was something of an oddball. Production began in October 1956 and continued until December 1968, with a total of 46,750 examples constructed. The *Munga* was used by the West German and Netherlands Armies. *Simon Thomson*

RIGHT: This *Munga* is acting as escort vehicle for a convoy of main battle tanks. *Warehouse Collection*

The name *Munga* is a contraction of '*Mehrzweck Universal Geländewagen mit Allradantrieb*', which translates to 'multi-purpose universal off-road vehicle with all-wheel drive'. Six-seat (*Munga 6*) and eight-seat (*Munga 8*) variants were also produced from 1962, both with a tailgate at the rear.

A total of 46,750 examples were constructed, and the vehicle was used by the West German Army and the border police service, as well as by the Netherlands Army, and the British Army in West Germany. Civilian versions were also available and there was a licence-built version produced in Brazil. Similar 4 x 4 field cars were also produced in small numbers by Goliath and Porsche.

Austin Champ

It has often been said that, like a camel, the Austin Champ was 'a horse designed by a committee'. And, with inbuilt features that included independent suspension by torsion bars at all four wheels, a gearbox that offered five speeds in forward and reverse, a measure of built-in waterproofing that made even the simplest maintenance tasks a nightmare, and radio screening of all of the electrical equipment, it was certainly sophisticated. Too sophisticated, some might argue.

Although series production did not start until 1952, work on what became the Champ had started as far back as 1945. When the vehicle finally appeared in its finished form it was not without problems. For example, although the standardised Rolls-Royce engine, which produced 69bhp (51kW) from a capacity of 2,838cc (173in^3), was apparently good for 200,000 miles (320,000km) and was a superb piece of work – unfortunately, it was also extremely expensive and way too well engineered for what was, essentially, a replacement for the Jeep. And, the back axle, which included the transfer gears, proved to be particularly troublesome.

ABOVE: Prototyped by the Nuffield Organization and manufactured in quantity by Austin between 1952 and 1956, the FV1801 Champ was perhaps a little too complex for the technology of the period, leading to reliability being sacrificed. *Warehouse Collection*

RIGHT: The Champ supposedly incorporated all of the lessons that had been learned during the Second World War, offering the best possible cross-country performance, by virtue of independent suspension at all four wheels; 24V radio-screened electrical system; in-built wading performance; two-speed generator on some variants; and five speeds in forward and reverse gears. *Simon Thomson*

ABOVE: Inheriting virtually nothing from the earlier Champ, the Gipsy was Austin's answer to the Land Rover. A number were submitted for military trials, but there were no series purchases; it was, however, favoured by the Home Office for civil-defence duties. *Warehouse Collection*

The open-sided body was slightly too high to allow ease of entry, and it lacked a tailgate at the rear – but, at least there were factory-made doors and side curtains that provided a weathertight, if claustrophobic, interior. Like the original Jeep, the windscreen could be opened or folded forward.

The Champ was produced in cargo and radio versions, with around 12,000 examples constructed between 1952 and 1956, at an average price of £1,200 per vehicle. A number were exported to Australia, and a very small number were produced for the civilian market with an Austin A90 engine.

The last examples were withdrawn from British Army service in 1966 in favour of the Land Rover.

Austin Gipsy

Following the relative failure of the Champ, Austin bounced back in 1958 when it attempted to steal the Land Rover's market with the Gipsy. In its Series 1 incarnation, the Gipsy featured 'Flexitor' rubber independent suspension designed by Alex Moulton, although by the time the Series 4 appeared in 1968, the independent suspension had been largely abandoned in favour of leaf springs and live axles. Power came from a 62bhp (46kW) four-cylinder engine, with a capacity of 2,199cc (134in^3), driving through the typical 4F1Rx2 transmission.

Like the Land Rover, there were both long- and short-wheelbase versions produced, but, unlike the Solihull wonder, the body was of steel construction, and had a propensity to rust.

Total production amounted to a modest 21,208, with several hundred going to the Auxiliary Fire Service as civil defence mobile fire column vehicles. A number of militarised Series 4 Gipsies were also trialled for the British Army at the Fighting Vehicles Research & Development Establishment, but there were no series purchases.

DAF YA-054

In 1951, DAF constructed two prototypes of the YA-054, a 4 x 4 field car powered by an American Hercules JX4C six-cylinder engine. With a power output of 60bhp (45kW) from 3,100cc (189in^3), the engine was coupled to a three-speed main gearbox combined with a two-speed transfer case. The drive-line followed an H pattern, with a central differential feeding the drive to distribution boxes located on either side of the vehicle, from which individual drive shafts provided power to the four wheels. Unusually, it was the rear-wheel drive that could be disengaged if it was not required.

There was torsion-bar suspension at the front, with coil springs at the rear, using trailing arms in both cases.

It was an ugly little beast, but elements of the Jeep can be seen in the cut-away sides, the angular mudguards, and the

LEFT: Powered by a US-built Hercules J4XC engine, the DAF YA-054 was prototyped in 1951–52 for possible use by the Netherlands Army. Just two examples were built. *Warehouse Collection*

folding windscreen. But, despite performing well in trials, there was no series production, and the DAF was passed over by the Royal Netherlands Army in favour of the Willys M38A1.

Delahaye VLR-D

At the end of the Second World War, the French Army received around 8,000 surplus Jeeps. At the same time, the *Ministère de la Défense* started to investigate the possibility of developing a wholly-French replacement, and in 1947, the *Direction des Etudes et Fabrications d'Armement* (DEFA) drew up a specification for an advanced vehicle with dry-sump lubrication, a four-speed gearbox, manual differential locks, and independent torsion-bar suspension.

DEFA approached the big three of the French automotive industry as well as various smaller enterprises, but the only company that showed any real interest in the project was the *Société des Automobiles Delahaye* and on 4 August 1949 two prototypes of the Delahaye VLR-D (*Véhicule Léger de Reconnaissance, Delahaye*) were unveiled. The design was standardised a year later, and a contract was placed with Delahaye for an initial 4,400 examples.

ABOVE: Production of the Delahaye started in 1951 and continued until 1955, with a total of 9,623 examples constructed. It was replaced by the Hotchkiss M201. *Warehouse Collection*

LEFT: The French-built Delahaye VLR-D fell into the same trap as the Austin Champ, sacrificing reliability for technical sophistication. *Warehouse Collection*

The production vehicle, now described as VLR-D *Modèle 51*, was decidedly Jeep-like with a simple flat engine cover, flat-topped angular front mudguards, an opening and folding windscreen, and cut-away body sides. The spare wheel and jerrycan were mounted on the back panel, and there was a folding canvas top.

Under the bonnet, there was a four-cylinder Delahaye Type 182 engine of 1,992cc (122in^3), producing 65bhp (48kW), featuring steel wet-liners in an aluminium crankcase, and dry-sump lubrication. The four-speed gearbox had an overdrive top gear, and there was a two-speed transfer case with a single lever to engage four-wheel drive and low-ratio gears; the axles were equipped with manual differential locks. Both front and rear axles consisted of trailing arms supported on lateral torsion bars, with a self-levelling feature at the rear.

As the first vehicles entered service, problems began to surface. It was suggested that the independent suspension made the vehicle difficult to handle, resulting in roll-over accidents. Worse still, problems were experienced with the differential locks, which either failed to disengage properly or actually managed to lock themselves – either way, the result was drive-line failure. There were lengthy investigations, but, in a final desperate attempt to cure the problem, the French Army disabled the locks altogether.

Delahaye modified the original design, with the VLR-D *Modèle 53* appearing in 1953, and a further modified version, described as the COB, was being developed when Delahaye was taken over by Hotchkiss in 1954.

Total production of the VLR-D over a four-year period amounted to 9,623 examples.

Like so many others, DEFA had failed to recognise that the utter simplicity of the Jeep was actually its greatest strength. In believing that they could design a better vehicle they fell into the same trap that had led to the development of the Austin Champ in Britain.

Fiat *Campagnola*

A prototype for what became the Fiat *Campagnola* appeared in 1950, intended for use as a civilian multi-purpose utility vehicle, rather like the Land Rover. However, it was quickly adopted by the Italian Army who referred to it as the AR51 (*Autovettura da Recognizione*). Improved versions were launched in 1955 (AR55) and 1959 (AR59).

RIGHT: Although it is seen here equipped as a police vehicle, and was originally introduced as a civilian multi-purpose vehicle, the Fiat *Campagnola* was equally at home with the Italian Army. *Warehouse Collection*

BELOW: Introduced in 1951, the military variant of the *Campagnola* was originally designated AR51; this was replaced by the AR55 in 1955 and by the AR59 in 1959, each with detail improvements. *Warehouse Collection*

ABOVE: Launched at the Amsterdam Motor Show in 1948, the Land Rover Series I was heavily derived from the original Jeep. Although originally seen as a stopgap until the development of the Champ was completed, the Land Rover eventually became the British Army's standard light utility vehicle. *Simon Thomson*

LEFT: Hardtop-equipped Land Rover Series I marked as a reconnaissance vehicle of the Home Office Civil Defence Corps. *Warehouse Collection*

RIGHT: Although the Red Army received more than 20,000 Jeeps during the Second World War, the GAZ (Gorkovsky Avtomobilny Zavod) plant also came up with the curious-looking GAZ-67 in 1941. Production continued until 1953, by which time the total number constructed had reached 62,843. *Simon Thomson*

BELOW: Similar to the US Army's M606, and dating from 1953, this licence-built Mitsubishi/Willys CJ3B-J4 was powered by a Japanese Mitsubishi JM63148 four-cylinder petrol engine based on the Willys Hurricane. *Mitsupicture*

The engine and transmission consisted of a Fiat four-cylinder unit, producing 56bhp (42kW) from 1,901cc (116in^3), coupled to a four-speed gearbox and two-speed transfer case. At the rear there was a live axle suspended on semi-elliptical leaf springs, but the front suspension, which consisted of coil springs enclosed in an oil bath housing, was a notable departure from the norm. The open four-seat bodywork was typical of the period, with a folding windscreen and open-fronted mudguards, but the doors could be clipped back in the open position to aid a speedy exit.

Production continued until 1973, when it was replaced by the *Nuova Campagnola*.

Land Rover Series I

Although it was certainly based on the Jeep, it seems astonishing now to think that Rover apparently did not see the potential for the Land Rover as a military vehicle, but rather considered it as a dual-purpose utility that would be equally at home on the road or in the fields. The British War Office thought differently and snapped up a total of 13,500 vehicles, out of a total production of 217,327, eventually using the Land Rover to replace the Austin Champ.

The first Land Rover appeared at the Amsterdam Motor Show in 1948. Recognisably derived from the Jeep, it was powered by a 1,595cc (97in^3) 50bhp (37kW) four-cylinder engine that was coupled to both front and rear axles via a four-speed gearbox, two-speed transfer case, and a free-wheel device to prevent drive-line wind-up. The free-wheel feature was quickly dropped to give a conventional drive-line, with the front axle now being selectable. The engine capacity was increased to 1,997cc (122in^3) in 1951, bringing the power output up to 52bhp (39kW). There were live axles, front and rear, suspended on semi-elliptic springs, and both long- and short-wheelbase variants were produced.

The bodywork was very basic, consisting of largely-flat panels, but, like the post-war Jeep, there was a hinged tailgate at the rear, and one advantage that the Land Rover did have over the Jeep was the fact that the body panels were aluminium, thus reducing the propensity to rust.

As regards the legendary quality of the ride, the Series I was every bit as firm and unforgiving as the Jeep. Curiously, *Soldier* magazine seemed to believe that the Land Rover was more comfortable, leading one to wonder whether they had actually ridden in one.

The original Series I was eventually superseded by the Series II, IIA and III, and then by the Defender, all of them quite recognisably derived from the original Series I and its inspiration – the Jeep.

THE REST OF THE WORLD

In Japan, alongside licence-built Mitsubishi Jeeps, there was also the Toyota BJ and the Nissan Patrol, both of which were introduced in the early 1950s, and both of which could easily be mistaken for Jeeps. And, while undoubtedly less Jeep-like than those vehicles already described, consider the Soviet-built wartime GAZ 67, the post-war GAZ/UAZ 69 and 469, the Czech Skoda 973P and 1100 VO, the joint Polish-Czech Borsuk, and the Rumanian UMM M-461. Whew!

But, despite all of these vehicles clearly being inspired by the Jeep, we're drifting further and further away from the original philosophy.

Chapter 9

Post-war Civilian Jeeps

'The Jeep is now being built in the USA with light-truck and estate-wagon bodies, but these are unobtainable in this country at present.'

COUNTRY LIFE MAGAZINE, 6 FEBRUARY 1948

The US Government started to dispose of pre-standardised Jeeps almost as soon as the MB/GPW went into production and, by late 1941, Hiram Berg of Chicago, later to become the self-styled 'King of Jeeps', had purchased large numbers of the Bantam BRC-40, Ford GP and Willys MA. Berg was even said to be supplying them to the British Army.

After VE-Day all Jeep contracts were cancelled and, as soon as the war was over, the US and British Governments started to dispose of large amounts of Jeep stock. Nevertheless, thousands of Jeeps remained in service, while others were loaned, leased or sold to the armies of the newly-liberated nations.

BELOW: Two-door Jeep station wagon conversion with a horizontally-split tailgate. The manufacturer remains unknown but the vehicle was apparently produced at Eaton Mews, Kensington. *Warehouse Collection*

Others were put up for sale to civilians at government auction sites in the USA, in Britain and across Europe, and in Australia and New Zealand. And the availability of Jeeps on the civilian market, no matter how battered, started a trend for conversions.

CIVILIAN MODIFICATION

As Europe tried to drag itself back to some sort of normality after 1945, plenty saw business opportunities in the acquisition and sale of military surplus. Companies began to pop up across Britain and Europe that specialised in supplying Jeeps and Jeep parts, with many also devising Jeep conversions that they believed would make the vehicle more acceptable to a civilian market that had been starved of new vehicles.

BELOW: The photograph was simply annotated 'Swiss friends' on the rear, which tells us very little, but clearly the Jeep is in private hands and there seems to be a racing motorcycle carried in the rear. *Warehouse Collection.*

ABOVE LEFT: A pair of heavily modified, and somewhat battered, surplus Jeeps that appear to be used for delivering take-away food from the Snack Shack Grill. *Warehouse Collection*

ABOVE RIGHT: The Automobile Association first deployed Land Rovers in London in 1949. Although these are said to have been among the first four-wheel vehicles used by the Association, which had hitherto favoured motorcycle combinations, Jeeps were also used as patrol vehicles at around the same time. Of course, this is nothing more than a converted Second World War Jeep. *Phil Royal*

The precedent for converting Jeeps had already been established during the Second World War, when servicemen with too much time on their hands had built enclosed bodies for Jeeps using things like discarded aircraft wing tanks, cockpit covers, and 1930s saloon cars. It wasn't long before it seemed that everyone was at it, some even cutting the chassis and extending the wheelbase to provide extra seating, or a larger cargo area. Eventually, Jeep-based ambulances, buses, farm tractors, dumpers, recovery vehicles and even railroad repair trucks began to appear, all of them using surplus Jeep chassis.

ABOVE: Making their first appearance in 1944, early Willys prototypes for what was to become the production CJ-2A Universal Jeep were named 'Agrijeep'. Note the side-mounted spare wheel necessitated by the use of a hinged tailgate. *Warehouse Collection*

LEFT: An Agrijeep undergoing land trials in the Netherlands; note the short truck cab. *Warehouse Collection*

ABOVE LEFT: A 1946 advertisement from Philadelphia-based Jeep dealers Turner Motors for the 'amazing 4-function vehicle'. *Warehouse Collection*

ABOVE RIGHT: This Willys leaflet promotes the use of the Universal Jeep around the farm. The material is undated but, judging by the illustrations, which include a CJ3B, it cannot have been published any earlier than 1953. *Warehouse Collection*

LEFT: In 1947–48, Paris-based company Duriez took a Jeep chassis and turned it into this forward-control *Canadienne* estate car for a price of 125,000 Francs. The company also produced other conversions. *Warehouse Collection*

In France, a company called Jeep-Duriez, based in Paris, developed a forward-control estate-car conversion in 1947/48, described as '*un Canadienne*'. The stated payload was 1,650lb (750kg) or nine persons, and the vehicle sold for 125,500Ffr. The company also produced a forward-control truck and a smaller normal-control estate car dubbed the 'Baby-Jeep-Duriez'. Carosserie Arnault built a similar wood-framed station wagon, which was also described, in the French style, as *Canadienne*, a term which apparently covered all such timber-framed vehicles. A garage proprietor in the Vosges area added a fifth wheel to turn his Jeep into a tractor for use with semi-trailers. And, in 1948, an enterprising Italian firm also transformed the little Jeep into a tractor for semi-trailer, using it to haul a 20-seater bus body.

Similar conversions were also produced in Belgium, and in Austria, where the Jeep was particularly favoured by fire-fighters. And, of course, no one should need reminding that the Philippines Jeepneys were originally based on Second World War Jeeps.

Back in Britain, there was more than one firm offering Jeep conversions. In New Malden, Surrey, a company called Farmcraft Coachbuilding produced, among other designs, a Jeep-based timber-framed shooting brake, somewhat in the style of the yet-to-be launched Morris Minor Traveller. Farmcraft also produced a long-wheelbase 30cwt pick-up truck. In nearby Kingston-upon-Thames, Wick Autos offered a variety of Jeep conversions including a handy little truck with a drop-down tailgate, with prices starting at just £275. FWD Motors, also based in Kingston, produced a kind of 'A40 Jeep', which grafted the rear end of an Austin A40 pick-up onto the front end of a Jeep, to which they added a steel-panelled hardtop. John Burleigh (Automobiles) of Kensington extended the wheelbase by almost 2ft (610mm) and built a fully-enclosed body of aluminium-panelled ash, which left very little of the original vehicle remaining. Intended for use as a dual-purpose farm utility vehicle, the price was £550.

The coachbuilding company Willenhall produced a very tidy-looking fully-enclosed two-door Jeep-based estate car with a side-hinged rear tailgate. The *art deco* grille lent a particularly stylish touch. Other similar timber-framed machines were produced by the Blue Star Garages Group, and by an anonymous company in Eaton Mews, Kensington – perhaps the forerunners of current Jeep dealers, Belgravia Garage.

The undoubted kings of the conversion game in Britain were Metamet, based in Belsize Lane, London NW3. The name was derived from 'metal and metal' and the company was originally run by an engineering firm called C.J. Stewart & Co, but was subsequently owned by Sergei Crulew, a Polish *émigré*, and his son, Steven, and remained in business into the 1980s. As well as offering the standard military surplus Jeep, the company's 1954 brochure also included no less than ten different Jeep conversions, including the top of the range 'Five in One' model, so-called because it offered five configurations – 'one', hood up, no sides; 'two',

ABOVE: The New Malden-based Farmcraft company offered this Jeep-based shooting brake. *Warehouse Collection*

LEFT: This is the Burleigh 'utility Jeep', which has had the wheelbase extended by some 20in (508mm) before being fitted with an ash-framed metal-panelled three-door body, which looks rather like a Jeep that has been swallowed by something a bit larger. *Warehouse Collection*

ABOVE: West Midlands-based Willenhall Coachcraft produced this Jeep-based estate car. Others produced by this company, including one example supplied to the Earl of Shrewsbury, were unaltered forward of the windscreen. *Warehouse Collection*

LEFT: A rear view of the Willenhall estate car. *Warehouse Collection*

completely enclosed with hood, doors and side screens; 'three', completely open; 'four', hood down, sides up; and 'five', sunshine roof. Other conversions included a pick-up truck, a van, and an agricultural utility vehicle.

Of course, there were also one-off conversions – for example, a British aircraft engineer used almost the entire bodywork of a 1937 Chevrolet to turn his Jeep into a stylish, if somewhat truncated, automobile, and a USAAF sergeant employed the belly tanks of a P-38 Lightning fighter to build a body for his Jeep, combining this with a front grille made from an ammunition rack. And, how about a Jeep onto which has been mounted the cab and rear bed of a Volkswagen *Typ 2* transporter? Or a Willys MB to which has been grafted the body of a Renault 4L (www.drivebysnapshots.com/jeep-r4-conversion/)?

Thanks, in part, to the efforts of these companies and individuals, thousands of Jeeps have survived to the present day – although, sadly, very few remain in post-war converted form.

ABOVE: It's amazing how much of a difference is made by fitting a better-shaped top. Of course, it doesn't look quite like a Jeep anymore but, presumably, that was the point. *Warehouse Collection*

BELOW: Based in Daleham Mews, Belsize Park, Metamet were the kings of the Jeep conversion game in Britain, even producing a simple sales publication that illustrated and described ten different Jeep conversions. *Warehouse Collection*

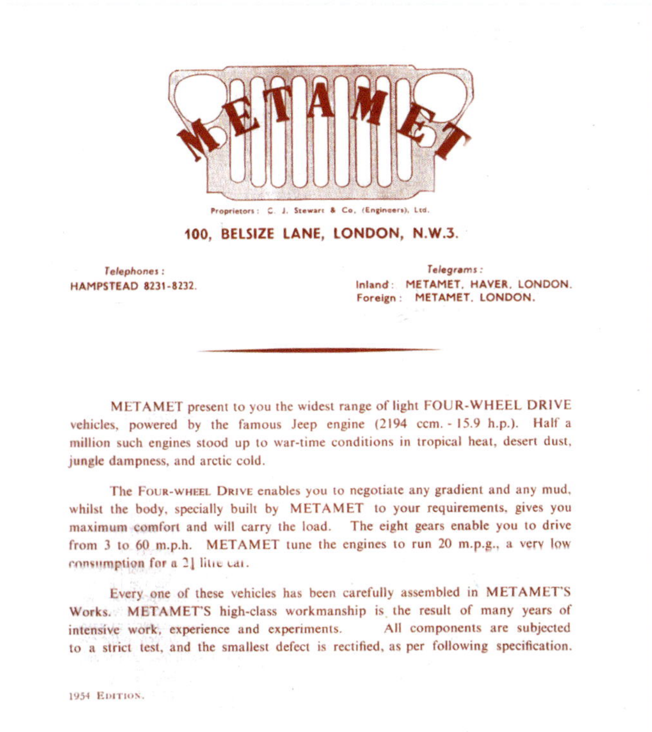

METAMET

Proprietors: C. J. Stewart & Co. (Engineers), Ltd.

100, BELSIZE LANE, LONDON, N.W.3.

Telephones:
HAMPSTEAD 8231-8232.

Telegrams:
Inland: METAMET, HAVER, LONDON.
Foreign: METAMET, LONDON.

METAMET present to you the widest range of light FOUR-WHEEL DRIVE vehicles, powered by the famous Jeep engine (2194 ccm. - 15.9 h.p.). Half a million such engines stood up to war-time conditions in tropical heat, desert dust, jungle dampness, and arctic cold.

The FOUR-WHEEL DRIVE enables you to negotiate any gradient and any mud, whilst the body, specially built by METAMET to your requirements, gives you maximum comfort and will carry the load. The eight gears enable you to drive from 3 to 60 m.p.h. METAMET tune the engines to run 20 m.p.g., a very low consumption for a 2½ litre car.

Every one of these vehicles has been carefully assembled in METAMET'S Works. METAMET'S high-class workmanship is the result of many years of intensive work, experience and experiments. All components are subjected to a strict test, and the smallest defect is rectified, as per following specification.

1954 EDITION.

ABOVE: Metamet's top of the range model was the so-called 'Five in One', which offered five configurations – 'one', hood up, no sides; 'two', completely enclosed with hood, doors and side screens; 'three', completely open; 'four', hood down, sides up; and 'five', sunshine roof. By the same token, you could call a standard Jeep 'Three in One'! *Warehouse Collection*

JEEP KICK-STARTS THE SUV CRAZE

In passing, I have often read that many attribute the enthusiasm for SUVs (sport utility vehicles) of the last decade or two to the Range Rover, which made its first appearance on the market in 1972. However, in much the same way that the original Jeep eventually brought you the Land Rover, I would contend that it is much more likely that the craze started with the Jeep Wagoneer of 1962.

Chapter 10

Originality and Restoration

'Beware the perils of inappropriate or over-restoration.
A classic car is only original once – and if lost, that originality cannot be regained!'

URBAN WISDOM

From a mechanical viewpoint, the Jeep is a simple, straightforward machine in which it is difficult to hide faults. There is some scope for concealing rust in the body panels, but the lack of interior trim means that everything is literally on show – you can see both sides of most panels and what you see is generally what you get. You don't need to be an expert; you just need to know where to look and to keep your eyes open and your wits about you.

And if the vehicle is incomplete, or in poor condition, remember that every part is available, literally off the shelf. Okay, not every part will come in its original wartime packaging but nevertheless, modern repro parts are generally of good quality and often take advantage of recent advances in materials and technology. Leather oil seals, for example, are often replaced by modern lip-type synthetic rubber seals, which may be less accommodating of worn contact surfaces, but which don't dry out on vehicles that are only rarely used.

LEFT: Under-bonnet view of the M201. Major differences between this and the Second World War offering include 24V electrical equipment, screened ignition system, and twin batteries, necessitating repositioning of the air cleaner. *Christophe Muller*

ABOVE: Although the original design brief made no mention of aesthetics, the Jeep is an attractive vehicle with no bad angles. And, when well-restored, is a thing of rare beauty. *Simon Thomson*

RIGHT: Enterprising enthusiasts have constructed replicas of the more unusual Jeep variants, including the Bantam prototype, the Willys MT-TUG, the Nuffield airborne Jeep (seen here), and SAS and airborne Jeeps. *Simon Thomson*

ORIGINALITY

In the classic-car world, the term 'originality' is much over-used and has become pretty much devoid of any real meaning. The moment a vehicle starts to be used, it begins to wear out, and once the first factory component has been replaced, that vehicle can no longer really be said to be original – and any Jeep that has been through an army rebuild programme can certainly never be described as original.

True originality is a virtual impossibility.

However, it may be legitimate to describe a vehicle as original if all of the parts remain correct for the month and year in which the vehicle was constructed, even if they are replacement parts, or even if those parts that have been replaced have been changed on a strict like-for-like basis, regardless of the date of manufacture.

Back in 1999, American Jeep enthusiast Lawrence Nabholtz produced a comprehensive guide to the changes made to both Ford and Willys Jeeps during the five-year production run.

Entitled *The Military Jeep: an Illustrated Guide to its Features and Evolution, 1941–1945*, the book is now hard to find, but it does provide the keen restorer with all of the detail that is necessary to understand how a Second World War Jeep left the factory – no matter that trying to find exactly the right variation on what will often be very minor parts will sorely test your patience.

As William Shakespeare once said, 'that way madness lies'. Real originality still remains an expensive dream.

A far more sensible approach to the restoration of a Jeep is to try to replicate how the vehicle might have been operated and maintained at a specific period during its service career. After all, no army has any interest whatsoever in maintaining a vehicle in what an enthusiast would regard as 'original' condition, but has every interest in keeping the thing running. A Jeep that has been restored to a 'genuine' military condition should include only genuine military parts. It could be argued that it is perfectly acceptable to use French or original American parts during the restoration of a Hotchkiss M201 since this is what the French Army workshops would have done, but it is not acceptable to use French-manufactured parts on any American Jeep, especially one that is presented as being of the Second World War era.

Remember, no military vehicle should be fitted, for example, with generic after-market parts. But, having said that, when the French Army issued *Bulletin Technique No 448/AU* in 1967, advising how to fit flashing indicators, many M201s found themselves wearing AXO A307 lights that would have looked perfectly at home on a Citroën 2CV.

ABOVE: Beautifully restored – note how the use of new canvas, including the windscreen cover, makes a huge difference to the appearance of a Jeep. *Simon Thomson*

So, you must make up your own mind about how far you want to go and whether or not you consider modern reproduction parts to be acceptable, but beware of telling another man that his Jeep is not original.

PROVENANCE

When searching for a Jeep to buy, you should be aware of the existence of the 'Americanised' Hotchkiss. Now, there's nothing wrong with the French Jeep – indeed, there are those who believe that the thicker chassis, 24V electrical system and more compliant ride make it a better bet, but there certainly used to be a significant price difference and one that was large enough to encourage the unscrupulous to attempt to disguise the origins of a French Jeep.

Although the French wheels, instruments and lighting equipment can be easily changed, there are one or two areas that are a little more difficult to hide. For example, the reinforcement in the chassis channels just ahead of the radiator cross member should be a sure indication that you are, at least, looking at a French chassis; and note that no American-built wartime Jeeps ever had a 24V electrical system no matter what the seller may tell you. Look for the starter switch mounted on the centre of the dash (or evidence that there has been such a thing), and the presence of spurious holes to the left-hand side of the dash that have no apparent function, but which indicate that various M201-specific switches have been removed. There is also a small square tooling cut-out at the centre of the scuttle top where the flange is folded over onto the dash panel on the wartime bodies; this is not present on the Hotchkiss body and is not easy to fake convincingly. Similarly, if the internal body supports just ahead of the doorway cut-outs are angular in shape then the body, at least, is almost certainly that of an M201.

If you do end up buying a French Jeep that has been 'Americanised', remember that it is really neither one thing nor the other. In your heart you will always know that it is 'wrong' and anyone looking at it, who knows his stuff, will also know that it is not what it seems. In the long run you will almost certainly be unhappy with it and it will cost money to put it back to its original condition. Worse still, many of the smaller French components, which may have been replaced during a previous ownership, are actually harder to find than their American equivalents. It took me 15 years to find a French decontaminator, and I have been searching for 25 years for the correctly marked French choke and hand throttle cables.

RESTORATION

Make no mistake, as with most vehicles, restoration is a costly business. At the time of writing (2021) a well-restored Jeep can cost upwards of £25,000. If your budget is more modest, vehicles can still be found at prices way below this and parts availability is such that there is no reason why any Jeep cannot be restored. Engines, transmissions, wiring looms, instruments – everything remains available and even the most badly rusted-out body tub can be repaired or replaced. But, remember, that in the long run, the cost of restoring a poor example will inevitably exceed the cost of buying a vehicle that has been well restored by someone else. It is good advice to buy the best example that you can afford and let the previous owner bear the cost of restoration. And if you buy well, you may find that your Jeep is actually a sound investment.

If you must restore, and are keen on maintaining a genuine military appearance, be wary of over-restoring your vehicle or of buying a Jeep that has been over-restored.

Proper restoration involves dismantling the vehicle right down to its individual parts and then making a decision regarding every worn, rusted or damaged component. Inevitably, there will be bent or rusty panels that will need to be straightened, replaced or repaired by skilful patching, and all of what may prove to be many coats of paint will need to be stripped from the components. And before refinishing, a decision will need to be made regarding the exact shade of paint that will be used. Once all of this work has been completed, the long, slow job of re-assembly can begin, but you will need to make a decision regarding the re-use of old fasteners – and if you own a Ford GPW, and you are really picky, then the question of whether or not to use 'F' script bolts will also need to be made.

BELOW: Step 1 for a serious restoration is to remove the body. *REME*

ABOVE: Underside view of the floor beneath the driver's foot well. The top-hat sections are particularly prone to rusting-out and on this body tub the spot welds have been drilled through and the top-hat sections removed to allow replacement. Note how rust remains in areas that the blast cleaning was unable to reach. *Christophe Muller*

Unfortunately, it is not at all easy to produce a convincing impression of a military vehicle in service.

Remember, Jeeps were not perfect when they left the factory and, for example, the various spot welds and body seams should not be filled. Similarly, slight imperfections in the appearance of the body panels are perfectly acceptable and some over-spray on the engine is in order. Unnecessarily fussy detailing, for example lining up the flats on the cylinder head bolts, using rubber or timber protection for the floor panels, or using modern laser-cut self-adhesive lettering where there were originally stencils, is an absolute 'no-no'.

When trying to decide how the vehicle should be finished and detailed, consider the pattern of wear on items that are frequently handled by the driver and crew, for example the edges of the body cut-out where the driver braces himself to get in or out, the pedals, the floor panels (particularly below the pedals), and various items of switchgear. Take a look at some 'real' military vehicles in service and note particularly the multiple coats of, often, indifferently-applied paint, and the total lack of attention to detail.

The problem with traditional restoration, particularly with an item as utilitarian as a Jeep, is that it is impossible to maintain any links that the vehicle has with its history or its service past. Unless you are extremely clever, all of the vehicle's original character will be gone – it may be a thing of beauty, but it will have lost its soul.

Perhaps a better approach, and one which is particularly apt if the vehicle remains sound and still has many of its original features, is to give serious consideration to maintaining it in what has come to be called 'oily rag' condition. This means that, for safety reasons, all of the running gear has been restored, but the inevitable knocks and scrapes of a hard service life are preserved, with the paintwork maybe exhibiting surface rust, and with even the upholstery deliberately worn. In other words, the vehicle looks as though it has received nothing more than a wipe-over with an oily rag.

BELOW: A Hotchkiss M201 looking almost good enough to eat! *Christophe Muller*

RIGHT: In most aspects of mechanical work 'cleanliness is next to Godliness'. *Warehouse Collection*

BELOW: Welding techniques, particularly for thin or rusted metal, have improved considerably since the end of the Second World War. *IWM, NA21592*

BELOW: With the body removed it is so much easier to gain access to the engine, transmission, suspension and axles. This photograph is one of a series taken to illustrate a REME exhibition special whereby two teams stripped and rebuilt a pair of specially prepared Jeeps that were driven into the arena and driven out again at the end. The winner was the team that completed the task in the shortest time. *REME*

ABOVE LEFT: Back in the 1950s and 60s, there were plenty of people selling surplus Jeep parts, often producing useful illustrated parts lists like this one from the Transportation Parts Co based in New York. *Warehouse Collection*

ABOVE RIGHT: Priced at just one shilling (5p), this parts list was produced by Universal Car Distributors based in Chiswick. *Warehouse Collection*

TOP RIGHT: Although Willys did supply a number of hardtop enclosures after the war, there never really was an official hardtop for the Jeep. However, there were plenty of locally produced examples and this restored US Navy Jeep is fitted with a very professional and attractive aluminium enclosure. *Simon Thomson*

BOTTOM RIGHT: If all else fails… . *REME*

PARTS AVAILABILITY

The availability of parts for rebuilding and maintaining Jeeps remains excellent, with many original 'new old stock' (NOS) parts from the original American manufacturers still available, often in the original wartime packaging. There are also original parts of French manufacture as well as modern reproduction items, including body sheet metal, upholstery, service items, and many of the smaller specialised military components that inevitably went missing during the years that 'old Jeeps' were considered valueless.

Although the standardised Jeep was effectively a product of Willys-Overland, Jeeps were built by both Ford and Willys and the parts produced during the Second World War are identified using either the Willys part numbers, which are prefixed 'WOA', or the Ford part numbers, which carry the prefix 'FM-GPW' or, occasionally, 'FM-GP', but there is no commonality in the number part of the code. Willys parts generally carry no manufacturer name, although some Ford-made parts were identified with the company's script 'F' character.

Sadly, life is not so easy for the enthusiast of the Ford GPW, because many of the original Ford-built components are no longer available.

Jeep parts that were manufactured in France are identified with a part number, which is prefixed 'HO' but, even where the part is common to the equivalent US-made part, the number part of the code is different. Some French-made parts are also marked with the brand 'WOF', signifying 'Willys-Overland France' – not 'Willys or Ford' as I once heard someone say.

Aside from areas where the MB/GPW and M201 Jeeps differ, such as the ignition and electrical systems, all parts manufactured for the M201 will also fit the MB/GPW although, of course, originality will be compromised.

Remember that the easy availability of parts is both a blessing and a curse. On the plus side, it means that no Jeep is beyond practical repair, but the downside of this is that almost any Jeep in Britain and Europe will include pattern parts, or parts produced by Hotchkiss, thus destroying originality. The same is equally true of Jeeps in the USA, although there are probably fewer Hotchkiss parts over the water.

N.A.S. QUONSET POINT
5
U.S.N.
249342

Epilogue

'The Jeep is quintessentially a utilitarian vehicle – a reliable tool whose primary function is transport, on- or off-road.'

MUSEUM OF MODERN ART, NEW YORK, 1951

In the last couple of decades interest in the Second World War period has grown enormously. Every weekend throughout the summer months enthusiasts gather to re-enact this period in history as a way of paying tribute to the servicemen and women who brought the world back from the brink of darkness. And, as the passage of time takes its inexorable toll on the surviving veterans, there has been huge interest in the annual commemoration of events such as the D-Day landings.

At the same time, historically accurate films and TV series such as Steven Spielberg's *Band of Brothers*, have shown a new generation the part that the American Jeep played in liberating Europe all those years ago. And, with a total production of more than 600,000 vehicles, it is hardly surprising that thousands of Jeeps have survived despite so many being butchered in the 1950s and 1960s – a time when old military vehicles were considered to be little more than junk.

A well-restored Jeep is an instant evocation of the war years – a visual link back to that time when the forces of freedom were pitched against the forces of tyranny.

LEFT: Jeep enthusiast George Kimmins bears a striking similarity to General George S. Patton … and thus provides the perfect Jeep accessory! *Simon Thomson*

RIGHT: Henry Reed's poem, 'The naming of parts', gently ridicules the military obsession with order, and opens (and closes) with the line, 'To-day we have naming of parts'. This still from a US Army training film illustrates what might be called 'the measuring of parts'. *Warehouse Collection*

TECHNICAL SPECIFICATION

Manufacturers: GPW, Ford Motor Company; MB, Willys-Overland; M201, Hotchkiss-Delahaye, later Hotchkiss-Brandt and then Thomson Houston Hotchkiss Brandt
Production: MB/GPW, 1941-45; M201, 1956-66
Number produced: GPW, 277,825; MB, 361,339; M201, 28,093.

Automotive details
Engine: Willys Go-Devil L4-134 Type 441 or 442; 2,199cc (134in^3); four cylinders; bore and stroke, 79 x 111mm; petrol; side valves; power output, 65bhp (48kW)
Transmission: 3F1Rx2; 4 x 4
Suspension: live axles, front and rear, on semi-elliptical springs, with telescopic shock absorbers
Brakes: hydraulic
Electrical system: MB/GPW, 6V (some later vehicles were converted to 12V); M201, 24V.

Dimensions
Length: 132¼in (3,360mm)
Width: 62in (1,575mm)
Height: top up, 69¾in (1,772mm); top down, 68in (1,722mm); windscreen folded, 52in (1,321mm)
Wheelbase: 80in (2,032mm)
Track: 49in (1,245mm)
Ground clearance: 8¾in (222mm)
Fording depth: unprepared, 18in (457mm).

Weight
Unladen weight: MB/GPW, 2,453lb (1,115kg); M201, 2,552lb (1,160kg)
Payload: 800lb (364kg)
Gross weight: MB/GPW, 3,253lb (1,479kg); M201, 3,366lb (1,530kg)
Maximum towed load: 1,000lb (455kg).

Performance
Turning circle: 35ft (10.675m)
Approach angle: 45°
Departure angle: 35°
Maximum gradient: 60 per cent
Maximum drawbar pull: 1,930lbf (877kgf)
Maximum speed: transfer case in high ratio, 65mph (105km/h); transfer case in low ratio, 33mph (55km/h)
Fuel tank capacity: 12.5gal (57 litre)
Fuel consumption: 20mpg (US) (8.56km/litre)
Cruising range: 300 miles (486km).

IDENTIFICATION

Chassis number

On MB Jeeps the chassis number will be found stamped into a zinc-plated steel tag that is riveted to a plate welded across the open face of the left-hand main chassis member between the bumper gussets. The chassis number for a Ford GPW is stamped directly onto the top face of the left-hand main chassis member between the mounts for the engine and the shock absorber. For a Hotchkiss M201, the number is stamped into the upper face of the right-hand main chassis member just behind the bumper gusset, and is often painted red.

In all cases, the number is also stamped onto the data plate that is riveted to the glove-box lid but, since new blank data plates are readily available, and equally readily stamped, this number should be treated with some caution.

Casting dates

All Ford Jeep engines carry a date code that indicates when the block was cast. This can help with establishing the date a particular Jeep was built but, of course, it is as well to remember that engines can, and often did, get replaced.

On early engines this code was located on the right-hand side of the engine block, close to the lower rear corner, and the code uses a single alphabetic character to represent the month (A = January through M = December) and a numeral to represent the day. Additional digits were appended to indicate the mould number from which the casting was made. From August 1943, the code was moved to just below the distributor and a third numeral was added to represent the year (eg, F4-311 decodes as June 4 1943, with '11' representing the mould number).

Military registration and census numbers

All Jeeps that served with the US forces were assigned a unique registration number by the military accounting/procurement department. The numbers were assigned to the vehicles in blocks according to the contract and were stencilled onto the sides of the engine compartment lid as the vehicles rolled out of the door at the end of the assembly line. The changing of the registration number was strictly prohibited by military regulations.

Unfortunately, there isn't a perfect correlation between the registration number and the vehicle chassis number because the numbers did not go hand-in-hand. For US Army vehicles, the number, which starts with '20' followed by six digits, is prefixed 'USA'; early examples also included a 'W' between the two parts of the number (eg, USA W 2015324) but, from about 1942 this practice was discontinued. An 'S' suffix indicated that the electrical system of the Jeep in question had been screened to prevent radio frequency interference. US Navy and US Marine Corps Jeeps were numbered under a different system, with the numbers prefixed 'USN' and 'USMC', respectively.

Jeeps in service with the British Army were assigned a registration number, which was prefixed 'M' to indicate that the vehicle was considered to be a car. The prefix 'L' or 'Z' was assigned to trucks, or lorries, 'P' was for amphibians, and 'H' was used for tractors; other letters were reserved for armoured vehicles, self-propelled guns and trailers. The actual numbers were assigned in blocks according to contract, the lowest number recorded is M4589425, which was assigned to a Bantam BRC-40, while the highest number was M6270724, which was the last of a series of 1,000 Ford GPWs. The registration number for vehicles in Canadian Army service was prefixed 'CM'.

Chassis numbers

	Bantam BRC	Willys MA, MB	Ford GP, GPW	Hotchkiss licence MB, and M201
1940	BRC-60.01 to 70	see note 1	see note 2	-
1941	BRC-40.2647 to 2651	MA.78401 to 79990	GP.8524 to 16603	-
	-	MA-4WS.85501 to 85550	GPW-4WS, see note 3	-
	-	MB.100001 to 108598	-	-
1942	-	MB.108599 to 200022	GPW.1 to 90837	-
1943	-	MB.200023 to 293232	GPW.90216 to 170336	-
1944	-	MB.293233 to 402334	GPW.170660 to 246405	-
1945	-	MB.402335 to 459851	GPW247172 to 277825	-
1956	-	-	-	00001 to 00882
1957	-	-	-	00883 to 04060
1958	-	-	-	04601 to 06653
1959	-	-	-	06654 to 09349
1960	-	-	-	09350 to 13075
1961	-	-	-	13076 to 17599
1962	-	-	-	17600 to 21961
1963	-	-	-	21962 to 25336
1964	-	-	-	25337 to 26927
1965	-	-	-	26928 to 27385
1966	-	-	-	27386 to 27614

Notes

1 If the Willys Quad prototype of 1940 was numbered, that number was never recorded
2 Similarly, the two Ford Pygmy prototypes of 1940 were probably not numbered
3 Ford built 50 four-wheel steer GPs; the chassis numbers are not known.

RIGHT: Alan Clark (1928–99) was a Conservative Member of Parliament as well as being a keen and extremely witty motoring author and diarist. Among his many motorcars, Clark had owned a surplus Jeep and once was heard to observe that 'no-one drives a Jeep for more than 60 miles for pleasure' – many enthusiasts would beg to differ! *Simon Thomson*

In 1949, all British military vehicles were renumbered using a six-digit alpha-numeric series; Jeeps were assigned numbers in the series 09YH21 to 99YH99 and 00YJ01 to 89YJ99, although not all possible numbers in the series were issued.

Until mid-1960, the registration number of all French Army Jeeps, regardless of origin, consisted of a six-digit number, usually separated into two groups of three digits. The number was stencilled onto the front bumper and onto a registration plate at the rear. From about August 1960, a new seven-digit registration system was introduced that included the year that the vehicle was issued, the arm of service, and whether the vehicle was new or rebuilt.

Dates of delivery

The data plates on the Second World War Jeep include a so-called 'date of delivery', which indicates the day on which the government approved that particular vehicle as meeting the requirements of the relevant contract, thus accepting it for service.

Both the US Army and the US Navy maintained inspection teams at the Willys-Overland and Ford plants to oversee production. For the Army, the inspection and approvals operation was originally run by the Quartermaster Corps, but was turned over to the Ordnance Corps in August 1942 when that department took on the role of military procurement. For the US Navy, this role was undertaken by the Navy's Bureau of Ordnance.

Once the vehicles had been assembled, all wartime Jeeps were subjected to a test for the efficiency of the radio suppression equipment. The majority were also given a short test drive and a small percentage were singled out for more extensive road testing or, in some cases, for some dismantling or other inspection. Inevitably, this process took some time and, although the date of delivery was usually the date on which the Jeep was completed or, in some cases, a day or so later, in extreme cases, the date could be as late as five days after the completion of assembly. The delay was caused by the amount of time needed to pass the vehicles through the inspection process, and the volume of vehicles being produced for inspection at that time.

SERVICE HISTORY

There is a Jeep on display at London's Imperial War Museum in which it suggested that the vehicle's provenance can be traced back to the Second World War and to the nurse who drove it throughout the war. There may also be others elsewhere, but these are very much the exception. Enthusiasts who claim that they have the 'first Jeep to come ashore on D-Day' or that they own 'the Jeep that General Patton used in France' are fooling themselves and no one else. In many cases, it is not even easy to discover which army or arm of service operated a particular Jeep, and unless genuine unit markings are found under the original military paintwork – and this is only possible through very careful rubbing down – it is virtually impossible to trace the military history of any specific Jeep. The paperwork simply does not exist.

As regards physical evidence, there may be rebuild plates on the vehicle, or on major components such as the engine or axles, which will give some clue as to its origins and its dates in service. And, in the absence of markings, it may be possible to make an educated guess as to the role of a Jeep, at least at some stage during its service career, through the position of holes or brackets that might suggest the vehicle had been fitted with stretcher carriers, a radio or a gun mount. But remember that most Jeeps were used as general purpose and reconnaissance vehicles and this evidence is unlikely to exist in every case.

If you are really lucky, you may be able to find a photograph of your Jeep in service.

After almost 70 years it is very unlikely that any surviving Jeep will not have been rebuilt, at least once during its military career and perhaps once more in the hands of a collector, and it will almost certainly have lost its integrity during this process. Be sceptical of claims of 'matching numbers' and be wary of chassis numbers stamped into seemingly-new data plates.

References

'Since the design of the Jeep – as the US Army ¼-ton truck has become universally known – was finalised in 1942, the vehicle has been produced by Ford and Willys to the same blueprints. As the vehicle is of severely utilitarian design there are no special difficulties in servicing it... no special tools are required other than a set of SAE spanners.'

THE MOTOR TRADER MAGAZINE, 15 SEPTEMBER 1943

Over the last couple of decades, interest in Second World War Jeeps, and by association, the post-war M201, has grown by leaps and bounds, with prices, of even barn finds, easily keeping pace. The days of cheap Jeeps are probably well behind us.

BELOW: In 1943, Lieutenant-General John C.H. Lee, SHAEF Services of Supply, stated that 'in all my travels I have never seen a Jeep that would not run' and what could be more pleasant than a leisurely Jeep run along a coastal road. *Simon Thomson*

RIGHT: If present, the identification plate will help to give basic information on the Jeep, as well providing data on the serial number and date of delivery; there will also be reference to the supporting documents. However, blank plates are easily available, which means that you need to make a judgement on whether or not the plate is original. *Warehouse Collection*

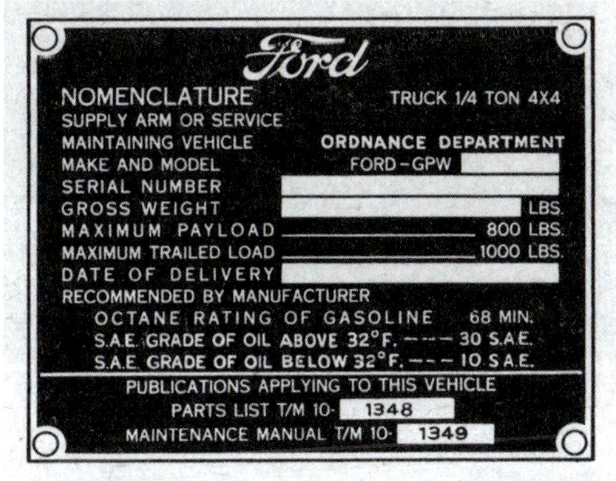

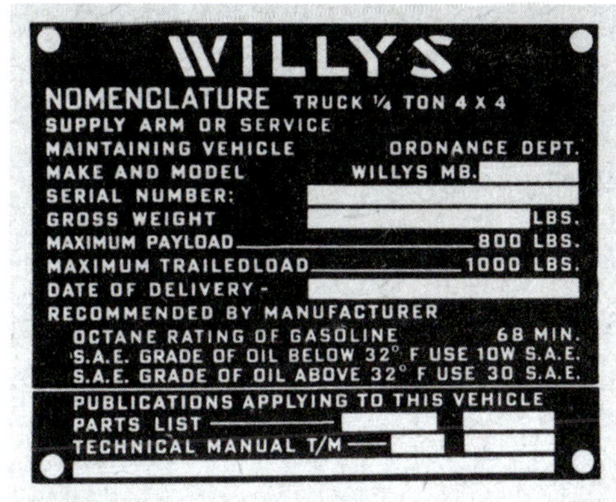

At the time of writing (2021), restoration costs can easily amount to £10,000, and perhaps as much as £20,000, and well-restored Jeeps are now regularly changing hands at north of £25,000. And the Percival Motor Company recently advertised a 1963 Hotchkiss M201 at £28,750, which, if it was achieved, was certainly something of a record.

But, on the plus side of the equation, these high prices mean that the Jeep has become mainstream, with new suppliers and information never more readily available.

INTERNET

The best website for Jeep information is www.g503.com. An excellent resource for Jeep enthusiasts, it was conceived, created, written, produced, directed and is currently maintained, watered and sun-shined by Ron Fitzpatrick Jeep Parts. And, you will find that Kaiser-Willys (www.kaiserwillys.com) also contains a wealth of useful information.

It is also worth checking out the Historic Military Vehicle Forum (www.hmvf.co.uk) which, although more broadly based, frequently covers Jeep-related topics.

MILITARY DOCUMENTATION

Like most military vehicles, the Jeep is the subject of an extraordinarily large volume of paperwork. Indeed, many enthusiasts actually seek out and collect official documents, manuals, photographs and other literature relating to their chosen vehicle. The major official military publications are listed below, as well as some of the more interesting minor items.

Tracking down copies of these items is not as difficult as might be imagined.

Willys MB, Ford GPW

Assembly instructions

- Form 3679-1. Instructions for unpacking and assembly of boxed vehicle. Ford truck,
- ¼-ton, 4 x 4, Model GPW
- Instructions for unpacking and assembly of boxed vehicle. Willys truck, ¼-ton, 4 x 4, Model MB.

BELOW: Collecting Jeep-related documentation can be both rewarding and instructive. *Warehouse Collection*

Lubrication order

- LO 9-803. ¼-ton, 4 x 4, truck (Willys-Overland model MB and Ford model GPW).

Operation and maintenance

- TM 9-803; TM-9-803-4; TM-10-1103; TM-10-1207; TM-10-1349; TM-10-1513, change 1. ¼-ton, 4 x 4, truck (Willys-Overland model MB and Ford model GPW).

Maintenance manuals

- TM 10-1205. American Bantam model BRC, ¼-ton, 4 x 4, truck
- TM 10-1207; TM10-1349; TM10-1513, changes 1-3. Ford truck, model GPW, ¼-ton, 4 x 4; Willys truck, ¼-ton, 4 x 4, model MB
- TM 9-1803A. Ordnance maintenance: engine and engine accessories for ¼-ton, 4 x 4, truck (Willys-Overland model MB and Ford model GPW)
- TM 9-1803B. Ordnance maintenance: power train, body, and frame for ¼-ton, 4 x 4, truck (Willys-Overland model MB and Ford model GPW).

Maintenance allowances

- ORD SNL 7 G-503. Organizational maintenance allowances for truck, ¼-ton, 4 x 4, command reconnaissance (Ford model GPW, Willys model MB)
- ORD SNL 8 G-503. Field and depot maintenance allowances for truck, ¼-ton, 4 x 4, command reconnaissance (Ford model GPW, Willys model MB)
- ORD SNL 8 G-503. Field and depot maintenance allowances for winterization equipment for truck, ¼-ton, 4 x 4, command reconnaissance (Ford model GPW, Willys model MB).

Modification work orders

- TB 9-803-1 to TB 9-803-9; TB 9-803-FE-1 to TB 9-803-FE-8. ¼-ton, 4 x 4, truck (Willys-Overland model MB and Ford model GPW)
- TO 19-75AE-5. ¼-ton, 4 x 4, truck (Willys-Overland model MB and Ford model GPW). To convert electrical system from 6 volts to 12 volts on certain specified vehicles.

Miscellaneous instructions

- TB ORD-92, 146, 147, 161, 163, 284, 353, 354, 362, 369, 570, 621; TB ORD-FE-25, 45, 57; FSM WO-G503-W1 to W9, and W9C1. ¼-ton, 4 x 4, truck (Willys-Overland model MB and Ford model GPW).

Parts lists

- ORD SNL 9 G-503. List of all service parts for truck, ¼-ton, 4 x 4, command reconnaissance (Ford model GPW, Willys model MB)
- TM 10-1100. Parts price list for (Ford) special model GP 80in wheelbase, four-wheel drive (4 x 4), 2- and 4-wheel steering
- TM 10-1186, change 1. Master parts list for Willys truck and trailer, models MA and MB, ¼-ton, 4 x 4, truck, and model MB-T, ¼-ton trailer
- TM 10-1206, changes 1-5. Parts price list for Willys truck, model MB, ¼-ton, 4 x 4
- TM 10-1206, changes 1-5; TM10-1512. Ford truck, model GPA, amphibian. Willys truck, model MB, ¼-ton, 4 x 4
- TM 10-1323. Master parts list for Ford truck, model GPW
- TM 10-1348, change 1; TM-10-1264. Ford truck, model GPW, ¼-ton, 4 x 4.

Radio installation

- TM 11-2715. Installation of radio equipment in truck, ¼-ton, 4 x 4
- WO code 11852. Wireless station C45 in trucks, ¼-ton, CT, FFW, 4 x 4, Austin; or trucks, ¼-ton, GS, 4 x 4, Ford/Willys or Land Rover.
- SRDE pamphlet 734A. Provisional installation and waterproofing instructions for wireless station no 19HP in cars, 5cwt, 4 x 4 (American Jeep).

Hotchkiss M201

Parts list

- MAT 3072/1, MAT 3072/2, MAT 3072/3. Catalogue des pieces détachées pour la voiture de liaison de ¼-tonne, Hotchkiss M201, toutes modèles.

Technical bulletins

- Bulletin technique 448/AU. Aménagement de l'equipment electrique pour le rendre conforme au code de la route. Voiture de liaison de ¼-tonne, Hotchkiss M201, Willys-Overland modèle MB et Ford modèle GPW
- Bulletin technique 468/AU. Renforcer la paroi gauche de la caisse. Voiture de liaison de ¼-tonne, Hotchkiss M201, porte-engins SS10
- Bulletin technique 469/AU. Montage d'un protecteur d'interrupteur a clé fixe du circuit de batterie. Voiture de liaison de ¼-tonne, Hotchkiss M201
- Bulletin technique 482/AU. Déserrage des vis de fixation des plateaux-supports de mâchoires de frein. Voiture de liaison de ¼-tonne, Hotchkiss M201, Willys-Overland modèle MB et Ford modèle GPW
- Bulletin technique 482/AU, modification no 1. Remplace le dessin no 3 par le dessin ci-joint. Voiture de liaison de ¼-tonne, Hotchkiss M201, Willys-Overland modèle MB et Ford modèle GPW
- Bulletin technique 482/AU, modification no 2. Déserrage des vis de fixation des plateaux-supports de mâchoires de frein. Voiture de liaison de ¼-tonne, Hotchkiss M201, Willys-Overland modèle MB et Ford modèle GPW
- Bulletin technique 492/AU, 493/AU. Transport du filet de camouflage synthétique garni modèle 1962 no 1. Voiture de liaison de ¼-tonne, Hotchkiss M201, Willys-Overland modèle MB

ABOVE: It is rare to be able to find original photographs showing a specific Jeep in service, or better still, in action. However, when deciding how to mark a completed restoration, carefully following all of the details of a period photograph will help to preserve the illusion of period. *Simon Thomson*

- Bulletin technique 631/AU. Aménagement de l'equipment electrique pour le rendre conforme au code de la route. Voiture de liaison de ¼-tonne, Hotchkiss M201, Willys-Overland modèle MB et Ford modèle GPW
- Bulletin technique 684/AU. Montage du support de radiamètre DOM 410. Voiture de liaison de ¼-tonne, Hotchkiss M201
- Bulletin technique 737/AU. Montage de la bache nylon avec rideaux at portières. Voiture de liaison de ¼-tonne, Hotchkiss M201, Willys-Overland modèle MB et Ford modèle GPW
- Bulletin technique 787/AU. Installation d'une baie MEDOVIC. Voiture de liaison de ¼-tonne, Hotchkiss M201.

Technical description

- MAT 2835. Notice technique de conduite et d'entretien de la voiture de liaison de ¼-tonne Hotchkiss type M201 4x4 24V et 6V.

User guide

- MAT 3152, 2701. Guide d'entretien de la voiture de liaison de ¼-tonne a 4 roues motrice.

Workshop manual

- MAT 3072/1, MAT 3072/2, MAT 3072/3. Manuel de réparation de la voiture de liaison de ¼-tonne, Hotchkiss M201 4x4 24V.

ABOVE: A 'Military Police' Jeep marked as belonging to the 50th (Northumbrian) Division. *Simon Thomson*

USEFUL CONTACTS

Military Jeep dealers and sources for parts

This list has been checked and updated since the first edition of this book (2010), but don't forget that, these days, Jeeps often crop up for sale on e-Bay and, of course, can also be purchased direct from a previous owner through military vehicle clubs or national magazines, or from sales websites such as Milweb (www.milweb.net), or the French site www.leboncoin.fr

United Kingdom
Allied Forces Canvas
Unit 1, The Elms
Rockhampton
Berkeley
Gloucestershire GL13 9DR
01454 261100
www.alliedforcesltd.com

Atlantic Jeepart
Brooklyn Farm, Chapel Lane
Sissinghurst
Cranbrook
Kent TN17 3NU
01580 720797
www.atlanticjeepart.co.uk

Dallas Auto Parts
Cold Ash Farm
Long Lane
Hermitage
Berkshire RG18 9LT
01635 201124
www.dallasautoparts.com

East Coast Jeeps
Tugby Orchards
Wood Lane
Tugby
Leicestershire LE7 9WE
07523 903021
www.eastcoastjeepsuk.com

Jeeparts UK
The Old Coach Yard
Little Tey
Colchester
Essex CO6 1HX
01206 210356
www.jeeparts-uk.co.uk

Jeffrey Engineering
Berry Court Farm
Pluckley Road
Smarden
Kent TN27 8RQ
01233 770007
www.jeffreyeng.com

John & Mary Worthing
Spout House
Orleton
Ludlow SY8 4JG
01584 831239
www.canvasco.com

MV Depot
Drury House, Main Street
Helperby
York YO61 2PW
07731 314145
www.milweb.net/dealers/trader/mvdepot

RR Motor Services
Unit 13, Hope Farm
Gibbons Brook
Sellindge
Ashford TN25 6HH
01233 820219
www.rrservices.co.uk

WHB Jeeps
The Garage
Ayr Road
St John's Town of Dalry
Castle Douglas DG7 3SW
01644 430208
www.whbjeeps.co.uk

Willys World War 2 Jeeps
26 Doman Road
Yorktown Business Park
Camberley
Surrey GU15 3DF
07788 751436
www.willysworldwar2jeeps.com

Australia
Milspares
Shed 4, 7 Johnstone Road
Brendale
Queensland 4500
(+61) 488 111 184
www.milspares.net.au

MV Spares
41 Porters Road
Kenthurst
NSW 2156
(+61) 296 542 412
www.mvspares.com

Austria
Augum Parts
Müroll Gewerbepark
Badenerstrasse 15
Traiskirchen 2514
(+43) 676 6760 327
www.shop.augum-parts.com/de

Camo – Günter Ctortnik
Industriestrasse 20-22
Himberg
A-2325
(+43) 223 584 233
www.camo.co.at

Belgium
Desmet
Antwerpse Steenweg 455
B-9040 Sint-Amandsberg
(+32) 9 228 33 66
www.desmetjeep.com

Canada
Willys Acres
3224 Line 7 North
Coulson
Oro-Medonte
Ontario L0L 2E0
(+1) 705 835 5739
www.willysacres.com

France
Crazy Jeep Stock
13 Chemin des Touleyres
Bize Minervois 11120
(+33) 468 48 23 59
www.crazyjeep-stock.com

Jeep Sud-Est
ZA de Chalançon
431 Allée Louis Montagnat
Vedène 84270
(+33) 490 39 56 27
www.jeepsudest.com

Jeep Village
380 Avenue de Stalingrad
Chevilly Larue 94550
(+33) 141 73 23 23
www.jeepvillage.com

Jeepest Eurl
La Ferme
12 Grand Rue
Menil aux Bois 55260
(+33) 329 89 03 03
www.jeepest.com

Lys Tout Terrain
32 Route de Clarques
Therouanne 62129
(+33) 321 38 57 01
www.lys-tout-terrain.com

Military Classic Vehicles
ZA Synergie
Route d'Isigny
Grandcamp Maisy 14450
(+33) 233 44 44 44
www.military-classic-vehicles.fr

Greece
Army Spare Parts
Ionos Dragoymi 38
Ionia
Thessalonika 57008
(+30) 231 07 82 58 1
www.army-spareparts.com

Netherlands
Bram Van Buuren Jeeps
Beijerdstraat 9A
4112 NE
Beusichem
(+31) 345 50 1800
www.bramvanbuuren-jeeps.nl

Eagle Jeep Parts
Rijneveld 86A
2771 SX
Boskoop
(+31) 629 28 4368
www.jeepsandlandies.nl

Jemax Jeep Parts
Romeinseberg 3
5296 LA
Esch
(+31) 411 60 4188
www.jemax-jeeparts.nl

Staman International Trading
Transportweg 4
7442 CT
Nijverdal
(+31) 548 61 0432
www.jeeparts.nl

H O Wildenberg
Remmerden 44
3910 AB
Rhenen
(+31) 317 61 8218
www.wildenbergparts.com

Willem Keizer
Semsstraat 8
9501 GA
Stadskanaal
(+31) 622 39 3941
www.keizer.nl

Sweden
Classic Jeep Parts
Skymningsvagen 4
Vasterljung
S-610 75
(+46) 7075 15843
www.classicjeepparts.com

USA
Army Jeep Parts
6500 Beaver Dam Road, Unit B
Levittown
Pennsylvania 19057
(+1) 215 269 5014
www.armyjeepparts.com

Beachwood Canvas Works
39 Lake Avenue
PO Box 137
Island Heights
New Jersey 08732
(+1) 732 929 3168
www.beachwoodcanvas.com

Brent Mullins Jeep Parts
1303 Cherokee Drive
College Station
Texas 77842
(+1) 979 690 0203
www.mullinsjeepparts.com
Daryl Bensinger
2442 Main Street
Narvon
Pennsylvania 17555
(+1) 610 286 9545
www.dlbensinger.com

Kaiser Willys Auto Supply
114 Bolton Court
Aiken
South Carolina 29803
(+1) 888 648 4923
www.kaiserwillys.com

Midwest Military
16075 State Highway 13 South
Prior Lake
Minnesota 55372
(+1) 952 440 8778
www.midwestmilitary.com

Nelson's Surplus Jeep Parts & Military Tires
1024 E Park Avenue
Columbiana
Ohio 44408
(+1) 330 482 5191
www.nsjp.biz

Peter DeBella Jeep Parts
1319 Pulaski Street
Riverhead
New York 11901-4821
(+1) 631 874 8660
www.debellajeepparts.com

Ron Fitzpatrick Jeep Parts
PO Box 2453
Grants Pass
Oregon 97528
(+1) 541 582 4035
www.g503/parts.com

RAPCO Parts Company
1201 US-81
Bowie
Texas 76230
(+1) 940 872 2403
www.rapcoparts.com

Surplus City Jeep Parts
4514 Pacific Heights Road
Oroville
California 95965
(+1) 530 533 2500
www.surpluscity.com

Vintage Military Vehicles
PO Box 1562
Fort Collins
Colorado 80522
(+1) 970 217 3859
www.vintagemilitaryvehicles.com

White Owl Parts Company
2539 Hillcrest Road
Kinston
North Carolina 28504
(+1) 252 522 2586
www.whiteowl.com

APRIL, 1943 AUTOMOBILE ENGINEER 131

THE G.P. WAR TRUCK

An Interesting Design Built for the U.S. Government

OF the many vehicle types produced essentially for military purposes few have aroused as much general interest as the American General Purpose War Truck. Officially designated the Model G.P.W. truck $\frac{1}{4}$-ton 4 by 4, and popularly known as the "Jeep." They are being built in large quantities to U.S. Army requirements. The Ford Motor Company and the Willys-Overland Motors are the makers, the model referred to in the following notes being a Ford product.

The main object of the designers was to produce a vehicle capable of serving with the U.S. Army in any part of the world. It had to be able to extricate itself from any difficult situation with ease and certainty, to negotiate almost impossible gradients, and force a way through, or over the roughest country. These objectives will account for the many departures from orthodox automobile practice. As is now generally known, the Jeep is quite small. It is remarkably compact, its wheelbase and track being only 6ft. 8in. and 4ft. $0\frac{1}{4}$in. respectively. It is thus but slightly larger than the original Austin Seven. Nevertheless, it is powered by an engine developing over 60 b.h.p. It has six speeds, four wheel drive, yet weighs little more than one ton.

Engine

The bore and stroke are $3\frac{1}{8}$in., and $4\frac{3}{8}$in. (79·375 mm. and 111·125 mm.) giving a total swept volume of 134·2 cu. in. or 2,199 c.c. for the four cylinders. This corresponds to a rating of 15·6 h.p. S.A.E., the maximum output at 3,600 r.p.m. being 60 b.h.p. The maximum torque of 105 lb./ft. is produced at 2,000 r.p.m.

The engine is of the L-headed type, with the valves arranged parallel to the cylinder bore. A single casting forms the cylinders and crankcase, the normal rigidity of the monobloc construction being increased by carrying the lower half flange well below the centre line of the crankshaft.

Generous water spaces extend for the full length of the cylinder bores and particularly around the valves and valve ports. A detachable head is, of course, employed. This is a close-grained grey iron casting retained by fifteen studs. As in the case of the cylinder block, the water passages in the head are of generous proportions, with adequate cooling around the sparking plug bosses and over the combustion chambers. The greater part of the combustion chamber is arranged over the valves, leaving a minimum clearance between the piston top and the combustion chamber roof. The compression ratio is 6·48 to 1.

Rigid transverse webs in the block casting support the main bearing housings the caps of which are secured by setscrews. Non-adjustable steel backed white-metal bearings carry the three journal crankshaft, which weighs 41·5 lb., and is machined from a drop forging. Grain direction thus follows the throws and the four integral countershafts. By the use of a short and robust crankshaft, the torsional vibration of the engine is reduced to a minimum.

After being machined, the crankshaft is balanced statically and dynamically, and afterwards balanced dynamically together with the flywheel and clutch as a complete assembly. Crankshaft end thrust is taken by the front main bearing flange. A wick type oil-seal on the rear main bearing prevents leakage of oil into the dry-plate clutch, and also checks loss when the vehicle is parked on a steep incline.

All the steel-backed bearings are produced to fine limits for assembly in the crankcase without line reaming. No adjustment is provided and a running tolerance of 0·001in. is allowed for all main and big-end bearings. Shims at the front main

ENGINE.—*Four cylinders, bore and stroke $3\frac{1}{8}$ in. × $4\frac{3}{8}$ in., capacity 134·2 cu. in. (2,199 c.c.). S.A.E. rated 15·6 h.p., compression ratio, 6·48 to 1, maximum b.h.p. 60 at 3,600 r.p.m., maximum brake torque 105 lb./ft. at 2,000 r.p.m. Side valves, three bearing crankshaft, aluminium alloy pistons, pressure lubrication to main bearings, big ends, camshaft and valve mechanism. Cooling by pump and fan, temperature regulated by thermostat. Carter downdraught carburettor. Ignition by coil and distributor.*

CLUTCH.—*Single dry plate 8in. diameter.*

GEAR BOX.—*Three forward speeds and reverse. Second and top gears synchromesh. Ratios, top direct, second 1·564 to 1, first 2·665 to 1, reverse, 3·554 to 1. Transfer unit ratios 1 to 1 and 1·97 to 1.*

REAR AXLE.—*Fully floating, hypoid bevel drive, ratio 4·88 to 1.*

FRONT AXLE.—*Three-quarter floating, front wheels driven from transfer box by cardan shaft and constant velocity universal joints.*

BRAKES.—*Lockheed hydraulic on four wheels. Handbrake operates contracting band on transmission drum.*

SPRINGS.—*Semi-elliptic front and rear, chromium alloy leaves with rebound clips. Hydraulic shock absorbers.*

STEERING.—*Variable ratio cam and twin pin lever.*

The Model G.P.W. $\frac{1}{4}$-ton 4 × 4 truck.

ABOVE: In April 1943, the *Automobile Engineer* magazine published a technical appraisal of the Jeep. *Warehouse Collection*

CATÉGORIE VÉHICULES TOUS CHEMINS	CODE E.M.A. 2222-16
GENRE V.L.T.T.	G.A.P.C.E. — MARQUE ET TYPE 882371 074735

Constructeur : Hotchkiss. — Type : M 201. — Année :

Manuel technique : — Charge utile :

Nombre de places : 2.

Nombre de personnels équipés pouvant être transportés en plus de l'équipage : 1.

Emploi : (aménagement défini en vue d'équiper le véhicule pour le transport et le service à bord du canon US de 106 SR.-M 40 monté sur affût M 79 et rendre possible son parachutage).

DONNÉES POUR L'EMBARQUEMENT ET LE STOCKAGE.

Les mêmes que pour la VLTT; code EMA : 2222.21.

DONNÉES PARTICULIÈRES POUR LE TRANSPORT PAR FER.

N'engage pas le gabarit. — Indication de la grenade : λ

DONNÉES PARTICULIÈRES POUR LE TRANSPORT PAR AIR.

Charge par essieu : — à vide { AV : AR : — en charge { AA : VR :

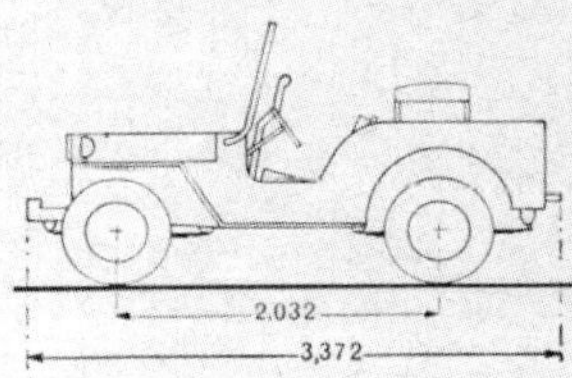

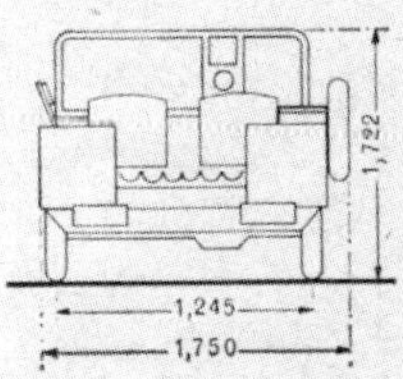

DONNÉES POUR LE RAVITAILLEMENT EN CARBURANT ET INGRÉDIENTS.

Les mêmes que pour la VLTT, code EMA : 2222.21.

DONNÉES POUR L'EMPLOI.

Vitesse maximum du véhicule sur sable : 40 km/h.

DONNÉES TECHNIQUES.

(Les mêmes que pour la VLTT, code EMA : 2222.21, sauf pour les parties mentionnées ci-dessous).

Roues : la roue de secours est fixée sur la caisse à l'extérieur du dit côté.

Suspension : ressorts AR à 11 lames et AV à 10 lames.

Pneus : ce véhicule doit obligatoirement être équipé en pneus de 650 × 16.

Système électrique : le dispositif d'allumage fonctionne sous une tension de 6 volts.

ABOVE AND RIGHT: French data sheets giving the basic details of the MB/GPW and the Hotchkiss M201 equipped with a recoilless rifle. *Warehouse Collection*

CATEGORIE TOUS TERRAINS
GENRE VL

CODE E.M.A. 22 22 21
N° DE NOMENCLATURE 213-419 612 341

Constructeur : **Willys ou Ford.** — Type : M.B. ou G.P.W. — Année :
Manuel technique : TM 9803 ou M 201.
Nombre de places : 5.
Nombre de personnels équipés pouvant être transportés en plus de l'équipage : 3.
Emploi : Transport de personnel ou de matériel léger.

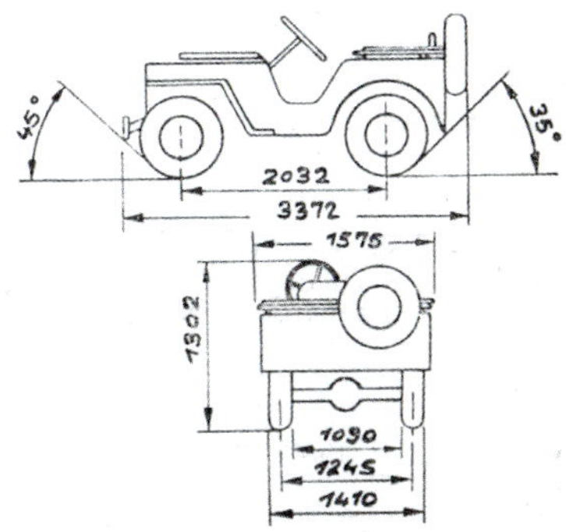

DONNEES POUR L'EMBARQUEMENT ET LE STOCKAGE.

Empattement : 2,032 m. — Voie : *avant :* 1,245 m ; *arrière :* 1,245 m.
Dimensions hors tout : *longueur :* 3,372 ; *largeur :* 1,575 ; *hauteur :* 1,722.
Distance entre les bords extérieurs des pneus ou chenilles : 1,410.
Distance entre les bords intérieurs des pneus ou des chenilles : 1,090.
Distance du centre de l'essieu avant au centre de l'essieu arrière (ou axe des boggies arrières) :
Distance entre les centres d'essieu ou de boggie arrière :
Surface de la projection horizontale du véhicule : 5,30 m2.
Surface totale des pneumatiques ou chenilles au contact du sol : 50 cm2.
Cubage du véhicule pour embarquement : *maximum :* 9,370 m3 ; *minimum :* 6,970 m3.
Poids en kg : *à vide :* 1 060 ; *en charge :* 1 476.
Poids total (sans équipage) tous pleins faits : 1 113 kg.
Pression sur le sol : *à vide :* 2,2 kg/cm2 ; *en charge :*
Quantité de carburant à maintenir dans les réservoirs : 1/4 de capacité ; 14 l.

DONNEES PARTICULIERES POUR LE TRANSPORT PAR FER.

N'engage pas le gabarit ; N° du feuillet du carnet de croquis : néant
Indication de la grenade : 1.

DONNEES PARTICULIERES POUR LE TRANSPORT PAR AIR.

Charge par essieu : *à vide*	Avant : 545 kg Arrière : 515 kg	*en charge*	Avant : Arrière

DONNEES PARTICULIERES SUR L'APTITUDE A FRANCHIR LES OUVRAGES D'ART.

N° de classe attribué :

DONNEES POUR LE RAVITAILLEMENT EN CARBURANT ET INGREDIENTS.

Carburant utilisé : essence. — Indice : 68 minimum.
Consommation moyenne sur route dure (Litres aux 100 km) :
— *avec charge remorquée :* — *sans charge remorquée :* 14.
Consommation moyenne tous terrains (Litres aux 100 km et horaire) :
Avec charge remorquée : ; sans charge remorquée :
Consommation moyenne d'huile horaire :
Autonomie sans nourrice organique (km sur route) : 400.

Contenance en litres

Réservoir à carburant : 56,8	Différentiel : 1,18
Dispositif de refroidissement : 10,4	Boîte auxiliaire : 1,42
Carter du moteur : 4,75	Pont avant : 1,18
Boîte de vitesses : 0,70	Pont arrière : 1,18
Boîtier de direction : 0,23	Convertisseur :
Dispositif de freinage :	Démultiplicateur :
Filtre du carburateur :	

Huile utilisée

	Eté	*Hiver*
Carter moteur :	SAE30	SAE10
Autres organes :	SAE90	SAE80
Freins :	LFA	LFA

TRUCK, COMMAND RECONNAISSANCE, ¼-TON, 4 x 4
(Ford, Model GPW; Willys, Model MB)

NOTE: ALL DIMENSIONS SHOWN ARE IN INCHES

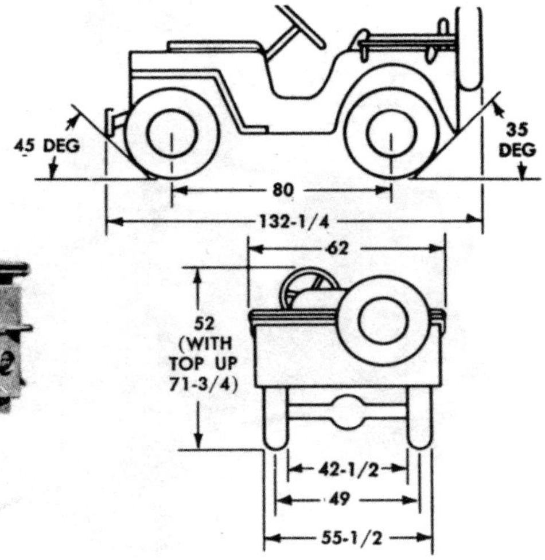

RA PD 137858

Technical Manuals: 9–803, 9–1803A, 9–1803B, 9–1825B, 9–1826A, 9–1827C, 9–1828A; **Supply Catalog:** SNL G–503.

Classification: Standard.

Purpose: To transport command and reconnaissance personnel and light cargo.

GENERAL DATA

Crew — 2; Passengers (including) crew 5
Weight (lb) — Net 2,450
- Payload — off highway 800; on highway 1,200
- Gross — off highway 3,250; on highway 3,650

Live-axle gear ratio — 4.88 : 1
Axle load (lb):
- Empty — front 1,240; rear 1,210
- Loaded:
  - Off highway — front 1,390; rear 1,860
  - On highway — front 1,465; rear 2,185

Tires — Ply 6; Size 6.00 x 16; Pressure (psi) 30
- Tread, center-to-center, front — (in.) 49

Shipping dimensions, uncrated — (cu ft) 247; (sq ft) 57
Vehicle dimensions:
- Ground clearance — (in.) 8¾
- Pintle height, loaded — (in.) 21

Electrical system — (volts) 6
- No. of batteries — 1
- Type of ground — negative

Fuel octane rating — 68
Capacities:
- Fuel — (gal) 15
- Cooling system — (qt) 11
- Crankcase, refill — (qt) 4
- Transfer — (qt) 1½
- Transmission — (qt) ¾
- Axles (each) — (qt) 1¼

Brakes:
- Manufacturer; Bendix — Type; hydraulic
- Parking brake, type — transmission

Transmission:
- Forward speeds — 3
- Gear ratio — High 1:1; Low 2.665 : 1

Transfer:
- Speeds — 2
- Gear ratio — High 1:1; Low 1.97:1

PERFORMANCE

Computed grade ability in lowest gear, loaded — (percent) 58
Turning radius (ft) — right 18; left 18½
Fording depth — (in.) 25
Fuel consumption, loaded — (mpg) 19
Cruising range, loaded — (mi) 285
Allowable speed, recommended — (mph) 65
Maximum recommended towed load:
- Off highway — gross-(lb) 1,000
- On highway — gross-(lb) 2,000

ENGINE

Manufacturer: Willys — Model 442
Type — L-head, 4-cycle; No. of cylinders (in line) 4
Displacement — (cu in.) 134.2
Bore — (in.) 3⅛
Stroke — (in.) 4⅜
Compression ratio — 6.48 : 1
Governed speed — not governed
Brake horsepower (max w/std accessories) — 54 at (rpm) 4,000
Torque (max) — 105 lb-ft at (rpm) 2,000

ADDITIONAL DATA

Live axles, type — hypoid, full-floating
Transmission, type — synchromesh

151

ABOVE: Data sheet for the MB/GPW Jeep taken from the US Army publication TM 9-2800-1 dated February 1953. *Warehouse Collection*

ABOVE: If you are looking for the unusual, what could be better than this bomb-disposal Jeep with its distinctive red-painted areas of the body. *Simon Thomson*

Index